PENGUIN BOOKS

THE PRODIGAL TONGUE

Lynne Murphy is Professor of Linguistics at the University of Sussex. Born and raised in New York State, she studied linguistics at the Universities of Massachusetts and Illinois, before starting her academic career in South Africa and Texas. Since 2000, she has lived in Brighton, England, where she has acquired an English husband, an English daughter, and an alter ego: Lynneguist, author of the award-winning blog *Separated by a Common Language*.

Praise for *The Prodigal Tongue*

"The war of words waged between Americans and Brits has been filled with dour pedantry on both sides—which is what makes Murphy's book such a welcome and refreshing revelation. Murphy playfully and expertly pokes at the linguistic chauvinism displayed on both sides of the Atlantic, slyly overturning false assumptions and explaining the linguistic ins and outs of each other's speech with candor and humor. She pulls back the curtain not just on our language, but our shared quirks, loves, and frustrations, and in the process, extols our linguistic differences as part of the rich history of English and the nations that speak it. With wit and expertise, *The Prodigal Tongue* calls all English speakers home to a language big enough for both fries and chips, bumbershoots and brollies."

—Kory Stamper, author of *Word by Word*

"How did we get our knickers in such a twist? The British sneer at 'creeping Americanisms' that are neither creeping nor American. Meanwhile, their cousins in the US have an inferiority complex about their English and lust after those plummy British accents. Enter Lynne Murphy, a linguist who has a foot in each culture and a unique understanding of the Great Divide."

—Patricia T. O'Conner, author of *Woe Is I* and, with Stewart Kellerman, *Origins of the Specious*

"Forget the usual bumbershoots and lifts and lorries—Lynne Murphy's book on the difference between English in America and English in England is full of much more interesting things. Did you know that increasing numbers of Brits are saying 'haitch' instead of 'aitch' for the name of the letter H? Or that Americans are using the subjunctive ever *more* lately? Or that James Corden was advised when he started hosting *The Late Late Show* that Americans find 'willy' and 'shag' cute but not 'half-cut' and 'knackered'? You'll be chuffed as nuts on every page."

—John McWhorter, author of *Words on the Move* and *Talking Back, Talking Black*, and host of Slate's *Lexicon Valley*

"Moving beyond facile stereotypes about British and American English, [Lynne Murphy] delves into subtle linguistic nuances with wit and aplomb. *The Prodigal Tongue* is a wonderful reading experience for anyone interested in understanding the true nature of these two distinct 'nationlects.'"

—Ben Zimmer, language columnist for *The Wall Street Journal*

THE PRODIGAL TONGUE

The Love–Hate Relationship
Between British and American English

LYNNE MURPHY

PENGUIN BOOKS

PENGUIN BOOKS

An imprint of Penguin Random House LLC
375 Hudson Street
New York, New York 10014
penguin.com

Excerpt from "On the Loose in London" by Dave Barry.
Used by permission of Writers House LLC.

LIBRARY OF CONGRESS CATALOGING-IN-PUBLICATION DATA
Names: Murphy, M. Lynne, author.
Title: The prodigal tongue : the love-hate relationship between American and
British English / Lynne Murphy.
Other titles: Love-hate relationship between American and British English
Description: New York : Penguin Books, 2018. | Includes index.
Identifiers: LCCN 2017057417 (print) | LCCN 2018002135 (ebook) |
ISBN 9781524704889 (ebook) | ISBN 9780143131106 (paperback)
Subjects: LCSH: English language—Social aspects—United States. |
English language—Social aspects—Great Britain. | English language—Variation—United States. | English language—Variation—Great Britain. | English language—Psychological aspects. | English language—Usage. | English language--History. |
BISAC: LANGUAGE ARTS & DISCIPLINES / Linguistics / General. |
LANGUAGE ARTS & DISCIPLINES / Linguistics / Historical & Comparative. |
LANGUAGE ARTS & DISCIPLINES / Reference.
Classification: LCC PE2808 (ebook) | LCC PE2808 .M87 2018 (print) |
DDC 427/.9—dc23
LC record available at https://lccn.loc.gov/2017057417

Printed in the United States of America
1 3 5 7 9 10 8 6 4 2

Set in Arno Pro

For Arden,
who says tomato *both ways*

CONTENTS

I

THE QUEEN'S ENGLISH, CORRUPTED

> If there is a more hideous language on the face of the earth than
> the American form of English, I should like to know what it is!
> Baron Somers, in the House of Lords (1979)[1]

Americans are ruining the English language. I know this because
people go out of their way to tell me so. I am a magnet for such
comments—an American who dares to teach English Language
and Linguistics at a British university and who has the chutzpah
to write about American and British language differences on the
internet. But you don't need me to tell you about the wrecking ball
that is American English—the talking heads of Britain have been
pointing it out for years. English is under attack from American
words that are "mindless" (the *Mail on Sunday*),[2] "ugly and pointless" (*BBC Magazine*),[3] "infectious, destructive and virulent" (the
Daily Mail).[4] American words "infect, invade, and pollute" (*The
Times*).[5] Even Prince Charles has assessed the situation, warning
that American English is "very corrupting."[6]

Perhaps you had thought someone or something else was causing English's demise. Maybe it's inarticulate young people, bent on
creating a future English that consists of little more than strings
of *so like kinda this and stuff*. Or is technology responsible? BBC
journalist John Humphrys likens text-messagers to Genghis Khan;
they are vandals who are "pillaging our punctuation; savaging our
sentences; raping our vocabulary."[7] Business jargon is another

1

likely suspect. Don Watson, in his book *Gobbledygook*, argues that management-speak expressions "sterilise the language and kill imagination and clarity."[8] In fact, the plain-language promoters at Clarity International blame business jargon for the financial crisis of 2008—the language of banking had become so meaningless that customers could not understand the risks they were signing up for.[9]

But look closer and you may decide that all these dangers to English are just symptoms of a linguistic malady whose ground zero is the United States. For instance, if young people are ruining the Queen's English, should we blame them, or blame America? The United States invented 20th-century childhood, which continues to shape culture worldwide in the 21st century. The seen-but-not-heard Victorian girls and boys of Britain have been replaced by the American inventions of the *teenager* and the *tween*. Children born in Essex or Edinburgh or Aberystwyth live part of their lives in a virtual America, home of hip-hop, Disney princesses, caped superheroes, and fast food. The situation is bad enough that in 2007 the British media regulator Ofcom (the equivalent of the US Federal Communications Commission) called for a national debate on the proliferation of American children's television on British screens. "We don't want our children growing up with American accents," proclaimed former BBC *Play School* presenter Baroness Floella Benjamin.[10] It may be too late. British young people, like their American counterparts are, like, ending their statements as if they were, like, questions?

And the youthful English speakers are not all that young anymore. As Oscar Wilde observed: "The youth of America is their oldest tradition. It has been going on now for three hundred years."[11] More than a hundred years after Wilde's quip, the lines between childhood and adulthood have become blurred by adults' refusal to put away childish things, with the US leading the way. The American invention of the word *kidult* underscores the point. In kidulthood, grown-up speech becomes more casual: no one wants to be called *Mister* or *ma'am*. We feel free to mumble our *gonna*s and *lemme*s. And everything is *awesome*.

Technology and business are similar stealth American invasions into global English. American technology spills foreignisms throughout the anglophonic world. We talk of *uploads*, of *microwaving* food, of *personal computers*. The technologies crossed oceans and so did the words. Microsoft Word asks British users to set the font "color." Facebook teaches us to *unfriend* people and *unlike* things, then puts a grumpy red line under perfectly good English spellings like *practise* with an *s* and *travelled* with double *l*. This increasingly technologized, globalized world brings us business jargon, the language of optimism and obfuscation. Surely *going forward, reaching out, and leveraging our real-time client synergy* is the fault of go-getting, pop-psychologizing American suits.

We can actually quantify the horror that American English arouses. After using a thesaurus in order to find adjectives meaning 'good,' 'useful,' 'bad,' and 'useless,' I searched the internet for the phrase *a(n)* _____ *Americanism*, inserting the synonyms into the blank. I'm happy to report that on that particular day the worldwide web knew of 227 *lovely* Americanisms, 73 *apt* ones, and even 5 *elegant* ones. But the top six not-so-flattering adjectives are slightly more numerous. (I've lived in England long enough to have mastered the ironic understatement.)

The internet's top six adjectives
modifying *Americanism*

Flattering		Not-so-flattering	
227	Lovely	Ugly	7,780
231	Nice	Horrible	4,780
100	Useful	Vile	3,610
73	Apt	Awful	1,700
25	Delightful	Dreadful	963
5	Elegant	Nasty	373

That's nearly thirty times as many not-so-flattering adjectives as flattering ones, just looking at the top six. After the top six, the flattering list stops, but the not-so-flattering one goes on. And on.

American English—the language of my childhood, my dear mom and dad, the teachers who introduced me to Shakespeare; the language of *Sesame Street*, Barack Obama, Maya Angelou, and Mark Twain—is Linguistic Public Enemy Number 1 in much of the English-speaking world. So far we've seen it described as a pollution, a disease, a destructive force, an aesthetic horror. The repetition of these refrains in my adopted country makes it difficult for me to maintain a stereotype that Americans hold dear: that the British are a polite and intelligent people.

Is American English really a disease that infects other languages, particularly the mother tongue of England? Or are we seeing the influence of linguistic hypochondriacs, diagnosing idiocy and destruction where there is none? Are Americanisms evil pollutants that disintegrate minds? Or do they inoculate English against a wasting atrophy? The answers to these questions are more complicated than the linguistic Chicken Littles ("The sky is falling! The language is imploding!") are willing to admit.

This book provides an arsenal of facts and an armful of interpretations that, I hope, might heighten our enjoyment of our common language and our pride in it. What if, instead of worrying about the "ruination" of English by young people, jargonistas, or Americans, we celebrated English for being robust enough to allow such growth and variety? What if instead of judging people (including ourselves) on the basis of pronunciation or grammar, we listened to what they had to say and enjoyed how they said it? What if instead of tutting, we marveled? Humor me with that for the length of this book. Then, if you must, you can go back to complaining.

Statements like "British is best" or "American is simpler" are just too glib to do our language justice. The ideas to be pilloried in the following chapters include:

- One kind of English is more pure than another.
- One kind of English is more precise than the other.
- American and British English differences amount to just a few spellings and some funny words.
- British English is older than American English.
- American and British English will soon be indistinguishable.
- English can be hurt by speaking it wrong.

Maybe you hold some of those beliefs. You certainly know people who do. They're harder beliefs to hold once you've looked closely at the full range of linguistic differences and similarities. These differences are superficial and deep, simple and complex, blatant and sneaky: the spelling of *colo(u)r*, the pronunciation of *garage*, the meaning of *frown*, whether you eat *mashed potato* or *mashed potatoes*. They touch on the language's relationships with time, with the landscape, with other languages, and especially with social class and self-image. They raise questions about what we value in our language. Is tradition more important than efficiency? Do we judge good English by what authorities say about it or by how people actually talk? Is it better to have many different ways to "English," or would we be better off with a more uniform language?

I'm not going to try to answer those questions for you. In fact, if I get my way, you may be more unsettled about these issues than when you picked up this book. Whether you value tradition or innovation, efficiency or poeticism, localness or universality, you may find that those things are harder to pin down once you dig deep into the mire that is English.

Anti-Americanism(-ism)

There is no such thing as American English. There is English.
And there are mistakes.

@QueenUK (not Her Majesty)[12]

When it became clear that American independence (on American terms) was inevitable, King George III vowed to "keep the rebels harassed, anxious, and poor, until the day when, by a natural and inevitable process, discontent and disappointment [are] converted into penitence and remorse."[13] But with other colonies to manage and Napoleon coming on the scene, the harassment did not last long. Today, with our bloody tax-and-governance dispute well behind us, the Anglo-American "special relationship" is one of the strongest allegiances in the world. David Cameron and Barack Obama took time in 2012 to write in the *Washington Post*:

> The alliance between the United States and Great Britain is a partnership of the heart, bound by the history, traditions and values we share. But what makes our relationship special—a unique and essential asset—is that we join hands across so many endeavors. Put simply, we count on each other and the world counts on our alliance.[14]

Notably absent from their list of what binds us is language. We can only guess how much Cameron cringed when he saw a *u*-less *endeavor* in a piece he had coauthored. No one is really sure who first quipped that the two countries are "separated by a common language," but our linguistic differences have long been noted and stewed over. In 1756, just after the publication of his great dictionary (but before there was a United States), Samuel Johnson referred to "the trace of corruption" in the language of an American book he reviewed. That he enjoyed the book at all is a testament to its author's skill and elegance, for as a loyal subject of the monarchy Johnson was no fan of the uppity colonists: "Had we treated the Americans as we ought, and as they deserved, we should have at once razed all their towns and let them enjoy their forests."[15]

All its life, the United States has had European naysayers. In the past century, distaste for America and its exports has been couched in terms of resistance to American cultural imperialism. Before that, it was America's radical rejection of the old inheritance-based roots of power that struck fear and disgust in the hearts of many. European anti-Americanism was born out of "astonishment over the new society [...] in which for the first time social stratification had no value," according to Dutch historian Jan Schulte Nordholt. Titles and family connections were much less important in the new country; what mattered was what an individual could achieve and accrue in their lifetime. "Soon one of the fixed stereotypes about America was that everything there was determined by money and everything could be had for a price."[16]

It may be hard for us in individualistic, democratic, western societies of the 21st century to appreciate how unsettling American independence was. These days, we roll our eyes at the Declaration of Independence's contention that "all men are created equal" and point out that its authors kept slaves. But for many 18th-century Europeans, the complete rejection of monarchy, aristocracy, and state religion looked like something very dangerous indeed. How could authority come from the people, when the people might very well have parochial interests, uneven education, and different ideas about God? Many, like Samuel Johnson, thought it ungrateful and unseemly that American colonists protested British laws and taxes, considering that they had benefited from the British crown's protection in disputes with other colonial powers and Native Americans in the New World.

Feelings against America were (and are) in no way limited to British monarchists. Even those who admired the United States' democratic project came to doubt the value of its people and their products. Charles Dickens had hoped to find in America less social stratification than he knew in London. Instead, he found nitwits. "I do not believe there are, on the whole earth besides, so many intensified bores as in these United States."[17] Many have suspected that the immigrants who populated the new country were not the best and the brightest that Europe had to offer, but were instead, as American journalist H. L. Mencken described them, "incompetents who could not get on at home."[18] The immigrant mélange of America could not be trusted to bring refined manners, learned culture, or the best English (among other languages) to the New World.

But those who worry about the déclassé Americans tend to be those who have the most invested in (and the most to gain from) the traditions and language that are associated with the British upper classes. The anti-British-establishment United States, its products, and its ideas were more popular with the commoners-cum-working classes of Europe than with those further up the social ladder. That hasn't really changed. At the close of the 20th century, journalist Alexander Chancellor observed that the British upper class has been "generally more anti-American than the working class because it felt more directly affronted by America's assumption of Britain's former role as a world power."[19]

European distaste for all things American often has an air of befuddled paternalism to it: How can a culture exist without a history? Those from more ancient cultures might look upon the United States as a parent might judge a toddler. The tot might be adorable and precocious in saying his ABCs, but he's still just a child. We're not going to hang his finger paintings alongside the *Mona Lisa*. His ideas and language are limited by the extent of his tiny experience, and so we don't have to take them too seriously. But then reality kicks in: that New World upstart is actually an influential player. And those words he spouts: Are they some kind of stealth weapon against all that is good and true in English?

From anti-Americanism-ism to amerilexicophobia

For shame, Mr Jefferson! [. . .] we will forgive all your attacks, impotent as they are illiberal, upon our national character; but for the future, spare—O spare, we beseech you, our mother-tongue!

European Magazine and London Review (1797)[20]

What crime against English had Thomas Jefferson committed that raised such ire in London literary circles? How did he "perpetually trample upon the very grammar of our language"? He had (it seems) invented the word *belittle*. Jefferson had been incensed by the Count de Buffon's theory that the wildlife and people of the New World (including the transplanted Europeans) could only ever be inferior in size to those of Eurasia, and so he wrote:

So far the Count de Buffon has carried this new theory of the tendency of nature to belittle her productions on this side of the Atlantic.[21]

Belittle, as Jefferson used it, literally meant 'make small.' In the end, Jefferson made a buffoon of Buffon, sending him a moose in order to demonstrate the majesty of North American creatures.[22] The count retracted his anti–New World theory, but the British distaste for the New World word continued for more than a century, with Fowler's *Dictionary of Modern English Usage* (1926) describing *belittle* as an "undesirable alien."

These days, British attitudes towards the US are generally mild and relatively positive (though subject to ups and downs depending on who sits in the White House). In 2014, 66% of Britons claimed to have a "favourable" view of the United States, compared with

51% in Germany, 34% in Greece, and 19% in Turkey.[23] But Britain is the worldwide hub of **anti-Americanism-ism**, prejudice against parts of the English language that are believed to be American. American words stir stronger emotions than linguistic imports from France or India or Germany or Ireland or South Africa or Australia. Call a scarf a *pashmina* and it's fashionable. Call a soup *pho* and it's trendy. Talk about *cupcakes* instead of *fairy cakes* and British folk write letters to the editor. I'm not kidding: one such letter in a food magazine recounted the horror of being thanked for "cup cakes." The cakes were certainly fairy cakes, the letter writer noted, because "I don't like cup cakes." The magazine editors decided that was good enough reasoning to make it Letter of the Month.[24]

Anti-Americanism-ism seems to be out of the reach of liberal tolerance or political correctness. When *Time Out* magazine listed the five worst sounds in London, American accents—"the ear-violating, soul-piercing, knob-shrivelling shrillness of their voices"—came second.[25] Apparently the only sound worse than *me* is the clicking of the mouse that chains you to your desk at work.

Scratch a prejudice and you can usually find a fear, and any psychopathology worth its paragraphs deserves its own pseudo-medical terminology. I could call it *amerilinguophobia*, 'fear of American language,' but that would anger the purists who protest that hybrid words like *tele**vision*** and *auto**mobile*** are cross-bred abominations of *Greek* and **Latin**. I am reminded of a T-shirt that proclaims

Polyamory is wrong!
It is either multiamory or polyphilia
but mixing Greek and Latin roots?
Wrong!

Whether the T-shirt is worn by purists or parodists, I wouldn't want to attract their attention with my miscegenation of *linguo* from the Latin for 'tongue' and *phobia* from the Greek for 'fear.' So let's call it **amerilexicophobia**, 'fear of American words', echoing the Greek *lexikos* 'pertaining to words.' Besides placating the purists, it's probably more accurate. American words are what British language purists talk most about and fear most viscerally. The accents may (now and again) be tolerated, and the grammatical differences may not be noticed, but fear of American words has gripped the arenas of British society where language is discussed.

There is a peculiarly inverse relation between fear of immigrant people and fear of immigrant words. British public attitudes are strongly against immigration these days, with 75% wanting immigration reduced.[26] My eighteen years' expatriation in the UK has been punctuated by cabbies or fellow shoppers or Scrabble opponents expressing their thoughts about immigration:

> **British Near-Stranger:** *Blah blah* immigration laws *blah blah* not right *blah blah* need to protect our jobs and culture *blah blah* Government's not doing enough *blah* . . .
> **Me:** Well, since the laws have let me in, I'm rather grateful for them.
> **BN-S:** Oh, clearly I'm not talking about people like *you*. Americans—you're our cousins.

While the far-right political parties spread fear about Romanians taking British jobs, about twice as many Americans as Romanians live and work in the UK. The most feared immigrants in the UK come from poorer countries and don't speak English at home. These immigrants certainly affect the economy—usually for the better. But their words have little effect on the English language because they are not spoken in English-speaking contexts and because the people speaking them have little power in Britain. Immigrants may bring words for foods (which some Brits will gobble up and others will ignore) and culture-specific traditions, but they do not affect the discourse of the boardroom or the evening news.

The most feared immigrant words are those that are English and particularly those that come from a rich and powerful country through its cultural exports. We American immigrants are not the problem—we learn to say *lift* (US *elevator*) and *aubergine* (US *eggplant*) like the other immigrants. The problem is the Americans in America, building their businesses, writing their books, performing their television shows, making their movies, posting their Facebook updates, fizzing their soft drinks, and exporting all those things to the rest of the world. Amerilexicophobia feeds on the perception that American English, like the country it comes from, is too powerful and *takes over*. It is the fear that one's own culture—the familiar foundations of oneself—is being displaced by language that is both foreign and, in its globalization, more generic. Australianisms and Indianisms don't inspire that kind of fear because they don't have that kind of power. The American role in the globalization of English is disconcerting for the nation that formerly exported the English language. The British Empire practically invented linguistic globalization.

As American English gained its power and worldwide audience, so did amerilexicophobia. It may be no coincidence that campaigns for an English "academy," charged with fixing the language in its most perfect form, came soon after the United States gained its independence. In the early days, new American vocabulary was regarded as a silly (and distasteful) colonial indulgence. Fast-forward to today and the British regularly hear American words in British accents and American voices on radio and television. For sufferers of amerilexicophobia, American English can no longer be dismissed. It is a threat. An invasive species that will choke and supplant the native wordlife.

From amerilexicophobia to amerilexicosis

The British [...] do not want to be happy; they want to be right.

Quentin Crisp

As history has shown again and again, the PREJUDICE + FEAR formula often equals MADNESS. Britain, the land of "Keep Calm and Carry On," reputedly conducts its moral panics with a bit more decorum and perhaps even rationality than the US does. Nevertheless, reason goes out the window when amerilexicophobia takes hold. Anti-Americanism-ism and amerilexicophobia transform into **amerilexicosis**: a pathologically unhinged reaction to American English. The symptoms of amerilexicosis include irritability, obsessive behavior, paranoia, and delusions.

Irritability can be seen in the regular appearance of anti-American-English diatribes in British media, with headlines like "Don't talk garbage!"[27] or the more wordy "For a country bereft of butchers...they've certainly butchered our language."[28] British expressions of irritability about American English are trivially easy to find, so let's turn to the obsessive behavior and paranoia.

The first case study of Amerilexicotic obsession follows from the British Broadcasting Corporation's annual *500 Words* story competition for children. Each year, after the prizes are awarded, the children's stories are added to the Oxford Children's Corpus. A linguistic corpus is a collection of texts of written or spoken language that have been systematically chosen and put into electronic format in order to allow for computer-assisted language analysis. The Oxford Children's Corpus is used to analyze trends in British children's language. The BBC News coverage of trends in the 2012 competition concluded with a heartening observation from competition judge and children's author Andy Stanton:

At a microscopic level, children's use of language is robust and imaginative. They know the value of a well-chosen word and the power of an original image.[29]

How did the BBC News headline writers sum up this message? Like this:

British children "turn to American English"

Just 11% of the article (two sentences; forty-two words) is about American English, and yet nothing *but* American English is mentioned in the headline. The article reassures us that children only use text-speak in stories when the characters are communicating by phone, but does not entertain the possibility that the children's American words were also used in apt and imaginative ways—for instance if Batman is on the *sidewalk* in Gotham City. The article gives other details of the children's stories that are reassuringly British. The most common character names were on-trend British *Lucy* and *Jack*. The story titles mention *Mum* and *poo* and *biscuits* (the kind that Americans would call *cookies*). Granted, one of the featured story titles was "I'm Not a Nerd, I'm a Superhero," but is there a better British word than *nerd* for this context? Couldn't that be a "well-chosen word"? Would British words like *boffin* or *swot* or *anorak* carry all the same connotations?

The phrasing of the headline gives away the horror: British children *turn to* American English. When *turn to* is used to mean 'choose a new direction in life,' the new path is rarely a wholesome one. You do not *turn to* a healthy diet or exercise or a better work-life balance. You (well, I hope not *you*) *turn to* alcohol, drugs, or a life of prostitution. The BBC led its story with insinuations about damage to children's language because they know that panic entices people to read news. Amerilexicosis provides ideal clickbait.

Obsessive paranoia is also seen in the *Telegraph* newspaper's reporting of preliminary findings from the Spoken British National Corpus 2014 (SBNC). This corpus consists of transcribed conversations from around the UK, a parallel to the spoken part of the 1993 British National Corpus (BNC). This pair of databases allows researchers to analyze how spoken British English has changed over the course of twenty years. The *Telegraph* headline and standfirst (= US *subhead*) read:

Cheerio pussy cat, hi there awesome English

Use of "cheerio" dying out as English language becomes more Americanised, with "awesome" gaining ground as the most characteristic emotive word[30]

The article bemoans the facts that *marvellous* is now less common than it was in the 1990s and that *awesome* is more common, giving the impression that *awesome* has forced *marvellous* out. But that's not what happened. By the time the 1993 corpus was collected, *marvellous* had largely been replaced by the also-characteristically British *brilliant*. The people who were still saying *marvellous* in 1993 were already quite old and by 2014 they were well on their way to extinction. Maybe the fading of *marvellous* is sad, but it is also completely expected, since evaluative words like these come and go generation by generation. By 2040, *awesome* will probably sound as dated as *groovy* sounds now.

Similarly, *cheerio* (which only came into the language around 1910)[31] did not die out because it was replaced by an Americanism. It was an informal term, mostly used by what are now very old people. Even in the 1993 corpus, only 190 instances of *cheerio* occur, compared to 1,775 variations of *goodbye* (*bye, bye-bye,* etc.). No Americanism has replaced *cheerio*, but that didn't keep the newspapers from linking the demise of *cheerio* to the rise of

Americanisms, again feeding the madness about Americanisms in British English.

Cambridge University's press release about the new corpus (largely reproduced in the *Telegraph* article) includes a table of words that distinguish the 1993 corpus from the 2014 edition:[32]

Typical of 1990s	Typical of 2010s
Fortnight	*Facebook*
Marvellous	*Internet*
Fetch	*Website*
Walkman	*Awesome*
Poll	*Email*
Catalogue	*Google*
Pussycat	*Smartphone*
Marmalade	*iPhone*
Drawers	*Essentially*
Cheerio	*Treadmill*

The table demonstrates not so much the effect of American English, but the effect of technological and lifestyle changes on the language. British *catalogue* has not lost ground to American *catalog*; it's the catalogues themselves that have been edged out by online databases and internet shopping. (*Chests of*) *drawers* have been replaced not by American *dressers*, but by IKEA wardrobes. (And where British folk do write about *drawers*, it's increasingly spelled *draws*.)[33] Only 18% of 16- to 24-year-olds eat marmalade (compared with 55% of their grandparents), while consumption of Nutella (not American) and peanut butter (OK, American) rises.[34] *Get* may be more common now than *fetch*, but *get* has been a British word since the Vikings brought it to England in the 12th century. Similarly, it requires a logical leap to claim that loss of the very British *fortnight* (derived from *fourteen + night*) is due to replacement by an Americanism. *Two weeks* is not an Americanism—it's just a longer way to say *fortnight* in English. It could be seen as part of a drift towards more wordy but transparent phrasings, like when *fortnight's* pal *sennight* (from *seven + night*) was replaced by *one week*. Facebook and iPhones are certainly American inventions, but *Facebook* and *iPhone* are the names of those things, not just the American names of those things. They do not threaten British English; they add to the number of things that British English speakers can talk about.

Distressingly, amerilexicotics can develop a more serious symptom: **delusions of America**. Consider this 2010 headline, also from the *Telegraph*:[35]

BBC criticised for creeping "Americanisms"

The article starts, "Radio listeners have noticed slang terms more commonly heard on the other side of the Atlantic creeping into common usage on BBC shows," and ends with:

A list of Americanisms
that have annoyed BBC listeners

Fess up instead of *confess*

The Americanisation of dates—*July the fifth* is now *July fifth* or *January the fifth* becomes *January five*

Take a look instead of *have a look*

Ahead of instead of *before*

Face up instead of *confront*

It's a big ask

It might of been instead of *It might have been*

An inconvenient fact about this list of Americanisms is that half the items are simply not Americanisms. The *Telegraph* got the country right for *fess up, July fifth, take a look,* and *ahead of.* But *face up* (*to*) has meant 'confront' since English author Daniel Defoe first used it in 1720. *It's a big ask* is an Australianism that's made its way north. Ten years ago I first heard that expression from an Englishwoman. I assumed it was British—until I got home and looked it up. But at least I looked it up. Unlike the folks complaining about "Americanisms."

The other two are a mystery. They are allegedly complaints about radio speech, but they are not spoken forms. While Americans might write a date as *January 5,* they do not say that things happened on "January five," but on *January 5th.* If BBC radio staff are reading it as *January 5,* they did not get the habit from America. *Might of* is a misspelling of the spoken form *might've*—an understandable mistake because they sound much the same. How did the listening public manage to discern that the radio presenters were *misspelling* the contraction that they were speaking? Even if the presenters did say *might of,* you cannot (with any knowledge or conscience) call the mistake an Americanism—as chapter 2 demonstrates.

Now, it is one thing that the British radio-listening public made some mistakes about American English, but it's another that a newspaper of repute reported them as facts without checking. While there are scare quotes around *Americanisms* in the headline, the article is not shy about accepting and promoting the view that the eight items *are* Americanisms. That is not just over-emphasizing the number of Americanisms in British English; it's hallucinating them.

The *Telegraph* article is not a one-off. The online *BBC Magazine* took suggestions from their readers for an article titled "50 of your most noted Americanisms."[36] This was reliably cited elsewhere on the internet as "50 of your most *hated* Americanisms." Half an hour with the *Oxford English Dictionary* will tell you: about a fifth of these were originally British.[37]

American Verbal Inferiority Complex

> The first step of an American entering upon a literary career was
> to pretend to be an Englishman, in order that he might win the
> approval, not of Englishmen, but of his own countrymen.
>
> Henry Cabot Lodge (1883)

While the British may suffer hypersensitivity, paranoia, and delusion when it comes to American English, American attitudes toward their own language are not much healthier. Many Americans suffer from American Verbal Inferiority Complex, or AVIC: a neurotic sense of low linguistic self-esteem, characterized by lack of linguistic self-worth and sometimes crippling verbal self-doubt.

This may be hard to believe. After all, inflated self-esteem has reputedly reached epidemic proportions in the United States. In fact, one study found that people from the UK think Americans have gone so far down the path of self-regard that we *all* meet the diagnostic criteria for Narcissistic Personality Disorder (though in reality the disorder has a low rate of occurrence in the US).[38] The United States would not exist if the colonists hadn't had the self-confidence to form a new nation, and American English wouldn't be what it is if Americans hadn't had the nerve to abandon older forms and make new ones.

In the early days of the country, commentators from both sides of the Atlantic felt that, give or take some rogue words, Americans on the whole spoke better English than the English. They were impressed that "the vulgar in America" could speak "much better than the vulgar in England."[39] But despite such adulation and the American veneer of confidence, the seeds of self-doubt were sprouting. Many learned Americans criticized the new American English dictionaries of the early 19th century, expressing horror at the "hurtful innovations" and "justification of the vulgar."[40]

Nowadays, pride in American English seems to have gone the same way as our pride in being a monarchy-free republic. The American public enthusiastically consumes news about every British royal birth, wedding, or death and fetishizes the *u* in *colour* as if it hadn't deserved the drubbing our ancestors gave it.

The gaps in American linguistic self-worth crop up in many little ways. "Everything sounds better in a British accent," they say. (In fact, you can buy several styles of T-shirt that say it.) Well-educated Americans are particularly susceptible to the belief that their American English is somehow wanting. A medical doctor writes on his blog that British *nappy* (derived from baby-talk for *napkin*) sounds "so much more civilized tha[n] *diaper*."[41] An American lawyer can't interact with an Englishwoman because her speech makes him feel embarrassed about his English ("I really tried to speak well, but I felt so inferior").[42] American professors note that their students write *whilst* (instead of *while*) and *grey* (instead of *gray*) in their essays, thinking these Britishisms will make them sound more intelligent.[43] Even I have to admit the satisfaction I feel (or is it *relief?*) when Britons compliment me on having a "soft" accent that isn't "too American."

Part of the reason that Americans associate Britishness with good English is that Americans tend to automatically associate Britishness with the English upper classes, with their private educations and distinct enunciation.[44] The American Anglophile hones their interests in manor houses, boarding schools, and the royal family. British television programs about the upper classes are broadcast on American public television in the *Masterpiece* and *Masterpiece Mystery* series. Meanwhile, British comedies and dramas about the working classes are either ignored in America or remade with American casts and locales; for example *Till Death Do Us Part* became *All in the Family, Steptoe and Son* became *Sanford and Son*, and *Shameless* was moved from Manchester to Chicago. Aspirational American audiences want to hear the accents of

English people they can admire. They're not really interested in identifying with struggling English folk.

AVIC is why Americans generally think people with English accents are more intelligent than themselves (and often, more intelligent than the English person actually is). It's why American critic Aristides thought that "a good English accent can still be worth an additional ten to thirty thousand dollars in annual academic salary."[45] It's why English people living in the US report "torn-up parking tickets, free subway rides, increased job opportunities, and better luck in singles bars"[46] on account of their accents. *"Visit a place* WHERE YOUR *accent* IS AN APHRODISIAC" is how the Las Vegas tourist board courts passengers of the London Underground.[47] AVIC is why Americans perceive Britain-related baby names as sounding the "smartest" and the "most sophisticated."[48] It's why many Americans will believe anything a Brit tells them about how the language should be.

A case in point: Lynne Truss's punctuation book *Eats, Shoots and Leaves* sold over 1.6 million copies in the US,[49] despite the fact that it promotes rules that contradict mainstream American punctuation style. A review in *The New Yorker* complained:

> The supreme peculiarity of this peculiar publishing phenomenon is that the British are less rigid about punctuation and related matters [. . .] than Americans are. An Englishwoman lecturing Americans on semicolons is a little like an American lecturing the French on sauces.[50]

So why do Americans buy the book? Well, besides the cute title and the engaging writing, Americans are fairly ignorant about the extent of American–British punctuation differences, while being fairly eager to defer to the English on linguistic and literary manners. In the US, being or sounding English gives one (to use a sociologist's term) "cultural capital," allowing upward social mobility regardless of financial means. It is therefore in English (and sometimes more generally British) people's interest to provoke American verbal insecurity by declaring the inferiority of American English. The American and British language neuroses feed each other.

Though Americans show classic symptoms of a verbal inferiority complex, some of the symptoms are found in anyone who is overly conscious of "correct" versus "incorrect" language. In America (or anywhere for that matter), inferiority-fueled linguistic overcompensation is often the source of hypercorrection, that is, applying rules where they shouldn't be applied—like saying *between you and I* instead of the traditionally correct *between you and me*. Insecurity may also fuel the American love for hard and fast rules about language, which has played a role in differentiating American English from British. Self-doubt can be a powerful motivator.

How to "save" English?

No one who has once taken the language under his care can ever again be really happy. That way misery lies.

Thomas Lounsbury,
The Standard of Usage in English (1908)

When sociolinguists study language attitudes—why people look down on some languages and dialects but value others—they generally come to the same conclusion: distaste or admiration for a particular way of speaking is just thinly cloaked distaste or admiration for the people who speak that way. Which accents sound sexy is pretty well correlated with which people are considered sexy even when their mouths are shut. While French accents used to dominate the "sexy accent" league table, Irish accents have now taken over in many surveys. Why? Because there are more good-looking Irish movie stars than there used to be. We like the people, and then the accent gets associated with things we like about those people. For American and British Englishes, stereotypes abound about intelligence, sincerity, refinement, sexiness, masculinity, and so forth. People link those stereotypes to how we speak. In this book, I'm saying: If you want to stereotype other people as intelligent, sexy, crass, or limp, I can't stop you. But leave English out of it. The language itself—in any of its forms—deserves better.

Complaining (just a little) about Americans like me complaining about English people complaining about American English, Giles Harvey wrote for *The New Yorker*:

> What most of these commentators fail to recognize, in any case, is that English people *enjoy* complaining about things, and that the content of any particular English person's complaint is rarely anything more than a pretext for the act of complaining. From Mr. Woodhouse to Basil Fawlty, *complaining about things*—the weather, the food, the trains—is what the English have always done best, and with the greatest eloquence and esprit.[51]

True enough. But if you're going to complain, I say: at least get your facts straight. If, on top of that, you can manage to avoid hypocrisy, all the better.

A few words about words

There even are places where English completely disappears
In America they haven't used it for years.
"Henry Higgins" in My Fair Lady[52]

I can't write about *American English* and *British English* without saying something about that choice of terminology. A famous quip holds that a language is a dialect with an army and a navy. On that basis, *American* should be a separate language from *English*. Not only do the two countries have separate armed forces, they've fought wars against each other. Still, though people first used *American* as a language name in the 18th century, it hasn't stuck. When former vice-presidential candidate Sarah Palin opined that immigrants should "speak American," it was seen by some commentators as an explanation for Palin's frequent incomprehensible utterances: she isn't speaking English after all; she's speaking *American*, a language that doesn't exist.[53] While some serious American linguistic commentators, like Noah Webster and H. L. Mencken, have written about *the American language*, they don't deny that it is English, and neither shall I.

So are American English and British English *dialects* of English? Well, yes, but I want to reserve the word *dialect* for the regional forms of the language *within* each country. So I have squashed together *national* and *dialects* to form **nationlects**, my own special term for what American English and British English (and South African English and so forth) are. Talking about nationlects is inherently oversimplifying. The English of either nation includes a range of regional dialects and other sociolects—forms of the language associated with particular social groups, such as African-American English in the US. In many cases here, I will be talking about the "standard" languages of the two places—the type of thing you find in dictionaries, classrooms, and news broadcasts. But those "standards" overlap and interact with the full variety of ways of speaking in the two countries. Words or pronunciations labeled *American English* may be original or particular to the US, but it doesn't mean that everyone in America says it that way. The same goes for *British English*.

Further problems for the term *American English* come from *American* as a descriptor. Most American-English speakers are happy calling themselves *Americans*. Still, complaints can be heard that using *American* to mean 'from the United States' is "arrogant" because there are other Americans than the ones who are in the US. That argument ignores the fact that many words are ambiguous, including many names. Arrogance doesn't come into it. Sometimes *New Yorkers* means people from the city; sometimes it means people, like me, from the state. Same with *American*. Sometimes it refers specifically to things associated with the United States of America, and sometimes it refers more generally to people and things associated with all of North and South America. It actually doesn't do the second job very often in English (it's a different matter in the languages of other former colonial powers),[54] and so I'm not going to let the potential ambiguity bother me. I hope it won't bother you. Some of the "American English" discussed in this book may well be found in other Englishes (especially Canadian), but my focus stays on the US.

The term *British English* is even worse, because *British* is both ambiguous and frequently misinterpreted.

Great Britain is an island, but not a country, and so *British* can refer to the people, places, and things of that island, be they English, Scottish, or Welsh. But the three nations of that island belong to a bigger country: the United Kingdom of Great Britain and Northern Ireland. Because *United Kingdom* does not have an adjective form, *British* does that job too. The result is that people from Northern Ireland hold British passports, even though they don't live in Britain and are not *British* in the 'island' sense of the term. (*British* can also refer to the British Isles, which includes the Republic of Ireland. This usage is not too popular with the Irish.) When I write about *British English*, I lean toward the 'island' interpretation of *British*, rather than the 'UKish' interpretation. Still, many things I say about British English may also be true of the English of the full United Kingdom, and some of those things will also be true of other Englishes, especially those in former British colonies.

Perhaps the biggest problem for the term *British English* is the tendency to associate *British* with England alone, or more particularly with certain linguistic properties of the southeast of England and the **Received Pronunciation** (**RP**) used by the elite (and the go-to accent of Hollywood villains).[55] Since the discussion here often focuses on the "standard" language, *British English* does often skew to England in this book. So, if 'the English of England' is what people tend to imagine when they hear the term *British English*, why not say *English English* instead? I have three reasons for refusing:

1. Vocabulary, grammar, and spelling are major points of discussion in this book, and in these cases we can mostly generalize across the whole of Britain. It's British English, not just English English, to talk of *motorways* (US *highways*) and *car boots* (US *car trunks*) and to spell *tyre* (on a car) and *calibre* (US *caliber*). Pronunciation has more variation, and so I try to be more precise when talking about accents.

2. *English English* gives the false impression that the English of England is one thing that is uniformly different from the Englishes of Scotland and Wales. But the Englishes of East London youth and Newcastle pensioners might well have less in common than the Englishes of the Queen and the leader of the Scottish parliament.

3. Lastly, and importantly, the doubling of the word *English* implies something that I don't want to imply.

I need to elaborate on that last point. Consider phrases like:

> *I didn't want a potato salad. I wanted a* salad-*salad*.
> *I'm a doctor, but not a* doctor-*doctor*.

We linguists call that kind of thing **contrastive focus reduplication**: repetition of a word or phrase to emphasize that you're using the word to refer to something specific and special. When we hear *salad-salad*, we assume that the salad orderer wanted a green salad, because we think of green salads as the best example of a salad, a "real" salad. A *doctor-doctor* isn't a PhD in linguistics, but someone who practices medicine. That's both the more usual way to use the word *doctor* and (for many people) the more respectable kind of doctor to be. And so, even if we don't intend to use *English English* to mean "real English" or "the best English," that impression is bound to leak through. The assumption that the English of England is "real English" is exactly the assumption that this book challenges. So we can't be having any of that. *British English* it is.

Now we come to the sensitive matter of who goes first. Should I write *American and British* or *British and American*? *UK and US* or *US and UK*? Sometimes the meaning of the sentence demands a certain order. But where the order doesn't matter, I use one order per chapter, and then reverse the order in the next chapter. Given my great respect for the alphabet, this first chapter has favored *American* and the next favors *British*.

Finally, which English is this book written in? The spelling and punctuation choices I've left to the copy editors; the American edition should follow American conventions and the British edition should follow the British way. The vocabulary and phrasing I can only describe as LynneMurphyish. My English got its start in the northeastern United States, but I've now lived over a third of my life in England (and a bit less than 10% of it in South Africa). My language is a **hodge-podge** (if I'm feeling American) or a **hotch-potch** (if I'm feeling British). While writing this book, I've kept a list of Americanisms and Britishisms that I've noticed myself using, which can be found at http://theprodigaltongue.com. If you notice others, you can let me know there.

2

THE WRONG END OF THE BUMBERSHOOT: STEREOTYPES AND GETTING THINGS WRONG

The present Earl of Marchmont [. . .] told me with great good humour that the master of a shop in London, where he was not known, said to him "I suppose, Sir, you are an American." "Why so, Sir?" (said his Lordship.) "Because, Sir, (replied the shopkeeper,) you speak neither English nor Scotch, but something different from both, which I conclude is the language of America."

James Boswell, *The Life of Samuel Johnson* (1772)

In 1987, British magazine *The Spectator* set a competition for its readers "to invent an exchange of letters between a Briton and an American in which the difference between the writers' mode of expression and meaning is excruciating and/or crucial."[1] The results disappointed the competition master:

I had hoped that the dividing nature of our common language would have given rise to a wealth of Anglo-American contrast and comedy, but the entries were few and there was a tired reliance on the half a dozen well-known words which can cause embarrassing confusion.

I know the feeling. How many times have I been told the story of someone's British auntie surprising American men with the request to *knock me up in the morning*? Possibly more times than there are actual aunties in Britain wanting to be woken up (and not wanting to be impregnated). If I had a penny for every time someone tried to explain to me why *fanny pack* is funny in England (because *fanny* refers to the vulva, not the derriere), I'd have enough money to buy top-grade earplugs and avoid hearing these tired examples of miscommunication again.

Perhaps the competition failed because people are just not very good at knowing what's British and what's American. Several dictionaries of British and American English are open in front of me. According to one, *stump orator* is a Britishism and Americans ask the time with *What time have you?*[2] According to another, *PIN number* is a Britishism, *kooky* is an Americanism, and *bookstall* is British for 'newsstand.' You may have guessed that I'm mentioning these because they're wrong—or at the very least, not entirely right. One of these books, *Understanding British English*, was written by an American whose claim to expertise was that she enjoyed British and Australian novels and had had two vacations (or, to be British, *holidays*) in England.[3] And so it includes Australianisms, expressions she may have heard one English person say once (but that no other English person has said before or since), and general English words that apparently hadn't been part of her vocabulary. Nevertheless, this book was successful enough to go through two editions. I am reminded of linguist Morris Halle's observation that "linguistics does have one thing in common with prostitution. In neither field can the professional hope to compete with the amateur."[4]

It's not uncommon for British or American people to report that they "know" the other English because they watch a lot of television or read a lot of books from the other country. That's the kind of blissful confidence about language knowledge that can only come from relative ignorance. Having lived with British English for nearly twenty years, I've had to grow a certain humility about the differences even as I grow more competent in identifying them, since I still have the daily privilege of discovering ever more. The overconfidence even affects the "experts." A recent academic study (by data analysts in Spain and the US) purported to demonstrate the "Americanization" of British English.[5] It looked at whether British people were writing "Americanisms" like *bell pepper* instead of "Britishisms" like *capsicum*. British readers will notice the problem right away: *capsicum* is Australian English. The British usually just call it a *pepper—sweet pepper* if they really need to distinguish it from a chilli. This glaring error (and many more minor discrepancies) did not discourage UK newspapers from running favorable "told you so!" stories about the study's findings of "Americanization."

So if published "experts" can't get things right, what chance do you have? When I talk about these issues in British schools and pubs I quiz the audiences on how well they can identify Britishisms and Americanisms. You can find those quizzes (and their answers) starting on page 345. (If you take the quizzes after reading the rest of the book, you'll have a much better score. If you take them now, I'll admire your courage.) The quizzes tend to demonstrate that our knowledge is lopsided. Words that we don't use are recognized as "foreign," but it's harder to know which of our "normal" words are strange for others.

But when you're talking with people from other places, you cannot second-guess every noun and verb you utter. You just talk and hope for the best. If others understand you, it might be because they know the same words and use them in the same way. Or they might understand you in spite of the linguistic differences. Or they might *believe* they got your meaning, when in reality they got a different one. You may never know what you communicated to them or how. For years after the Kinks released the song "Come Dancing," my teenage American friends and I thought that the line "Now she's married and lives on an **estate**" meant that the woman had married a rich man and lived in a manor house. That's not how British listeners (or the British band) would understand it. The song was saying that she lived in a housing development—an area where all the residences were built at the same time. More particularly, the Kinks' *estate* is probably short for **council estate**—the kind of government-owned housing that Americans might call **the projects**. My friends and I had "understood" the words, but hadn't understood the use to which songwriter Ray Davies had put them.

The dictionaries of British–American differences are not perfect, but the press coverage of the differences tends to be downright bad. In response, I have devised **Lynneguist's Law** (a corollary of my namesake Murphy's Law):[6]

Lynneguist's Law:

Any list of more than seven "Americanisms"
or "Britishisms" [not compiled by a trained
lexicographer] will contain nonsense.

Lynneguist's Law applies to the British–American dictionaries described above and especially to lists of "Britishisms" and "Americanisms" presented in the media. The errors are of various types. Sometimes the meaning is wrong, like when an American *Vogue* article claimed that **cheerio** is a British greeting.[7] Sometimes the lists mistake a regionalism for a "nationalism," like when a British newspaper lists "the" American pronunciation of **nuclear** as "nookyooler." (Not for me, it isn't.)

Sometimes they get a bit muddled by a complicated situation. For instance in the *BBC Magazine* list of "50 of your most noted Americanisms," an Ohio-based Englishman named Alastair contributed **eaterie**. (He didn't just note the word, he abhorred it.) I have searched the restaurant listings of Ohio and I have yet to find an *eaterie*. But this is not surprising, since the Frenchified spelling *eaterie* is the preferred British spelling of American **eatery**.[8] *Eaterie* has lived in British English at least since P. G. Wodehouse's Jeeves and Wooster characters were saying it in the 1920s, but it doesn't really exist in American. Poor Alastair doesn't know which English he's coming or going from. Neither does the *Vogue* journalist who thought *cheerio* meant 'hello.' Her "American" translation of the British word **off-licence** (which she or her editor spelled as *off-license* with an American *s*) is *liquor shop*—an odd hybrid of American **liquor store** with the more British word **shop**. (As it happens, *liquor shop* is what off-licences are called in India.)

The British media's error rate in lists of Americanisms runs somewhere between 20 and 50%, by my count. This list of pronunciations from the *Daily Mail* is a good case study:[9]

You say lootenant, we say leftenant . . .
two nations divided by a common language

	ENGLISH	AMERICAN
Advertisement	*Advertissment*	*Advertizement*
Lieutenant	*Leftenant*	*Lootenant*
Patriot	*Patriot*	*Paytriot*
Schedule	*Sheduel*	*Skedule*
Premiere	*Premiair*	*Premir*
Monarch	*Monak*	*Monark*
Era	*Eera*	*Error*
Bouquet	*Bookay*	*Bokay*
Neither	*Nyther*	*Neether*
Glacier	*Glassiar*	*Glaysiar*
Zebra	*Zehbra*	*Zeebra*
Semi	*Semee*	*Semai*
Buoy	*Boy*	*Bui*
Nuclear	*Newclear*	*Nukilar*
Garage	*Garaj*	*Garidj*

32

	ENGLISH	AMERICAN
The letter Z	Zed	Zee
Iraq	Irak	Eyerak
Lasso	Lasu	Laysoo
Vase	Varze	Vayze
Research	Risearch	Reesearch

The *Mail*'s attempts at phonetic transcription are inconsistent and incompetent at every level. Even taking a very generous reading of these fantastical sound-spellings, the list of twenty items includes six "American" pronunciations that have never come out of my American mouth, including the older "boo-ey" pronunciation for *buoy*. (I may be in an American minority on that one, though.) Some are just weird mistakes. Most Americans pronounce **vase** with an [s] sound, not the [z] that the *Mail* gives. In the case of **lasso**, it looks like the author vaguely remembered that Americans use a different vowel than Brits do—but then they just guessed at which of the two vowels it is. Some Americans pronounce the second vowel to rhyme with *too* and others pronounce it with a more Spanish-like *o*. But no one who knows the word pronounces the first syllable as *lay*.

In other cases, where two pronunciations exist, the *Daily Mail* assumes that the pronunciation that diverges most from standard British is standard American. Is the *Mail* being disingenuous when they claim that "Irak" is the British pronunciation of **Iraq** and the American pronunciation is "Eyerak"? Apparently they've never heard Barack Obama or Bill or Hillary Clinton say *Iraq*. (Maybe *eyerack*-sayers George W. Bush and Sarah Palin are more the *Daily Mail*'s style.) No matter how few or many Americans say "Eyerak" or "nukilar" (another of the *Mail*'s odd phonetic spellings), the *Mail* is willing to paint all Americans with that phonetic brush. And then there's that *garage* pronunciation. We'll come back to *garage*.

33

If an American newspaper were to attempt an equivalent list for British English, it might claim that "bovva" is how the British say *bother* or that the British stress the first syllable of *contribute* rather than the second (some do, some don't). I have to rely on a hypothetical list here because American media lists of UK–US differences rarely focus on pronunciation. Americans want to know about funny British words and phrases they can enjoy or puzzle at. These are supplied with titles like "17 British phrases Americans should start using" or "British phrases that baffle Americans." Tellingly, the "must start using" headlines tend to be presented on American news sites, and the "baffle" ones tend to be on British sites aimed at Americans. The American headlines encourage linguistic togetherness; the British ones hold American English at arm's length.

In contrast, British lists of Americanisms often have titles like "41 Things Americans Say Wrong" and include vocabulary, grammar, and pronunciation differences.[10] The greater British interest in (or horror of) pronunciations stems from the fact that most British people hear a fair amount of American English and therefore get the chance to notice the more obscure pronunciation differences. But not only is there greater opportunity to notice the differences, there's a greater *disposition* to notice. The British are conditioned to notice when others don't talk like they do because accent is an inescapable marker of social position in Britain. This fact inspired George Bernard Shaw's observation: "It is impossible for an Englishman to open his mouth without making some other Englishman hate or despise him."[11] Americans, on the other hand, are often a bit accent-deaf.

Lynneguist's Law applies equally to discussions of pronunciation, vocabulary, and usage. It sums up a symptom of our mental limitations: our minds work against us when we try to think about our own language. The limitations are for a good cause; if we didn't limit *something* in the very complicated processes of speaking, listening, reading, and writing, we'd not be able to speak fluently or to instantaneously comprehend what we hear. In the process of understanding speech, too much information is coming in too fast. As you listen to it, you hold the last few words you've heard in a "memory buffer." Once you can identify a likely meaning for that bit of the utterance, that meaning moves to longer-term memory storage and the buffer is cleared. The words aren't stored in your memory, but their significance is stored. This is why you might be able to remember the facts and the tone of what I wrote on the last page, but you can't recite the page. Occasionally, the phrasing itself will stick in your memory, but that's only when the phrasing is somehow memorable—for instance, because it was repeated a lot, because it was exquisitely beautiful, or because it made you scratch your head. Even in those cases, most people *believe* they remember the exact phrasing better than they actually remember it.

Since we don't store verbatim copies of conversations or paragraphs in our heads, when we "remember" something we've heard or read, we are really reconstructing it. And we're rubbish at reconstructing. One study of memory for "earwitness" testimony found that people could recall a tiny bit of a conversation immediately after hearing it, but by four days later they could not re-create the wording at all. In trying to recall the conversation they'd heard, people sometimes added information that hadn't been there in the first place. For instance, when trying to reconstruct a conversation about a crime, some remembered mention of money, even though nothing about money had been said. They "remembered" it because they used a stereotype about crime: that money often motivates misdeeds. In our case of recalling facts about British or American language, a listener may "remember" hearing words that they didn't hear or they may forget ones that they did hear. We do this because we are trying to make the memory accord with our beliefs about the other country or the other English.

I'm reminded of a forensic science lecture I attended in 2016. In the course of describing how a murder scene is investigated, a major crimes investigator from the Sussex Police paused to mention that he uses the word *homicide* not because he wants to be "trendy and American," but because that's the correct legal term that he has to use. It's only a murder when there is intention to kill, and police investigators must not prematurely conclude that such an intention existed. When I commented afterwards that that was an odd thing to say—of course *homicide* is not a borrowing from American English—two English people insisted to me that they had *only ever* heard that word in an American accent. And yet the Metropolitan Police in London have a **Homicide** and Major Crimes unit. They charge people with crimes under the **Homicide** Act of 1957. These English folk had probably heard the word in one or more British accents just a couple of weeks before our conversation, when the government released its annual **homicide** statistics and the various media outlets reported them, with headlines like "Homicides in England and Wales up 14%."[12] Contrary to my conversation partners' beliefs, the UK police have not come to say *homicide* after watching too many episodes of *Law & Order*. (It may feel like it's been on since 1957, but it hasn't.) *Homicide* is not the most common word for killing, but it's one that's used in any English.

Our beliefs about language (and about people) are steeped in **cognitive biases**—error-ridden ways of thinking that rely on bad assumptions and poor reasoning. Cognitive biases are the reason linguists like me work hard to find concrete evidence about the whats, whos, hows, whens, wheres, and whys of language. We know it's unwise to rely on our intuition or memory about how English is (or has been) because those memories are filtered through many layers of selective attention.

A basic cognitive bias that interferes with our observational powers is the **novelty bias**: we tend to notice things that are unusual or new; familiar things go unnoticed. If someone says something in an "unusual" way, it makes an impression. I have to imagine this is why British commentator Simon Heffer proclaims, in two books, that Americans prefer the word **repetitious** over **repetitive**—even though *repetitive* is around nine times more common in American text.[13] Linguistic oddities stand out and linguistic similarities don't stick with us, and so people deceive themselves into conclusions like "I've only ever heard *homicide* in an American accent" or "Americans don't say *repetitive*."

Those conclusions are also helped along by **confirmation bias**: the tendency to notice things that help support our preconceptions about a situation. People who think Americans are overly fond of technical terms instead of plain language are more likely to notice Americans saying *homicide* than Americans saying *murder* or than Britons saying *homicide*. People who think Americans "mangle" the language are more likely to notice it when Americans use **real** in place of the adverb *really*, as in **real good**—and to not notice that Brits also use adjective forms in adverb places, as in **dead good** and **proper drunk**. And Americans who think the British are adorably quaint will notice the **cheerio**s and **toodle-pip**s, while the much more frequent **goodbye**s fade into the background.

A related cognitive bias means that we tend to stereotype members of groups we don't belong to, but we see the individuality of people in our own group. This is called the **out-group homogeneity effect**.[14] Just as you are much more likely to hear an exasperated woman say, "Men! They're all the same!" than to hear an exasperated man say, "Men! We're all the same!" it's hard for Americans to think of themselves as "all the same," but easier for them to make generalizations like "The British are so polite."

Along these lines, not one but two British comedians—David Mitchell and John Cleese—have released online video rants instructing Americans that they are wrong in saying **I could care less** rather than **I couldn't care less**.[15] Why "Americans"? Some

Americans use *could care less*, but many don't—especially not in writing. There are more instances of *couldn't care less* in the Corpus of Contemporary American English than *could care less*, at a ratio of about 3:2. (Furthermore, *I couldn't care less* is originally an Americanism—so why should British comedians be the lords of how to say it?) I'm sure hearing *I could care less* strikes Cleese and Mitchell as sharply as it strikes me when I hear English people say *me mother* to mean *my mother*. But if I asked them, "Why do Brits always say *me mother*?" I'm sure they'd answer that only some people do this, and those people probably don't even do it all the time.[16] Well, right back at ya, comedians.

On top of being bad at identifying Britishisms and Americanisms, people are bad at talking about the nationlects. The word *slang* comes up constantly and inappropriately when discussing "the other English," as when Lifehack.org suggested "30 Awesome British Slang Terms You Should Start Using Immediately."[17] These "slang" terms included *fortnight* ('two weeks') and *car park* (= US *parking lot*). From the other end, we have examples like British singer-songwriter Lotte Mullan saying that even though she sings "American roots music," she won't use "American slang like *sidewalk*."[18]

Slang offers informal alternatives to the "normal" ways of expressing ideas. It only suits very casual contexts, and much slang is used only by the young. But *fortnight* and *car park* are the normal ways to express those ideas in Britain, as *sidewalk* is in the US. They might feel like slang to people from other places who have other, "normal" words for those things. If Americans were to start saying *fortnight*, it might feel like slang to them because they'd see it as a new, alternative phrasing. But it's not slang in Britain, so it is wrong to call it *British slang*. While I'm sure that Mullan and the writers at Lifehack didn't intend to demean the other English with their use of the word *slang*, they kind of did. Calling other people's normal language *slang* implies that their words are not proper, serious words. Those kinds of implications come through clearly in some of our stereotypes of each other's speech.

Silly, adorable, eccentric British

Me: Hi

English person: You mean you don't have SNELLYDORF HUFFLEDAMS? WHERE DO YOU PUT YOUR BROOKENSHIRES?

Me: Aight man have a good day

@minfiliawarde[19]

Since 2011, University of Delaware Professor Ben Yagoda has been writing *Not One-Off Britishisms*,[20] a blog that tracks British turns of phrase that are infiltrating American media. (*One-off* is one of those Britishisms.) Reflecting on his role as a one-man linguistic border patrol, Yagoda wrote a piece for the online magazine *Slate*,[21] wondering:

Why have we adopted **laddish** while we didn't adopt **telly** or **bumbershoot**?

Yagoda immediately faced a comment storm from Britons asking, "What on earth is a bumbershoot?" Why indeed would British people know **bumbershoot**, an early 20th-century American slang term meaning 'umbrella'? Yet in the collective American imagination, *bumbershoot* has become British. You might recall hearing it, minus the last consonant, in the Morris-dancing scene in *Chitty Chitty Bang Bang*, set in Edwardian England:

you can have me hat or me bumbershoo,
but you'd better never bother with me ol' bamboo.[22]

Morris dancing may be an English folk tradition, but the song-writers were American and so was the *bumbershoo*. Similarly, the American writers of the sitcom *Frasier* had their English character Daphne endorse the British *bumbershoot* myth:

Niles: Take my bumbershoot.
Daphne: Oh, isn't that nice, well at least someone appreciates my
   mother tongue.[23]

Investigating why Americans associate the Americanism *bumbershoot* with Britishness, Yagoda traced the misapprehension as far back as 1939, when the word was only a few decades old.[24] The *New York Times* had noted that umbrellas were key elements in caricaturing the British prime minister: "Mr. Chamberlain's 'bumbershoot' provides inspiration for British and American cartoonists," they wrote. Putting *bumbershoot* in quotation marks hinted to the reader that it might be Chamberlain's word. Soon *bumbershoot* was a fixture in descriptions of the British. As the 1940 book *War and Propaganda* noted: "To many upper-class Americans there was nothing so thrilling as having an Englishman around the house, complete with Oxford accent, school tie, and bumbershoot."[25]

Why did Americans get the wrong end of the *bumbershoot*? It probably helped that umbrella-carrying is a stereotypical British activity—so much so that British English *does* have a slang term for 'umbrella': **brolly**. But a crucial factor in the faux Britishness of *bumbershoot* is another American stereotype of British English: that it is full of preposterous words. American humorist Dave Barry sets the scene with this tale of touring London:

Often, when [Londoners] get to the crucial part of a sentence, they'll realize that they don't know the correct words, so they'll just make some silly ones up. I had a lot of conversations that sounded like this:

Me: Excuse me. Could you tell us how to get to Buckingham Palace?

British person: Right. You go down this street here, then you nip up the weckershams.

Me: We should nip up the weckershams?

British person: Right. Then you take your first left, then you just pop 'round the gorn-and-scumbles, and, Jack's a doughnut, there you are![26]

Matthew Inman had a go at the stereotype in a comic on how British people sound to Americans.[27] A white-haired, pipe-smoking, book-reading character spouts a speech full of sentences like "I'm chuffed as nuts to see you looking as humbly-jumbly as Her Majesty's watermelons!" The speech runs on nonsensically, peppered with real Britishisms like **chuffed as nuts** ('extremely pleased'), **rumpy-pumpy** ('sexual intercourse'), and **todger** ('penis') alongside fake ones, like *humbly jumbly, dingbangling,* and *throbbing wobbly.* They sound stereotypically British to Americans, with their silly rhymes and somehow comical sounds: lots of consonants from the front of the mouth, like /b/ and /f/, with the *o* and *u* vowels from the back of the mouth.* Not to mention the naughtiness (*nudge, nudge, wink, wink*). For further evidence, I invite you to revisit the subtitled scene in *Austin Powers in Goldmember* in which Powers and his groovy spy dad (played by Michael Caine) switch to "English English" in order to talk about "naughty things" in front of American women. "Are you telling pork pies and a bag of tripe? Because if you are feeling quiggly, why not just have a J. Arthur?"[28]

---

* A quick guide to some linguistic symbols I use: Slashes around a letter, like /b/, mean I'm referring to the sound rather than the letter. When I refer to letters, I use italics: *b*. Another linguist's trick is to use the slashes for the underlying sound in a word (the phoneme) and square brackets for the way the sound comes out in speech. So, for example, the first sound in *pot* is /p/ but when we pronounce it, we put a little puff of air after it, so we represent the actual sound as [pʰ]. That distinction between slashes and brackets will come in useful as the discussion turns to accents.

Stereotyping the British as silly might seem to conflict with the premise of American Verbal Inferiority Complex: that British English sounds educated and upper class. But the two stereotypes intersect, since the British upper classes are often regarded as somewhat preposterous—in the US as well as the UK. British commentators often mistake American fascination with the British aristocracy as a regretful longing for the monarchy that our ancestors so decisively rejected. The BBC's former US correspondent Justin Webb has perhaps a truer reading of the American obsession with royal weddings and the like: "They flock to see us make fools of ourselves."[29] My sister-in-law offers a case in point. Coming to England, all she wanted to see were castles and "old things," and she was duly impressed. But that didn't keep her from exclaiming, "That's ridiculous!" at the explanations of the rituals associated with the things she saw. Judges wearing wigs that look like ancient scouring pads, palace guards wearing eighteen-inch-tall bearskin hats, and a rich tradition of comedic cross-dressing—all are vaguely ludicrous, impressively convoluted, and definitely British. Maybe Americans enjoy associating the English with a bonkers aristocracy that says bonkers words (like *bonkers*) because doing so provides entertainment while reinforcing the idea that we're better off without such people in positions of power.

Gobsmacked ('shocked'), *wanker* ('jerk,' literally 'masturbator'), *argie-bargie* ('argument, row'), and *kerfuffle* ('commotion, to-do') are all Britishisms whose transatlantic migration Yagoda is tracking on *Not One-Off Britishisms.* There are silly syllables like *fuff*, not used in other English words. There's rhyming. There's naughtiness. They all seem delightfully British. And they're so cute that Americans eat 'em up.

Poppycock is another *bumbershootism*: an Americanism that sounds silly enough that Americans assume it's British. *Poppycock*, from the Dutch for 'doll's poop,' comes to English from Dutch settlers in North America—yet it's frequently heard in American impressions of upper-class Brits. *Urban Dictionary* lists it as "a British term for **bullshit**," though the example cited is from the very American band Nirvana. Those two "short *o*" vowels may be to blame. In an English "Received Pronunciation" accent, this *o* vowel is further back in the mouth, with a smaller mouth opening, than the "short *o*" in American English. When I say *hot* in my native US accent, the vowel sounds like "ah." The RP vowel (whose phonetic symbol is [ɒ]) just does not exist in most American dialects. So, if you want to make a word sound British, give it some short *o*'s and say it in an upper-class English accent. Those internet lists of "British phrases you should be using" are happy to supply such words, including **sprog** ('offspring'), **dogsbody** ('person who has to do grunt work'), **toff** ('upper-class person'), **gobby** ('loud-talking, blunt'), and **tosh** ('nonsense'). While that sound accounts for less than 5% of the vowels in a British English dictionary,[30] it is nearly 15% of the vowels on "75 simple British slang words you should probably start using."[31] The tragic fact about Americans who impersonate Brits saying *poppycock* is that they could have said **codswallop**, which also has two of those adorable short *o*'s, means the same thing, and is actually British.

Those lists of Britishisms that Americans "should" use are often very dated both because the authors know that their audiences expect and want "quaintness" in their British expressions and because much American contact with British culture is episodic, limited, and often in the form of historical drama. **How's your father?**, a *Mental Floss* list explains, is a "turn of the century" euphemism for sex. They don't mention it's the turn of the previous century. Cockney rhyming slang is of perennial fascination—birthdays bring me yet another Cockney dictionary from stateside friends, picked up from the impulse-purchase tables at chain bookshops. They would have me say that *I'm going out for* *some Britneys with me old china*, with *Britney (Spears)* meaning 'beers' and *china (plate)* for 'mate.' Never mind that the slang has long been "cultivated more assiduously in the media than in the East End of London."[32] It's a secret language, it's fun, and so Americans want it as part of their picture of England. These wish lists of Britishness don't tend to include the kind of slang that's used on the streets of London these days, like *bare* ('a lot of; very,' as in *I'm in a bare good mood*) or *cotch* ('to relax; to sleep'). The British vocabulary that Americans consume lives at Downton Abbey, 221B Baker Street, or Hogwarts. It doesn't come from the inner-city settings of soaps like *Coronation Street* or from the party animals of the *Geordie Shore*.

And Americans seem to like it that way—imagining that their British words come straight from the country manor, the Edwardian chimney sweep, or Her Majesty's Secret Service, not from the local hairdresser or the kids in the skate park. When James Corden was preparing to take over US institution *The Late Late Show*, the CBS network encouraged him to use "charming" British words, but stopped him from using others that they thought might "confuse" his audience. According to newspaper reports,[33] the charming ones included *willy* ('penis'), *bonkers* ('crazy'), *shag* ('have sex with'), and *squiffy* ('tipsy'). Some of these were already well known in America thanks to British-Canadian comedian Mike Myers, whose Austin Powers and Simon (a "cheeky monkey" of a boy on *Saturday Night Live* who liked to do "drawrings" in the "bahth") characters are silly, cute, and slightly obsessed with their willies. The ones on Corden's don't-say list included *knackered* ('worn out, tired'), *dodgy geezer* ('untrustworthy man'), *bladdered* ('drunk'), *half-cut* ('drunk'), *well-oiled* ('drunk'), and *trollied* ('drunk'). You may notice a theme there.

Advertisers in the US have cottoned on to the American love of unfamiliar British syllables and risqué content. It helps that rude

British words have an easier time getting past American censors than their American counterparts. Hygienic wipes have been made "fun" with the catchphrase *Let's talk about bums* (= US *butts*). A New York billboard campaign contrasted a British ale to a Belgian lager with the phrase *no bollocks* ('testicles,' = US *no bullshit*). And one of the most talked-about ads of the 2016 Super Bowl had Helen Mirren intoning the word *pillock* ('penis; idiot') to plug an American beer.[34]

Are British words inherently more silly, or do Americans just like to think of them that way? Certainly, unfamiliar things can seem silly, and the perception of silliness may be helped along by the fact that the British are known for not taking themselves too seriously—in contrast to Americans, whom the Brits generally think of as being "too earnest." British comedy—especially the British comedy popular in the US—is full of silly, camp, and sur-realist humor. Expressions like *lovely jubbly* and *mad as a box of frogs* seem to fit American tastes for Brit wit. But as with any of these linguistic generalizations, they are made without much self-reflection. Americans love to make up and say funny words too, like:

> *bloviate* 'talk, without much to say'
> *lickety-split* 'quickly'
> *gonzo* 'a subjective style of journalism'
> *hootenanny* 'an improvised folk concert'
> *mugwump* 'an independent politician'
> *discombobulate* 'come apart, put out of sorts'—and its recent
>   partner . . .
> *recombobulation*: 'the process of putting yourself back together
>   after clearing airport security'

And let's not forget the silliest American word of them all: *bumbershoot*.

Grating, sloppy American and careful, correct British

> Our Transatlantic friends do have one grievous fault: their misuse of the English language. If only they could be persuaded to bring the same ruthless rigour to bear on vocabulary as they do on dentistry, all would be well.
>
> "Constance Harding" in the *Telegraph* (2012)[35]

When I lived in South Africa in the 1990s, I got to be on the panel of SABC Radio's language program, *Word of Mouth*. Listeners wrote in with their linguistic questions and we tried to answer them. In my seventeen appearances on the show, only one question came up more than once (and more than twice): "Can we stop people using that horrible American pronunciation *conTROVersy*?" In the minds of the conservative-English-speaking South African audience, putting the stress on the second syllable was new and wrong, and therefore it must be American. But it's British. Very, very British. The British seem to be in as much denial about this fact as the South Africans, given this *Daily Telegraph* heading:

The "conTROversy" over changing pronunciations

To language purists they might grate, but new ways of pronouncing words are spreading in Britain thanks to the influence of US culture.

Mere centimeters below that headline, Jonnie Robinson, the British library's curator of sociolinguistics, is quoted as saying that the new pronunciation "does appear to be peculiarly British [. . .] there is no evidence that Americans are [saying] it."[36] South Africans and Britons who hear *conTROVersy* never hear it from Americans, but that doesn't seem to stop them from believing that Americans must be at fault. Surely, they reason, it is America that ruins words.

This takes us back to *garage* in the *Daily Mail's* list of British–American pronunciation differences. The list said that Britons pronounce *garage* as "garaj," but Americans say "garidj." But like *controversy*, their so-called American pronunciation is absolutely, entirely, and strictly British. It has to be, since it stems from the way that British (and not American) people pronounce recent two-syllable loanwords from French. Because British English stresses the first syllable GAR*age*, the second vowel "weakens" (as vowels do in unstressed syllables), causing the /a/ in -*age* to become less *a*-like. Because the weakened vowel takes the word further from French, the second *g* goes from the French "zh" sound to a more English "dj" sound. We can see the end of this process in words that English took from French in the Middle English period, including *village, marriage,* and *language. Garage* didn't come into English until the 20th century, and so the UK and the US were left to their own, separate devices in deciding how to pronounce this new borrowing. American English puts the stress on the final syllable, as it does generally with French loanwords: *gar*AGE. The first vowel can be weakened, but not the second one. The "garridge" pronunciation just isn't going to evolve from the American pronunciation any time soon.

So if the *Daily Mail* writer wasn't hearing Americans say "garridge," why did he think it was the American pronunciation? Simply because it sounded wrong to him. English people have been calling "garridge" a "vulgar pronunciation" for almost as long as they have been talking about garages.[37] If a pronunciation sounds wrong to some English people, then some of them will assume it's American.

And then there's the case of **might of** (instead of *might have* or *might've*), reported in the *Daily Telegraph* as an Americanism heard on the BBC. As someone who has read thousands of British students' essays, I can tell you: no one needs to import this mistake from another country. It is an understandable error that is reinvented regularly. The earliest examples of the errant *of* have been found in letters sent in England in the 1770s, as in "I should be very happy to of seen m."[38] From that point on, the *Oxford English Dictionary* lists plenty of examples from both sides of the Atlantic. These days, Britons write *might of, would of, could of,* and *should of* nearly twice as often as Americans do.[39] But since it's considered to be wrong, some British folk blame Americans. Thanks to American Verbal Inferiority Complex, some Americans do too.

Twitter provided one of my favourite examples of the "British is more correct" myth. Currently (as I'm writing this), if you go to the settings page on a Twitter account, you see this:[40]

Everyone's American-cultural-imperialism sirens are going at full blast now, right? Choose "English" and you get American spelling. Choose "English UK" and some spellings change; for example, *Center* on the settings page becomes *Centre*. But in 2016 there was another difference. If you had chosen "English," your profile page would show suggestions for "Who to follow." If you'd chosen "British English," the *who* grew an *m*: "**Whom** to follow." Was it that way because *whom* is British English and *who* is American? Absolutely not. *Whom* has been following the same gentle, centuries-long downward trajectory in both countries. It's a word that people think they should use, but most have no idea how to use it. A case in point is this overheard conversation from the London–Brighton train, reported on the *traindrops* blog:[41]

Manboy1: So what's the difference between *whom* and *who*?

Manboy2: *Whom* is more correct

Manboy1: So I should say *whom is that*?

Manboy2: No, it's only for plurals like *whomever*

Manboy1: Oh right, and like, *whom's is that*?

Manboy2: Exact.

It's not just the youth who are confused. The final print edition of the *Independent* newspaper ran a correction because they had used *whom* incorrectly.[42] This was in the same week they published "41 things Americans say wrong." You know, they say the British are good at irony.

Despite ample evidence that (a) Americans did not invent various "wrong" things said in Britain today, and (b) the British are no better at using "proper" grammar than Americans are, the "British is more correct" stereotype lives on. In the UK, it is a symptom of British Verbal Superiority Complex. In the US, it's a symptom of American Verbal Inferiority Complex. Tangled in with all this are different attitudes about language education and language standards (but that's the stuff of chapter 8).

Prudish American and unashamed British

> I can see the whole destiny of America contained in the first
> Puritan who landed on those shores.
>
> Alexis de Tocqueville, *Democracy in America* (1835)

When I was eleven, I felt as though I'd been saved. A new girl had transferred to our school, and I was no longer the last person picked for the teams in gym class. When you're really very bad at something, it can be a huge, shameful relief to know that someone else is worse at it than you. And this is my way of showing empathy for the British. Voted the most prudish in a pan-European poll,[43] the

British exercise a certain glee in pointing out any ways in which others might be more repressed. Hence the British stereotype of Americans as straitlaced and puritanical. Yes, American English is full of euphemisms that sound funny to the British. But are the British more forthright in talking about taboo topics? Let's not forget that *Victorian* is a synonym for *inhibited*—and the British invented Victorianism long after the Puritans had jumped ship to America.

Euphemisms for bodily functions? There are, if you'll excuse me, shitloads of them in both countries. When an unfortunate American tells their doctor *I have pain when I go to the bathroom*, they don't mean that they knock their head on the doorframe. A chain of meaning changes—semantic drift, we could call it—has led to this state. First, in the US, **bathroom** went from meaning 'the room with the bath in it' to 'the room with the toilet in it' because baths are almost always in the same room as toilets in American homes. (Some UK homes have separate rooms for the two.) That led to **go to the bathroom** becoming a less explicit way to say 'go to the room with the toilet in it, to use the toilet.' As a result, *bathroom* became more directly associated with smelly bodily functions, and so it can seem less than genteel, pushing Americans to use euphemisms for that euphemism, such as **restroom** and **powder room**. This is an example of what psycholinguist Steven Pinker calls "the euphemism treadmill"; pleasant words for unpleasant things become tainted by the unpleasantness of the thing, and therefore need to be replaced regularly.[44]

None of these are British ways to talk about toilets or excretion, and so we get exchanges like this one that I overheard between a security guard and two American tourists in London's National Gallery:

Tourist: Could you tell us where the restroom is?
Guard: Do you need a rest?
Tourist: Oh no—I mean the bathroom.
Guard: Why? Do you want to have a bath?

Tourists: *gasping for another word*
Guard: I can direct you to the ladies' toilets.

That guard knew exactly what those tourists were asking for, but he could not resist pointing out the literal meanings of the Americans' compound nouns in order to demonstrate his wit and his lack of shame in saying **toilets**. It's not that Americans find the word *toilet* itself unsayable, since it is the American word for the porcelain receptacle for human waste. In the UK or the US, you could say you *stood on the toilet* in order to change a lightbulb. But these days Americans use *toilet* for the porcelain object and not for the room in which the object is situated, so it seems too personal and overdetailed to ask for directions to *the toilet*. On the other hand, asking for the room in which the toilet sits seems less personal, since you could be asking to go to that room for any number of reasons—to brush your teeth, to blow your nose, to adjust your toupee . . . So Americans ask for the room, not the object, and no one is forced to contemplate bodily functions.

The British, of course, do the same. They don't stop a conversation to say "I'm just going to go defecate now." Just like Americans, they say where they're going, rather than what they'll be doing there. (In fact, according to an actual study on the matter, Brits are even more likely than Americans to just mention the room and not the errand.[45]) They say they're going to **the loo** or **the ladies'** or **the lavatory** (from the Latin for 'washing place'). Or *the toilet*—because in British English it does refer to a room. But before anyone congratulates the British for their directness in saying *toilet*, there are two things to know about it: (1) it's a euphemism; (2) it's an Americanism.

Toilet originally comes from French *toilette*. Way back in the 16th century, it referred to a piece of cloth used for wrapping up garments. (Notice the similarity to the fabric name *toile*.) By the following century, it referred to a cloth covering for a dressing

51

table, and then on to meanings related to dressing and putting on makeup. It was only in 19th-century America that *toilet* became a word for the room where one eliminates bodily waste, and later for the seat on which one does that business. Borrowed into British English in the 20th century, *toilet* (for the room) was initially considered an unwelcome invader, and *lavatory* was often suggested as a classier thing to say. But these days *lavatory* and other British terms like **privy** and **water closet** have lost out to *toilet* and the more infomal **loo**. What all these British words for poo places have in common is that they are euphemistic. They make reference to washing and water, but they don't mention naked bottoms and what comes out of them.

The British tendency to verbally tiptoe around these topics is so great that medical communication is compromised by prudishness. The BBC reported in 2010:

> Foreign nurses are receiving a crash course in euphemism after bewildered patients expressing the wish to "spend a penny" ['urinate'] found themselves being escorted to a hospital shop. Norfolk's Queen Elizabeth hospital has organised special "adapting to life in Norfolk" sessions for Portuguese staff whose otherwise excellent English results in too-literal translations of everyday expressions. Patients, particularly the elderly, face being met with incomprehension when [. . .] experiencing problems with their "back passage" ['rectum'].[46]

An American acquaintance in the UK was confused when her British doctor asked about her **waterworks**. Having never heard that euphemism for the urinary tract, she thought he was asking if she cried a lot. When I sit in my doctor's waiting room in England, I'm amused and a bit astonished to find posters about what to do if there is blood in your **pee** or **poo**. (See your doctor immediately!) The posters use nursery words for their serious message, while the equivalent American public-service advertisements say *urine* and *stool*. In the medical context, America avoids being crude by using scientific terms and medical jargon, while Britain uses euphemism and childish words.

Americans' animal-name choices can also seem prudish to some Brits: *rooster* rather than *cock* and *donkey* rather than *ass*. *Roach* now serves as a synonym for *cockroach* because 19th-century Americans lopped off the *cock*. (Yet somehow Americans still talk about *cockfighting* and *peacocks*.) But Americans weren't the first to see the connection between the animal names and the embarrassing human body parts. *Donkey*, formerly a slang word, was promoted to genteel British society by the start of the 19th century, when the pronunciations of *ass* (the animal) and *arse* (the body part) were becoming too close for comfort.[47] Jane Austen, Charles Dickens, William Makepeace Thackeray: all wrote *donkey*.

Rooster may also have got its start in Britain, as a Kent dialect word, though it has mostly died out. But don't let that fool you into thinking that the British are perfectly happy to call male chickens *cocks*. Instead, more and more Brits are resurrecting the word *cockerel*, formerly a word specifically for a young cock. By 1891 the *Oxford English Dictionary* had declared *cockerel* "archaic," but in the 21st century, *cockerel* is used almost as often as *cock* to refer to male chickens.[48] When I caught my child's English godmother saying *cockerel* for a bird whose age she wouldn't have known, she explained, "It just doesn't feel right to say *cock* in front of a child."

Nevertheless, it's still the Americans who have the reputation for changing words in an effort to avoid "sounding dirty." David Mitchell, an English comedian who trades on his erudition, has presented a "message from the Queen" to Americans via his video podcast.[49] The Queen, he says, is happy to let Americans use "her" words in their own ways, except for "the silly ones like *tidbit* because you think the syllable *tit* is intrinsically rude." Mitchell chose the wrong example. It is conservatism that has Americans saying *tidbit* rather than the British **titbit**—but it's linguistic conservatism, not sexual prudery. The original *tyd bit* (1641) or *tid-bit* (1701) had the *d*. *Tid* meant 'special.' So a *tidbit* might be the best bit that you saved for last. Somewhere along the line, *tid* was forgotten and the British started using *tit*—perhaps because it has connotations of smallness, as in the bird names *titmouse* and *titlark*.

That's another one where American prudery is often assumed. Several American species of titmice are now called **chickadees**, after their song. Meanwhile, the British like to shorten *titmouse* to **tit**. Do Americans say *chickadee* because they don't want to say *tit*? I doubt it. After all, the *tufted titmouse* is native to North America and called such. *Chickadee* offers a much more descriptive name than *titmouse*, which, after all, is not a mouse. (Along the same lines, Americans prefer **ladybug**—a word invented in Britain, by the way—over the less literal British **ladybird**.) Rather than American prudery, we may be seeing a British *tit* obsession. The phrase **tit-for-tat** had started as **tip-for-tap** and **go arse over tit** ('lose one's balance') had been **go arse over tip** until the British stuck their *tits* in.

Americans were eager Victorians. There's no doubt about that. American Victorians popularized the Latinate word **limb** in order to avoid saying *leg* and began sorting poultry meat into **light** and **dark**, so as to avoid saying *breast* and *thigh*. But across the ocean, the British started calling chicken legs **drumsticks** for the very same reason. There was just no escaping Victorian tastes.

So yes, Americans do bowdlerize the language sometimes. (Sometimes. Some of us are pretty good at using naughty words too.) But perhaps the real difference is simply in the variety of euphemisms, rather than in the urge to avoid taboo. For most of the "prudish" American words, there are similar British ways to avoid taboo topics and blasphemy. *Goddamn it* becomes American **doggone it** or **gosh darn it** and British **Gordon Bennett** (though

Bennett himself was a rich American whose drunken shenanigans outraged polite society on both sides of the Atlantic). English people were saying *by George* and *by Jove* well before Americans were saying *gosh* and *golly*—all to avoid saying *God*. American *gee whiz*, *Judas priest*, and *jeepers creepers* are all variations on *Jesus Christ*, but the Brits invented *crikey* to stand in for *Christ*. *Cor blimey* ('God blind me'), *bleedin' heck* ('bloody Hell'), *my goodness* ('my God')—all British euphemisms. They may not call it *cussing*, but the British have a long and rich history of avoiding it too.

Crass, pretentious, corporate American

The Americans, who are the most efficient people on the earth, [...] have invented so wide a range of pithy and hackneyed phrases that they can carry on an amusing and animated conversation without giving a moment's reflection to what they are saying and so leave their minds free to consider the more important matters of big business and fornication.

W. Somerset Maugham, *Cakes and Ale* (1930)

When it's claimed that Shakespeare coined 1,700 words, people think he's a genius. (He didn't, but that's another point.[50]) When a poet says that a telephone *squats*, we applaud the imagery. But when the boss's boss says *incentivize* or uses *action* as a verb, word lovers often become word haters. Allan Massie, writing for the *Telegraph*, argued that most Americanisms are "lively, useful and agreeable," but the "American language we really should guard against is the management-speak promoted by business schools to baffle outsiders."[51] Someone needs to tell Allan: you don't need Americans for management-speak. The first evidence we have of *incentivize* (spelled *incentivise*, in fact) appeared in the UK *Guardian* newspaper in 1968. The first evidence of *action* to mean 'to take action on' was in *The Times* (of London) in 1960. The only definite business Americanism in this paragraph is **boss**, from the Dutch *baas*, 'master.'

Still, there are good reasons to stereotype management-speak as American, and Massie was right to think of business schools. Americans invented the Master of Business Administration (MBA) in the early 1900s. In becoming an academic subject, business changed from something you *do* to something you *talk about*. A new jargon was born.

Business degrees were not easily exported to the UK; British academia and business were not so eager to get into bed with each other. Even a gift worth nearly £2 million in today's money could not persuade Cambridge University to appoint a professor of business in the 1950s.[52] British managers continued to learn their skills by working, rather than studying. While they had specialist vocabulary of their own, they had no reason to broadcast it beyond their workplaces. The first British business degrees were awarded in the 1960s, but they only started to be popular in the 1980s and '90s. Even then the British viewed them with great suspicion.

The Americanness of management-speak is not surprising if you consider some key differences in British and American values. In the 1970s, psychologist Gordon Allport asked English and American insurance clerks to complete the sentence: "The qualities I admire most in a person are . . ." In many ways the two nationalities were the same—for instance, equal numbers valued a good sense of humor. But a real difference emerged in the attitudes towards assertiveness. Thirty-one percent of American responses said (in some way) that they valued the ability to exploit or exercise control over situations. This might be expressed with Americanisms like **being a go-getter** or having a **can-do attitude**. Only 7% of English respondents mentioned any such thing. On the flip side, 30% of the English respondents, but only 8% of the Americans, admired people who exercise self-restraint.[53] Management-speak is the language of go-getting—of grabbing opportunities and having impact, starting with the effect on the language. People who advertise their go-getting aspirations by using management-speak can sound crass or self-important to those who prefer not to grab attention with new, action-packed words. And while management-speak is detested around the world, it's bound to be particularly unpopular in the land of **stiff upper lips** (an Americanism that the British have adopted with gusto).

Values bleed into language, and so American English might be "more active" than British in certain ways:[54] American English makes use of the agentive suffix *-er* with a wider variety of verbs, making new words like *A-lister*, *doomsayer*, and *fixer-upper*. While all Englishes make verbs out of nouns, American English feels particularly comfortable making compound verbs, squashing the object onto the front of a verb, as in *to table-hop*, *to time-share*, or *to fund-raise*. American business metaphors often hark to the American sense of the frontier—the language of gold mining (*pan out*, *hit pay dirt*), oil prospecting (*strike it rich*), and saloon gambling (*high stakes*, *win big*). It's the language of action and risk-taking.

Also from the frontier is the word *maverick*, which is used with different connotations in the UK and US. *Maverick* originally referred to an unbranded calf, but came to mean an unorthodox, independent-minded person. Reacting to a book with the title *Mavericks at Work: Why the Most Original Minds in Business Win*, the *Financial Times* of London spelled out the difference:

> To Americans, imbued with the frontier spirit, a maverick is an admirable person, independent in thought and action.
>
> But the *Shorter Oxford English Dictionary* offers this definition: "a masterless person; one who is roving and casual." A former British Cabinet minister recently was described as a "maverick voice." This was not meant as a compliment.

That frontier values are not shared transatlantically can also be seen in the British use of *cowboy* (as in *cowboy builder*) to mean a 'person without qualifications who competes against established traders or operators, providing shoddy goods or services' (OED). In modern American lore, cowboys are "good guys." Football teams are named after them, and cowboy characters or images are used to advertise blue jeans, fast food, and cigarettes (before cigarettes were demonized). The frontier may be lawless, but frontierspeople are hearty pioneers. Not having a master has never been a bad thing for Americans, and so Americans have created a passel of positive words for people who battle the frontier, including *trailblazer*, *groundbreaker*, and *pathfinder*. Negative-tinged business expressions deride those who don't have that independent spirit, for example *groupthink* and *drink the Kool-Aid* (alluding to the 1978 mass suicide by the Peoples Temple cult). In a sense, American willingness to create new words is a way of embodying that frontier spirit—though by the eightieth time you've heard a businessism, it sounds a lot less like independent, creative thinking.

Since business is competitive, many of its metaphors come from sports (or *sport*, to be British). Of course, different sports are popular in different countries, and so the metaphors often don't translate well.

UK

cricket	*close of play*	'end of the game/working day/negotiations'
	knocked for six	'shocked, surprised'
football (soccer)	*It's a game of two halves.*	'circumstances can suddenly change'
rugby	*hospital pass*	'act that puts recipient in a difficult, damaged position'

US

baseball	**step up to the plate**	'assume responsibility; take initiative'
	touch base	'contact, in order to communicate with'
	ballpark figure	'rough estimate of a number'
	inside baseball	'having an insider's expertise'
	knock it out of the park / hit a home run	'have a definite success'
football (gridiron)	**hail-Mary (pass)**	'last-ditch attempt'
	spiking the ball	'showing off about a success' (players bounce the ball on its tip after a touchdown)
	It's a game of inches.	'progress towards a goal comes in small increments'
basketball	**slam dunk**	'an inevitable success'
	layup	'a near-certain success'

Those who don't know the sport might not understand the metaphor. *Step up to the plate* is not infrequently heard in the UK, but some Brits seem to think it alludes to getting ready to eat, rather than taking the bat (at *home plate*) in baseball. When I first heard *hospital pass*, I guessed it meant 'permission to roam around a hospital,' analogous to American **hall pass**, the slip of paper that gives children permission to be out of the classroom. Instead, it alludes to a rugby-ball pass to a player who is certain to be tackled. Even without sports, metaphorical idioms can be hard to translate. A recent addition to British management-speak is **wash-up meeting**, for a meeting in which a project is reviewed and any loose ends are tied up. This works in the UK because after a meal, you **wash up**—that is to say, you wash the dishes. But in American English you **wash up** before the meal, because it means 'wash your hands.'

Opaque metaphors and neologisms can make communication more difficult—but this is only part of the reason people complain about management-speak. The other reason is that the expressions get used to death. Metaphorical phrases like *open the kimono* ('disclose the inner workings of a company') or *peel the onion* ('look at the layers of a problem') become less evocative and more clichéd with use.

And, speaking of clichés: you'll never believe what happened next! British English has taken on management-speak with the enthusiasm of a convert. If we look at the top nineteen "buffling" business terms, as found by a UK YouGov poll,[55] several are Americanisms that are now used more in Britain than in America. These include *pro-active, thinking outside the box,* and *blue-sky thinking*—the last of which occurs six times more often on British websites than on American ones.[56] No wonder the British are sick of it.

The British aren't just adopting American business clichés, they're inventing their own. Six of the top nineteen annoying businessisms are UK in origin: *at the end of the day, at this moment in time, singing from the same hymn sheet, 360° thinking, flag it up,* and *thought shower.* You might be scratching your head at that last one. Its presence in the "most annoying" list probably comes from people hearing about it on the news, not in real life. *Thought shower* had been briefly entertained (then widely mocked) as an alternative to the Americanism *brainstorm*—not so much because *brainstorm* was an Americanism, but because a borough council in Kent thought it might be offensive to people with epilepsy. (The National Society for Epilepsy called the coinage "political correctness gone a step too far."[57]) Other management clichés with UK origins include: *across the piece* ('throughout'), *cradle-to-grave* ('complete'), *not letting the grass grow* ('seizing opportunities now'), and *looking under the bonnet* ('seeing what makes something work').

American business culture has affected British culture, and British business culture has pushed management-speak in its own directions. Despite the distress about jargon, not everyone is convinced that the American cultural influence is a bad thing. UK *Guardian* columnist Jonathan Freedland suggests that importing American "can-do culture, partly fostered by the cult of business and enterprise" may rescue Britons from a "semi-feudal passivity" seen "in the habit of looking upward, waiting for those in charge to sort things out."[58] Expatriate author Toni Hargis calls this the British "yes, but . . ." culture.[59] Whether you think the British are better or worse off for importing aspects of American business culture, remember that many Americans are just as annoyed by management-speak as British people are, agreeing with Samuel Johnson that "Commerce, however necessary, however lucrative, as it depraves the manners, depraves the language." Let's not blame the Americans. Let's blame capitalism!

It's just hard to know

Like my dad, I often confuse American and British English. I guess I'm a crisp off the old distance along a street between two intersections.

@GlennyRodge[60]

The truth is, most people can only guess at where their words come from. Even for professional linguists, it's hard to make claims about "British English" and "American English" because it's hard to know what to count as one or the other. Using the word *pen* to refer to ink-based writing implements is General English, common to any English-speaking country. But what about **pen pusher** to mean 'low-level bureaucrat'? Here's where it gets tricky. The *Oxford English Dictionary*'s first citation for it is from California (1875). But nowadays, it's mostly the British who say *pen pusher.* Americans tend to say *pencil pusher*, first recorded in Massachusetts in 1881. Based on its origin, *pen pusher* is an Americanism. Based on who says it, it's a Britishism. This isn't a lonely example. *A shambles* (in its metaphorical 'scene of chaos' sense), *to skive* ('avoid work/play hooky'), and the phrase *know your onions* ('be well acquainted with a subject') are all American inventions that have taken root in the UK while mostly dying out in the US.

The lists of Britishisms and Americanisms found in the media and in amateur UK–US dictionaries tend to consider only the present: it's a Britishism if British people say it now and Americans don't. The result is that these lists become very dated very quickly. But once the "equivalences" are in print, they live on and on as a kind of fantasy. I learned in high school that the British call a room with a toilet a *water closet*. What my teacher didn't tell me (because he didn't know) was that use of that phrase had peaked in the early 19th century.[61] The *Oxford English Dictionary* says it's now archaic, historical, or euphemistic. Its initials *WC* might be found on toilet doors, but no one ever asks for the *water closet*. And yet today with very little effort I've found *water closet* listed as the "equivalent" of American *toilet* in a half dozen recent UK–US language comparisons,[62] even one with "21st century" in the title.[63]

3

SEPARATED BY A COMMON LANGUAGE?

We really have everything in common with America nowadays, except, of course, language.

Oscar Wilde, *The Canterville Ghost* (1887)

At the height of the British Empire, English intellectuals were taken with the notion of an "Anglo-Saxon race," tracing its roots to the Germanic peoples who settled in Britain after the Romans left in the 5th century. With self-satisfaction they concluded that their "race" was something special, illustrated by the strength of their culture over that of the conquered Celts, their early codification of individual rights with the Magna Carta in 1215, and their break with the Roman church in the 16th century. Belief in their own good example made appropriating other peoples' lands much easier to justify—and Americans of English stock were happy to share in this myth. But by the 20th century, talk of an *Anglo-Saxon race* had fallen out of fashion, and instead of genetic inheritance, it was language that seemed to unite us.

Thus we started to be called *the English-speaking peoples*, a term used with particular influence by two statesmen-historians, Theodore Roosevelt in *The Winning of the West* and Winston Churchill in *A History of the English-speaking Peoples*. President and prime minister turned to this language-based description of "our peoples" because other possible descriptions had become impossible. While the rest of the empire could still be called *British*,

Americans had severed that connection. The European population of the former British colonies was never entirely British anyhow; Roosevelt's paternal line stretched to the Dutch settlers of what was once New Amsterdam (later New York). During the 19th century, the ethnic de-Britification of white America sped up, due to massive and increasingly diverse immigration. The children of immigrants to the US from Germany, Scandinavia, Ireland, and Italy became English speakers, but would never be Anglo-Saxons. As Britain, its colonies, and its former colonies grew apart, language became the most prominent link between us.

The plural *-s* on *English-speaking peoples* hints that Roosevelt and Churchill wanted to establish our separateness as national or even ethnic groups, while hyping our togetherness in language. Are we really that together, though?

How different are we?

There has never been any major difference between British English and American English.

> Jonathan Culpeper, *History of English* (2005)[1]

There are two possible answers to the question *How different are American and British English?*

1. Hardly different at all.
2. Really very different.

Both of those answers are correct. The nationlects are similar enough that we consider them to be varieties of the same language, rather than different languages. Most of the vocabulary is the same and almost all the grammatical rules are the same. We can read each other's books and watch each other's films without too much trouble. People learning English as a second language find the differences to be small curiosities and occasional inconveniences, but rarely are they major barriers to learning.

On the other hand, they are different enough that Americans and Britons can tell within a few syllables if someone is not speaking "their" English. In speech, pronunciation is the most obvious difference, and it differs on at least three dimensions.

First, there's how we pronounce sounds—our accents. Accents of course vary immensely within the US and UK, never mind between the two countries. Though this internal variation makes it difficult to be specific about properties of "American accents" and "British accents," we can make a few broad generalizations.

Most American accents differ from most British accents in how they handle /t/ between vowels, as in the word *butter*. In the US it is generally pronounced as a "voiced alveolar tap": a quick tap of the tongue on the gum ridge behind the top front teeth. Because the vocal cords are vibrating during the tap, it sounds more like a [d] than a [t]. In the UK the /t/ in *butter* is usually a clearer [t] or sometimes, informally, a glottal stop (a closing in the throat, as you do in the middle of *uh-oh*).[2] Because I've lived among the non-tappers for twenty years and because I sometimes like them to understand me, I often fail to tap my /t/ these days. That little change alone is enough for American strangers to mistake me for English when I visit the US. (My English friends find this hilarious—or maybe horrifying.)

Another accent clue is **rhoticity**: the quality of having a pronounced [r] after vowels—though we need to be more cautious in generalizing about nations here. Much of England and Wales is **non-rhotic** these days; no [r] is pronounced in *car* or *farmer*. This leads to *r*-lessness being stereotyped as a difference between the so-called "American accent" and the so-called "British accent." But, of course, there are British *r*-ful accents: traditionally in the west of England and parts of Lancashire and certainly still in Scotland. And American has *r*-less accents in New England, metropolitan

New York, and the southeast. Still, r-less speakers in Hampshire don't sound like r-less speakers in New Hampshire. The r-less syllables of non-rhotic accents have different vowel qualities in the two countries, and American and British /r/s are a bit different in the rhotic accents as well.

Vowel sounds are much harder to generalize about. Americans perceive *bath* with a "broad" *ah* vowel as "British" or "English" or at least "not American," though a good portion of Britain (including parts of England) has a flatter vowel that's more (but not exactly) like the /æ/ vowel that Americans use in both *bath* and *bat*. Suffice it to say that vowels are shifty little creatures that differ within and between the two countries.

It's not just that we have different sounds and sound patterns. Sometimes we disagree on which words have those sounds or patterns. For instance, what are the first sounds in *schedule, herb*, and *ecological*? Which syllables do we stress in words like *shallot* or *capillary*? What are the first vowels in *boogie* and *privacy*, the middle vowel in *tomato*, the final vowel in *compost*?* These aren't different ways of pronouncing the "same sound," as we saw for accent differences above. Instead, Americans and Brits are treating these words as if they have different sounds in them. Take *privacy* for example. For most Americans, the *i* in *privacy* is pronounced like the *i* in *private*. For most Britons today, it's pronounced like the *i* in *privy*. Both dialects have both vowel sounds, but in *privacy* we've differed in how to perform the written *i* as sound. Some of these word-based pronunciation differences apply to sets of words. For instance *ecological, evolution,* and *economical* show a pattern in the pronunciation of the first vowel: usually "ee" in

---

* In case you don't know who you are—**American**: skedule, erb, eckological, SHALLot, CAPillary. *Boogie*'s first syllable is like *bookie*'s, *privacy* starts like *private*, to-MAY-to, *compost* rhymes with *post*. **British**: shedule, herb, eekological, shalLOT, caPILLary. *Boogie*'s oo sounds like *bootie*'s, *privacy* starts like *privy*, to-MAH-to, *compost* rhymes with *cost*. Some variation can be found within the countries, especially the UK, but these are the typical "dictionary pronunciations."

general British, almost always "eh" in American. Similarly, the *-ile* syllable in adjectives like *agile*, *fertile*, *hostile*, and *virile* sounds like *aisle* in British but rhymes with *lull* in American.[3] It's not that we don't have the sounds for pronouncing the words the other way. Our dialects have just designated the words as having different sounds.

How many US–UK word-pronunciation differences are there? One study found that 1.7% of the words in the *Longman Pronouncing Dictionary* have their emphasis on different syllables, such as *laboratory* as *LAB'ratory* in the US and *labOrat'ry* in Received Pronunciation.[4] That's a small percentage, but on the other hand, it's about a thousand words. And that's just the stress differences, not the different consonants, nor many of the different vowels.

The third kind of pronunciation difference is prosody—the "melody" of a phrase or sentence. Some call this "the most obvious difference" between the two Englishes.[5] When that melody is absent—as in a computerized monotone—it can be much harder to tell whether a voice is American or British. To give a couple of examples of prosodic difference, American questions are more likely to end on an upward swing in pitch than ones said in the southeast of England, and southeastern English sentences are more likely than American ones to start at a high pitch, with a steep fall within the sentence.[6] That said, the usual "tunes" of sentences probably differ more within Britain (perhaps even within the borders of England) than between the "standard" forms of American and British English.

* * *

While the differences in American and British are most immediately noticed in speech, the written language is more resistant to regional difference. Still, it's not too hard to tell which of the two countries these two banana-bread recipes come from:

Banana bread[7]

Move oven rack to low position so that tops of pans will be in center of oven. Heat oven to 350°F. Grease bottoms only of 2 loaf pans, 8½ × 4½ × 2½ inches, or 1 loaf pan, 9 × 5 × 3 inches.

Mix sugar and butter in large bowl. Stir in eggs until well blended. Add bananas, buttermilk and vanilla. Beat until smooth. Stir in flour, baking soda and salt just until moistened. Pour into pans.

Bake 8-inch loaves about 1 hour, 9-inch loaf about 1¼ hours, or until toothpick inserted in center comes out clean. Cool 10 minutes. Loosen sides of loaves from pans; remove from pans and place top side up on wire rack.

Banana bread[8]

Preheat the oven to 180C/350F/ Gas 4.

Sift the flour, bicarbonate of soda and salt into a large mixing bowl.

In a separate bowl, cream the butter and sugar together until light and fluffy.

Add the eggs, mashed bananas, buttermilk and vanilla extract to the butter and sugar mixture and mix well. Fold in the flour mixture.

Grease a 20 cm × 12.5 cm / 8 in × 5 in loaf tin and pour the cake mixture into the tin.

Transfer to the oven and bake for about an hour, or until well-risen and golden-brown.

Remove from the oven and cool in the tin for a few minutes, then turn out onto a wire rack to cool completely before serving.

The recipes are for slightly different breads and they were written by different people, so we have to be careful not to attribute all the differences to nationality. For example, one recipe says "beat until smooth" and the other says "mix well"—not because one is American and one is British, but because English gives us many ways to say the same thing. Still, the authors' nationalities are on show at several levels.

Starting with **orthography** (written form), the spelling *center* tells us straightaway that the left-hand recipe is the American one—it would have to be *centre* in British spelling. It's frustratingly tricky to count the US–UK spelling differences. In order to try, I looked at the five thousand most commonly occurring lemmas in a 4.5-million-word corpus of American English.[9] (*Lemma* is a fancy linguists' term for 'word in its basic form'—the form you'd find at the start of a dictionary entry. So if the word *hoping* is in the corpus, it was counted as an instance of the lemma *hope*.) Among these five thousand lemmas are fifty-five spellings that would usually be different in British text—about 1% of the word list. These included words in well-known patterns of difference, like *-o(u)r* (*color/colour, tumor/tumour*) and *-er/-re* (*center/centre, fiber/fibre*), and also one-offs like *artifact* (UK = *artefact*) and *gray* (UK = *grey*). But the story gets more complicated if instead of counting lemmas, you're writing a paragraph. If you add *-ed* to *travel* do you have **traveled** or **travelled**? If you put an *-ing* on *age* do you get **aging** or **ageing**? If you put *re-* on *interpret* should you have a hyphen or not? Then there are the compounds: should *hobbyhorse* be one word or two?

Personal preference also comes into play, as spelling variation exists within both countries. Dictionaries may tell you that *dialog* is an "American" variant of *dialogue*, and that much is true, but *dialogue* with the *-ue* is much more common in American spelling (except in the computer use: *dialog box*). Reading the British banana-bread recipe I wondered about the hyphenated *golden-brown*. My first reaction was: I wouldn't spell it like that—is that a British thing? But on closer investigation, *golden brown* gets a hyphen about 7% of the time in both countries. We have to put that one down to the personal preference of the recipe writer, not their nationality.

Punctuation also differs. While there's a fair amount of punctuation variation within either country, there are still noticeable trends that make texts look suspiciously American or British. How many commas should you use? Americans use more, especially for words or phrases that occur before the subject of a sentence. In everyday writing Americans would be likely to put a comma after "In everyday writing" in this sentence, while Britons would be half as likely to do so. Do you use single or double quotation marks, and should end-of-sentence punctuation come inside or outside the quotation marks? Britain usually goes with single and more often puts the **full stop** (= US *period*) outside the quotation marks if the quote is at the end of a larger sentence. America usually goes for double quotation marks and puts the period inside the quotation regardless. The recipes are not the best place to observe punctuation (there isn't much of it), but every page of this book has punctuation choices that go against the preferences and tendencies of one country or the other.

Next we come to the three types of **vocabulary** difference on display in the recipes. The most obvious type is when they use different names for things, as in the case of *baking soda/bicarbonate of soda*. A second kind of difference is when the two nationlects have the same words, but those words have different ranges of meaning. We see this where the American recipe bakes the loaf in a *pan*, but the British one refers to the same vessel as a *tin*. Both nationlects have the words *pan* and *tin*, but the boundaries of their meanings differ. American and British both use *pan* for the type that has a handle and goes on top of a heat source, but American is more comfortable extending its use to shallow baking vessels. *Tin* is used for more types of bakeware in British English than in American, where its use is mostly limited to the compounds *muffin tin* and *pie tin*. The third type of difference is in the frequency of an expression, where one way of saying things is more common in one nationlect than the other. Consider *vanilla* and *vanilla extract*. Dictionaries in both countries list 'vanilla extract' as a possible meaning for the word *vanilla*, but it's more common in

American English than in British to use *vanilla* to specifically refer to the flavoring that comes in a little bottle.

So for the thirteen objects or substances that are named in both recipes, three have different usual names in the two countries. We'd see even more differences if both recipes mentioned all the same items. The US recipe mentions a **toothpick**, meaning the type of object that is more commonly called **cocktail stick** in British English. When I found other British recipes that suggested testing the loaf by piercing it, the tool of choice was a skewer. This might reveal a cultural difference: the British recipe maker might assume that British bakers are more likely to own skewers than little wooden sticks, while toothpicks are a common kitchen item in American households (even for those who never pick their teeth). Other cultural differences in the recipes include the types of measurement used. These aren't strictly linguistic differences, but they have an impact on the language that is used. Americans generally measure by volume, using measuring cups for baking, while the British weigh their ingredients. When the BBC's *Good Food* website was at risk of closure, a tongue-in-cheek suggestion by @PaulMcMc on Twitter reflected the British perception of American measurements as old-fashioned and confusing:

> No BBC recipes? Just use an American internet one instead. "a sixth of flour, 3 groats of sugar, $1/7$ bucket of milk, 2 cubits of salt . . ."[10]

My favorite of the vocabulary differences in the recipe (an example of the second type) comes in the British instruction to "pour the cake mixture into the tin." My immediate American reaction to that is:

> What cake mixture? I haven't made a cake mixture. I thought this was a banana-bread recipe?!

American baking has a traditional category called *quick breads*, that is, breads leavened without yeast. Quick breads include banana bread, **zucchini** (= UK *courgette*) bread, and my mother's famous pumpkin bread, as well as American **biscuits** (which look a bit like British scones, but don't feel or taste like them) and what the British call *American-style muffins*, including blueberry muffins and bran muffins (though they've proved so popular in the UK that the *American-style* is usually left off these days). In an American cookbook, these recipes are located in the *bread* chapter. Banana breads and blueberry muffins are relatively new to Britain, and they came over without the larger QUICK BREAD category. They thus fell into the CAKE category.

Had the American recipe mentioned the substance that was to be poured into pans, the writer probably would have opted for **batter**. That wasn't an option in the British one, since British *batter* refers only to the very thin type used for making crepe-like English pancakes or Yorkshire puddings (an airy, savory baked delight that usually accompanies roast beef). And so the writer opted for *mixture*.

Now, maybe I've biased the differences tally by choosing recipes. There are few international treaties about home baking, and so American and British baking traditions have been free to develop separately. *Of course* some words differ. Instructions for making a nuclear reactor might well be more uniform across English-speaking countries. But then again, for most of us, baking is a more familiar activity than making nuclear reactors, and it's these everyday linguistic differences that affect us most. If Americans read international news stories from British newspapers, they'll find a few words or turns of phrase that are unfamiliar. If they read the local newspaper or the sports pages, they may well have to ask for some translation.[11]

So how different are the national vocabularies, really? The best reply to that question is a very British idiom: *How long is a piece of string?* If we count the words that only exist in one nationlect or the other, we'll miss the ones that exist in both but mean different things. If we count the words that have different dictionary definitions, we'll miss many subtle differences that the dictionaries missed. For instance, American and British dictionaries generally define the 'footwear' sense of *boot* in much the same way, but that doesn't reveal the fact that high-top athletic shoes are sometimes called *boots* in British but never in American English. A dictionary can tell you what a *street* or a *road* is, but it won't tell you that *road* is used in Britain in places where *street* is more normal in America—for instance when we talk about crossing one or living on one. Or should that be living *in* a street or road? Can we even count all the ways we differ in the use of prepositions like *on, in,* and *at*? I can't. At least not without several well-trained assistants and a computer with ample processing power.

Vocabulary differences *within* a nationlect can be greater than the differences between them. For example, one group of researchers looked for sets of noun synonyms (*merchant/trader, pants/ trousers, perspective/view,* etc.) in some large, comparable collections of American and British texts. They found that while American and British newspapers often use different vocabulary, American newspapers have more vocabulary in common with British newspapers than they have in common with fiction from their own country.[12] The researchers found some interesting transatlantic differences that might not have been apparent without their statistical approach—for example that Britons (in the 1990s) were much more likely than Americans to call a disease an *illness* and to call any desktop computer a *PC*. But since the study only considered a small set of nouns, it cannot give a good sense of the extent of vocabulary differences as a whole.

The editors at Oxford University Press are in the process of merging the databases for their British and American general-use dictionaries. Although the print dictionaries were about the same size, the current databases share only about 78% of their headwords—the words they define.[13] Not all the other 22%

are British-only or American-only (many factors affect what goes in a dictionary). Still, it's an interesting number coming from a single dictionary publisher. The lexicographer Laurence Urdang once estimated that if he were to Americanize a British dictionary or Briticize an American one, about 20% of the text would have to change for vocabulary, spelling, or grammatical reasons. Another lexicographer, Robert Ilson, looked at a small sample of definitions (*enjoy–enter*) in one publisher's dictionaries for learners of English, one for British English and one for American English.[14] While nineteen of the entries were essentially the same, ten had significant differences. I was once employed to Americanize British-written entries for the *Encarta Dictionary*, and none of these figures surprise me. I made a lot of changes to those entries.

Finally, **grammar**. Linguists have a saying: "Accent divides, syntax unites." English speakers from different places talk differently, but we're still speaking the same language, using the same rules. Sure, some words differ, but words come and go easily in a language. The grammar is English's sturdy foundation. There are few things about which you could say, "This is a possible phrase in American English, but an impossible one in British English." The banana-bread recipes give the perfectly reasonable impression that the grammar is much the same in American and British. But then again, recipes present a very limited view of grammar.

Transatlantic grammatical differences include things like:

	American English	British English
Could you join us?	*I could.*	*I could do.*
Which tense for recent events?	Mostly simple past: *We just ate.*	Mostly present perfect: *We have just eaten.*
Which verb form agrees with collective nouns?	Singular: *The band is on the bus.*	Plural (or singular): *The band are on the bus.*

While it's a small list, those differences are basic enough that they might pile up in a single text. Many other "grammatical" differences are linked to particular words:[15]

	American English	British English
Does the verb need a preposition?	Not necessarily: *I protested the cost.* *I appealed the ruling.*	Yes: *I protested **at** the cost.* *I appealed **against** the ruling.*
	Yes: *We agreed **on** a plan.*	Not necessarily: *We agreed a plan.*
Does it follow the -ed rule for past tense?	Yes: *The sun **shined**.** *I **spilled** the milk.* *I **spelled** it wrong.*	No: *The sun **shone**.* *I **spilt** the milk.** *I **spelt** it wrong.**
	No: *The shoe **fit**.* *I **dove** into the pool.** *I **snuck** into the room.**	Yes: *The shoe **fitted**.* *I **dived** into the pool.* *I **sneaked** into the room.**
Which "light" verb?[3]	*You **take** a bath/ shower/nap/look.* *You **get** some exercise.* *You **make** a photocopy.*	*You **have** a bath/shower/ nap/look.* *You **take** exercise.** *You **take** a photocopy.**

* indicates that both forms are used in significant numbers in that country

Sharing most of the grammar isn't enough to make American and British English look or sound grammatically the same. Very often one country uses one grammatical pattern more than the other does, and what we do with those patterns—which kinds of texts or discussions they're appropriate to—are other matters. Let's count those as differences of **style**. Which words and grammatical structures do we like to use most? How do we structure our interactions or our texts? While the same sentences may be perfectly *acceptable* to say in American and British, the choices speakers or writers make in putting thoughts into words can make them sound more American or more British. Nothing in their grammatical rules prevents Americans from saying *go on, then*, but they'd not be as likely as Brits to use those words to mean 'Yes, I'd like some of what you're offering, please.' While Brits like to put that adverb *then* at the ends of sentences (more than Americans do), they don't put the adverb *already* there much, while Americans do (*Get to the point already!*). We have the same words and the same phrase-making abilities, but we often apply them in different ways.

Newspapers provide many examples of different stylistic preferences. The first sentences of obituaries, for instance, provide the same kind of information, but with a different focus:[16]

New York Times[17]
Prince, the songwriter, singer, producer, one-man studio band and consummate showman, **died on Thursday at his home,** Paisley Park, in Chanhassen, Minn. He was 57.

Daily Telegraph[20]
Prince, who has died aged 57, **was to the pop music of the 1980s what David Bowie had been to that of the previous decade**, its sole authentic genius.

Boston Globe[18]
Prince, one of the most inventive and influential musicians of modern times with hits including "Little Red Corvette," "Let's Go Crazy," and "When Doves Cry," **was found dead at his home Thursday in suburban Minneapolis,** according to his publicist. He was 57.

The Guardian[21]
Typical of its prodigiously gifted composer, a multi-instrumentalist with a ferocious work ethic, **the 1984 album Purple Rain, and accompanying semi-autobiographical hit movie of the same name, launched** Prince, who has died aged 57, **on to the global stage.**

Variety[19]
Music icon **Prince**, who sold more than 100 million records during his storied career, **has died**. He was 57.

BBC News[22]
Prince—who's died at his home in Minnesota near Minneapolis at the age of 57—**wrote hundreds of songs for himself and other artists**.

I've highlighted the main clause (subject + verb phrase) of each of these sentences. The American sources make the fact of Prince's death the topic of the sentence. Information about who Prince was and what he did lies between the commas, as bonus information. Age at time of death is considered important enough to deserve its own sentence. The British obituaries prioritize the information about who Prince was or what he did. They mention death and age in relative clauses, set off by commas. American obituaries are written as news (of a death); information about the deceased is given as context for the story. The British ones are written as eulogies, with facts about the death added as asides. When British news sources report deaths, they often say the person *has **sadly** died*. That's something I may never get used to. Americans expect newspapers to sound more emotionally detached.

In other newspaper sections, one can find different stylistic preferences and traditions. In American business pages, stocks fall *to* a new price *from* an old one, but rise *from* an old price *to* a new one in the UK papers. In the sports section, British papers put the home team's score first; for Americans the winning team's score goes first. These differences in phrasing may reflect more general cultural differences. In the case of the stock prices and the obituaries, the American news focus is on *now*. Information about the past is put in the grammatical background.

* * *

So with all those differences at all those levels of linguistic consideration, we're left with the question: Do Americans and Brits
have the same language? Most people, including me, say yes.
Do we have the same culture? There people are more willing to
claim a difference. I'd say we have the same culture to much the
same extent that we have the same language. Our cultures are
based on the same foundations, and we share a range of values,
traditions, and assumptions about how the world works. Plunk a
Minnesotan in Shropshire or a Glaswegian in Texas, and they will
get some things wrong and offend some people. But they'll have
an easier time getting along than if you'd plunked them in Yemen
or Japan—and not just because of the language. For instance,
we share a tradition of breakfast, in which certain foods (eggs,
bacon, sausage, toast) are served on plates and consumed with
knives and forks alongside hot drinks. We eat at tables. Sometimes
we go to cafés. We call it "the most important meal of the day."
But the sausages have different spices, and the bacon is cut from
different parts of the pig. The relative consumption of tea and
coffee differs, and we disagree about which dairy products (if
any) to put in those drinks. We hold our forks differently. One
side cannot understand why anyone would want to eat baked
beans at such an early hour; the other cannot trust fluffy pancakes as a meal.

That's what our difference in language is like. We have the
same basic structures, but we perform the rituals in slightly different ways. Many, many slightly different ways. Still we mostly
understand what the other's going on about. We can appreciate
television from another English-speaking country without having
taken language lessons. We won't get all the jokes. We won't even
know that we've missed half the jokes. But we'll be able to follow
the plot.

Why are our Englishes so different?

How tame will his language sound who would describe Niagara
in language fitted for the falls at London bridge, or attempt the
majesty of the Mississippi in that which was made for the Thames?
        North American Review and Miscellaneous Journal (1815)[23]

What's the deal, America? Our English is more different from
British English than Canadian or Australian or New Zealand or
South African English are. The US also has more varied dialects
than those other "settler" Englishes have. Is it an accident that our
English is so different from the motherland's, or are Americans
trying to be difficult? A bit of both, as it turns out.

Any geographical obstacle provides the opportunity for different dialects to emerge. Highlanders often speak differently from
lowlanders, the urban differently from the rural. Rivers serve as
dialect boundaries, but bridges can bring dialects closer together.
Geographical obstacles don't come much bigger than oceans.
The 3,500 miles between Britain and its American colonies felt
even further in the days before steamships and flying machines.
The lack of voice recording or broadcast technologies meant that
English-speakers heard the English of those around them and no
one else. So when the language changed in one place, it would be
some time before the change made it to the other place, if it ever
made it there at all.

Geography forced American English to diverge from British
English. "The new circumstances under which we are placed,"
Thomas Jefferson remarked, "call for new words, new phrases, and
for the transfer of old words to new objects."[24] The Algonquian
languages of the northeast provided American English with many
of the words it needed for animals (**skunk, raccoon, chipmunk,
moose, opossum, caribou**), food plants (**hominy, succotash, pecan,
persimmon**), and indigenous artifacts and traditions (**powwow,**

wigwam, moccasin). Earlier European colonists in some areas provided the geographical vocabulary. From a Dutch word for a kind of cliff, Americans got *bluff*, which was the first known victim of anti-Americanism-ism, after English traveler Francis Moore called it "barbarous English" in 1735. From other colonial powers, American got Spanish *mesa* (for a type of plateau) and French *prairie*, *butte* (a type of flat hill), and *levee* for a river embankment. (An Englishman once proposed to me that Americans say *levee* because they're too prudish to say *dike* or *dyke*. Since *dyke* as slang for 'lesbian' came about two hundred years after Americans started saying *levee*, that hypothesis can be shot right down.)

When others' words weren't conveniently available for borrowing, early Americans exploited English's many means of making new words. Adding prefixes or suffixes to existing words gave us *rapids* (1744), *episcopalian* (1786; from the existing *episcopal*, 'relating to bishops'), and *deputize* (1811).[25] Adapting old words for new use resulted in *corn* specifically for maize (1608; *corn* previously referred to any grain), *clapboard* for the wedge-edged planks used in house building (1641, formerly a certain size of oak plank used for barrel making), *dime* for the ten-cent coin (1786, formerly 10% as a tithe to the Church), and *squatter* for a person living on land without permission (1788). Some of these words are now just as useful in other countries. That's not to say that American English did all the inventing and diverging. Separate from Americans, Britons started talking of *bookshops* (1762), *bank holidays* (1778), and *duvets* (1759). They started fondly calling people *lovey* (1684) and less fondly calling others *knobheads* (1738). And so the two nationlects started to drift apart.

Now, if geography were the only cause of linguistic differences, then Australian English should be three times more different from British than American English is, since it's three times further away. Time is another crucial factor. The first successful English colony in the New World was Jamestown (Virginia) in 1607. Thirty years later, Harvard College had been set up and the colonies would soon get their first printing press. When the American colonies declared their independence from the British crown in 1776, their population stood at about 2.5 million (one-third the size of the British population), and at least 85% were American-born. Some families had a five-generation history in the New World by this time, while Canada had been under British rule for only thirteen years. Australia, New Zealand, and South Africa were not yet twinkles in the empire's eye. American English thus had a 150-year head start on other Englishes outside the British Isles.

And they were 150 linguistically boisterous years. The English who founded the American colonies spoke Early Modern English (think Shakespeare). But by the time the United States came into being, English was in its Late Modern period (think Dickens—or Twain). The boundary between Early and Late Modern English is generally put at around 1750. Such boundaries are rather fuzzy; people didn't suddenly start talking differently on the first of January 1750. Nevertheless, they signal the closing down of some linguistic processes and the opening of others. The turn of the 17th century, when the first colonists were crossing the Atlantic, was a time of intense vocabulary growth. At the same time, existing words were asked to do more work—acquiring appreciably more meanings.[26] There was yet no Received Pronunciation, and many of the features of RP, like r-lessness after vowels, had not yet made themselves known. But these things began to change at the very time that people were hauling their dialects over the Atlantic. Thanks to local fertility and continued immigration from Britain, the colonies expanded from a population of about fifty thousand in 1650 to over a million in 1750, and then more than doubled again before independence.[27]

By the Early Modern period, spelling standardization had been going on for centuries. But it was still very usual for words to appear in various forms, even in a single document. The First Folio version of Shakespeare's *Romeo and Juliet* (1623), for instance, included three spellings of *devil* (none of which were *devil*) and four of *dew*.[28] Pronunciation and grammar varied even more—across regions and social classes. People learned the versions of the language that they heard in daily life, and they might have little idea of the grammatical fashions even a hundred miles away. There was no radio to hear "standard" English from, and not even a reliable dictionary in which to find the most common words. Several generations had learned English in America before Samuel Johnson published his influential dictionary in 1755.

Johnson's dictionary and several grammars from around the same time were the impetus for a new emphasis on prescribing "correct" and "incorrect" usage (which continues to plague us today). The linguistic changes-in-progress thus had the opportunity to carry on separately in the two countries, evolving in different directions or carrying on at different speeds in the two places, as we'll see in the next chapter.

Since 1776, life has changed a lot. And when life changes, language changes. People had to come up with ways to talk about trains and planes and automobiles—and about their parts, their functions, the infrastructures that have arisen because of them, and the activities we do with them. We needed nouns and verbs for communicating on a variety of technologies. Relationships shifted at home, at work, and in public, and we needed new ways to address people and to sound polite. Tastes changed, with some trends coming and going and others coming and staying. The chances that these cultural changes would have the same effects on English in Britain and its colonies were reduced by the geographical distances and the until-recent limitations in communication. If something was invented between the American Revolution and the Second World War, there is a good chance that Americans and Britons talk about it differently. But an additional engine for linguistic difference arose in the US: the politics of the relationship with Britain.

After the American Revolution, Britons continued to emigrate to America, but they were never again the top source of immigration to the US. The Brits went elsewhere. Between 1815 and 1850, eight hundred thousand Britons undertook the Great Migration of Canada. In the second half of that century, discovery of gold made Australia attractive, and after World War II the Australian government tried to ensure a white majority population by massively subsidizing the cost for Europeans to move. This led over a million Britons to become "ten-pound Poms," so-called after the price of the sea voyage. (*Pom*, short for *pomegranate*, was rhyming slang for *immigrant*. It remains an Australian epithet for British people.) Australia, Canada, and other parts of the British Empire (and later the Commonwealth) were thus exposed to more and more recent British English than Americans could get in the pre-television, pre-internet era.

And then there was the nastiness of the breakup between the US and Britain, involving an eight-year war with thousands of casualties (and then a further bloody row, 1812–14).[29] Canada, Australia, and New Zealand still have a monarch—the British monarch—unlike Americans, who rejected the British aristocracy and the British structure of government. This is important for language, not just because new words like *constitutionality* (1787) and *presidential* (referring to the hoped-for dignified demeanor of a president; 1804) were needed, but because rejecting the King's English was another way to reject the king. Some early Americans went as far as to suggest that French, Greek, or Hebrew should be the national language, just to spite the British. It was far more practical, however, to keep speaking and writing English, but with a patriotic twist.

Noah Webster, author of the first major dictionary of American English, was one of the clearest voices advocating linguistic separation from Britain. In Webster's words, Britain's linguistic preferences were not to be emulated because "the taste of her writers is already corrupted, and her language on the decline."[30] Americans needed to develop and celebrate their own ways of speaking and writing. According to Webster, looking to London for the "standard" of English was a self-sabotaging move. A new kind of English was needed to bring the disparate former colonies together as a nation—speaking in the same way so that regional differences in accent or vocabulary didn't lead the new Americans to think less of one another. "Our political harmony," according to Webster, required "a uniformity of language,"[31] and Americans should look to America for that language:

> [A] *national language* is a band of *national union*. Every engine should be employed to render the people of this country *national*; to call their attachments home to their own country; and to inspire them with the pride of national character. [...] Thus an habitual respect for another country, deserved indeed and once laudable, turns their attention from their own interests, and prevents their respecting themselves.[32]

Webster's *American Dictionary of the English Language*, published in 1828, was his magnum opus. A full dictionary to rival Johnson's, it recorded American English words, meanings, pronunciations, and spellings. However, it was his "Blue-Back Speller" (formally, *A Grammatical Institute of the English Language, part one*) that had put him on the map. First published in 1783, this spelling textbook sold more than sixty million copies over the next century, during which it was in continuous use in American schools.[33] New editions offered an increasing number of spellings that differed from those in Samuel Johnson's dictionary, the de facto standard in Britain.

Webster's linguistic patriotism was shared by early American politicians. John Adams, the second president, correctly predicted that America's use of English would help to propel the language past French as the global language of influence. He took

Americans' responsibility for English seriously and proposed a language academy on the model of the Académie Française "for refining, correcting, improving, and ascertaining the English language," adding, "perhaps the British king and parliament may have the honor of copying the example."[34] His successor, Thomas Jefferson, celebrated new American words and even invented quite a few of his own, including *indescribable*, *Anglophobia*, and *electioneering*.[35] Having experienced British snobbery about his own words, Jefferson noted the parallels in Britain and ancient Greece:

> will these [new dialects] adulterate, or enrich the English language? Has the beautiful poetry of Burns, or his Scottish dialect, disfigured [English]? Did the Athenians consider the Doric, the Ionian, the Aeolic, and other dialects, as disfiguring or as beautifying their language? Did they fastidiously disavow Herodotus, Pindar, Theocritus, Sappho, Alcaeus, or Grecian writers? On the contrary, they were sensible that the variety of dialects, still infinitely varied by poetical license, constituted the riches of their language.

However much presidents influence the language, they're not in charge of it and neither are dictionary makers or spelling-text writers. The general population had more mixed views about whether to look home or abroad for linguistic models and authorities.

Why aren't we more different?

Our language will be the same three hundred years thence [...] in spite of the exertions of Mr. Webster.

The Monthly Anthology and Boston Review, 1808[36]

In early 1776, as the American colonies contemplated independence, Benjamin Franklin predicted that unless Britain and the colonies could find a way to reconcile, our languages would become as different as Spanish and Portuguese.[37] In case any readers are under the impression that the Spanish and Portuguese do share a language, here's the beginning of British Airways' online information for diabetic passengers, in Spanish and Portuguese, respectively:[38]

En los vuelos de larga distancia, solemos servir la comida principal a las dos horas del despegue y después una comida más ligera aproximadamente dos horas antes del aterrizaje.	Em voos de longo curso, servimos normalmente a refeição principal até duas horas após a descolagem e, em seguida, uma pequena refeição até duas horas antes da hora de aterragem.

And, for comparison, here is the same information on their American and British websites:

On long haul flights, we usually serve the main meal within two hours of take-off and then a smaller meal within two hours of landing time.	On long haul flights, we usually serve the main meal within two hours of take-off and then a smaller meal within two hours of landing time.

That's their American translation on the left, by the way.

Franklin was not alone in expecting much greater divergence of the two Englishes. John Pickering, author of an early dictionary of Americanisms, foresaw a time "when Americans shall no longer be able to understand the works of Milton, Pope, Swift, Addison, and other English authors [...] without the aid of a translation."[39] Noah Webster thought American and British would be like two "rays of light, shot from the same center, and diverging from each other" so that future American English would be "as different from the future language of England, as the modern Dutch, Danish and Swedish are from the German or from one another."[40] A century later, this hadn't happened, but that didn't stop Henry Sweet (the real-life basis, some say, for Henry Higgins of *Pygmalion* and *My Fair Lady*) from declaring that within another century Americans, Britons, and Australians would not be able to understand each other. And yet here you are, reading the same book that people in another country are reading. (An author can hope.)

Unlike Spanish and Portuguese, which have been developing separately from their Latin roots for 1,500 years, American and British have only had 400 years to grow apart. How far could a language split in such a relatively short time? Other colonial situations give some clues. Think of Jamaica, for example, where (besides a standard Jamaican English) Patois or Patwa, an English-based creole language, has developed. See if you recognize the famous lines that have been translated into Jamaican Creole here:

Wi Faada we iina evn, mek piipl av nof rispek fi yu an yu niem.
Mek di taim kom wen yu ruul iina evri wie.

Creoles develop under very specific sociolinguistic conditions—the kinds of conditions that were created by the Atlantic slave trade.

1. Speakers of many languages need to communicate with one another.
   - Slave traders frequently made sure that groups of slaves were linguistically diverse in order to prevent them from plotting revolts. With hundreds of languages in West Africa, this was achievable.
2. Access to the language of power is uneven.
   - Few slaves had sufficient exposure to the English of the slave traders and slave holders to learn more than a basic vocabulary, but they had to learn some quickly. So they spoke a "pidgin" English—that is, English words with very little in the way of English grammar.

3. When a pidgin is passed on to subsequent generations, its grammatical form develops and solidifies and it becomes a creole.

- What arose in Jamaica was a language that combines a basic English vocabulary with pronunciations influenced by the native languages of its early learners, and a grammar that reduces the number of word forms used—such as *yu* for both *you* and *your* in the beginning of the Lord's Prayer. (Did you recognize that as the text on the previous page?)

The United States is home to a few creoles, including Gullah (still occasionally heard along the southeastern coast) and Hawaiian Creole English. But despite the multilingualism of the American colonies and later states, our English stayed basically English—not a creole—because the majority of English learners were not learning under the horrific conditions of slavery. Most immigrant groups had full access to standard Englishes. They became bilingual and passed on English to their children, so that by the third generation the language of the "home country" was typically lost to the family. Simplified pidgin forms of English may have been used at first between the English and various Native American tribes, but those pidgins did not need to develop into long-standing creoles because they did not need to serve as anyone's first language. Native Americans became multilingual, with English as one of their languages. Over time, the bane of English monolingualism has meant that most indigenous languages are threatened, if not extinct.

Maybe South Africa provides a better comparison than Jamaica. Dutch settlement in South Africa started around the same time as English settlement of North America. Yet the Dutch of South Africa turned into Afrikaans, rather than staying Dutch. Not only does Afrikaans have its own name, pronunciation, and lots of non-Dutch vocabulary, its grammar has diverged from Dutch in less time than American English has been around. To measure how different they are, researchers asked Afrikaans and Dutch speakers to listen to a news story about a runaway kangaroo, but the Afrikaaners heard the story in Dutch and the Dutch heard it in Afrikaans. When asked comprehension questions about the story, the Afrikaans speakers scored only 44% on their understanding of Dutch, and the Dutch speakers 62% for Afrikaans. When the same test was done for Scandinavian languages, Norwegian speakers on average scored 89% for comprehension of Swedish.[41] Given that both American and British reporters can be heard in each other's country's news broadcasts (without dubbing or subtitles), we can estimate that our scores for understanding each other would be even higher.

The English language in America had support, in the form of political and cultural connection, that Dutch in South Africa did not have. The Netherlands never colonized South Africa; the Dutch East India Company did. The trading company brought settlers from Holland, but also sailors from other parts of Europe and slaves from Asia and Africa. Since the Netherlands had no interest in colonizing South Africa, the contact between South African Dutch speakers and European ones was limited—even more so as the settlers moved inland. By comparison, the American population included a good number born in Britain for about two hundred years and had British government for most of that time. The contact between the two countries kept their Englishes alike.

The best comparisons for the relationship between American and British English are Latin-American and European Spanish, Brazilian and European Portuguese, or Canadian and European French. But still, comparing Latin-American Spanish to American English also gives hints to what could have changed for English but didn't. Pronouns, for one thing. Most European languages historically had multiple ways to say 'you': singular versus plural and formal versus informal. English was no exception, with *thou* (informal singular) and *you* (plural or formal singular). By the time the American colonies were being settled, *you* was well on its way to replacing *thou*—though *thou* was still around in religious and emotive situations and was used more generally in parts of the north of England and Scotland. One group stuck with *thou* even longer: the Quakers, who settled in numbers in Rhode Island and in the mid-Atlantic colonies (now the states of Pennsylvania, New Jersey, and Delaware). The Quakers later migrated southward and westward, and until the revolution (which challenged their pacifist principles) they were very active in American politics. So, infant American English had enthusiastic, widespread, and influential *thou*-sayers, and yet *thou* died the same death in the US as it died in England.

Compare this to Spanish, which formerly made singular/plural and formal/informal distinctions in its pronouns. Today the former 'polite singular you' *vos* is used in much of Latin America instead of (or as well as) the formerly more formal (but now informal) *tú*. Spain retains a distinction between formal and informal plurals *ustedes* and *vosotros*, while American Spanish has mostly lost *vosotros*. A similar pronoun division exists for European and Brazilian Portuguese. English speakers have come to compensate for our loss of the *thou/you* distinction by making new plural forms for the formerly plural *you*, but these remain regional and are rarely used in formal language. They include *y'all* in the American South, *yinz* (probably derived from Scots-Irish *you ones*) in western Pennsylvania, *youse* in Ireland and New Jersey, and *you lot* in informal British English. American *you guys*, though very informal, is the one to watch, as it's heard in many parts of the world now.

The pronoun differences across Spanish are a bigger deal than having different words for footwear or car parts. Linguists make a distinction between **open and closed classes** of words. The open classes are the areas of vocabulary that are considered to be prone to expansion and change—nouns, verbs, and adjectives. The differences between American and British English mostly lie in the open classes. The closed classes are things like articles (*the, a*), conjunctions (*and, but*), and pronouns. We rarely add new closed-class words to the language, and the ones we have resist change. Noun, verb, and adjective differences are superficial differences. Differences in the closed classes are more remarkable, more basic to the language. The American and British English differences are mostly very superficial. We have resisted the opportunities for deeper divisions, like pronoun differences. So we might say that American and British English are not even as different as American and European Spanish or Portuguese.

So were Ben Franklin and others being ridiculous when they predicted that American would cease to be English at some point? Franklin's comparison with Spanish and Portuguese works to the extent that the Roman Empire spread Latin around Europe and the British Empire spread English around the world. Give it another five hundred years and maybe English would separate like Latin did into what we now call *the Romance languages*.

But probably not. For one thing, the Latin that Roman soldiers took across Europe was not a standardized language. We now call it *Vulgar Latin* to distinguish it from Classical Latin, the more regular written form. By the 17th century, English had a solid written history and had already been through the big grammatical and pronunciation upheavals that distinguish it from other Germanic languages. For another thing, the British and Roman Empires worked differently. When the Romans came, saw, and conquered, they put their language in the hands (or mouths, as it were) of the conquered people. The English, on the other hand, were more interested in hanging out with other English speakers. (I can't help but think of the current English style of retirement in Spain—moving to a village full of other English retirees, speaking English and going to pubs and fish-and-chip shops.) The English settlers did not often integrate with indigenous peoples, nor did they invite the invaded to become full members of the English-speaking society.

This meant that in the American colonies English was mostly spoken by the children of English speakers, and a minority spoke it as a second language.

And since many of the early settlers were from southern England, so was their English. At the time, the southeast, particularly London, was increasingly the standard-maker for British English. American lexicographer Charlton Laird supposed that if the immigrants to America had come from the northwest, American and British would now be as different as Danish and Norwegian.[42] Still not as different as Spanish and Portuguese, but more different than today's American and British standards. Later colonial migration came from the north of England, Scotland, and Ulster, but that migration was mostly to the inland and southern parts of colonial America—rather than to New England and the coastal north, where the universities and dictionaries were founded and where Americans sought their linguistic standards. The non-southern dialects of Britain stamped their marks on Appalachian English and African-American Vernacular English in particular.[43]

The cultural and technological situation of the British Empire was terrifically different from what the Roman Empire had to deal with. The invention of the printing press in the 15th century sped up the creation of standard forms of language, and these spread further as literacy rose over the subsequent centuries. Because the written word was now easily shared, standards of spelling, vocabulary, and usage could be shared. The books that early Americans read were mostly from Britain—whether shipped over from London or reprinted locally. America and Britain thus remained tethered to the same written tradition. And since England had the longer tradition, many early Americans were uncomfortable with the idea that Americans should have their own standards for English usage. Citing the biblical Tower of Babel as a cautionary tale, the *Monthly Magazine and American Review* in 1800 argued that "books are the only adequate authority for the use of words" and good American English must be like those "whose dialect is purified by intimate intercourse with English books."[44] Alexis de Tocqueville experienced this in the early 1800s: "American authors may be said to live rather in England than in their own country, since they constantly study the English writers and take them every day for their models."[45] Though Webster's dictionary and spelling book sold well in the US, Americans had little interest in his grammars, preferring British authors. (Not only did they contain the language of the old country, they were cheaper, since American printers didn't have to pay royalties to English authors.) Despite Webster's efforts, it wasn't until the start of the 20th century that American linguists started talking about a "Standard *American* English."[46]

Though Webster had more impact on spelling, it was certainly not to the degree that he had hoped. He would have liked us to write more like he did in his *Essays and fugitiv writings* (1790):

> In the essays, ritten within the last yeer, a considerable change of spelling iz introduced by way of experiment. This liberty waz taken by the writers before the age of queen Elizabeth, and to this we are indeted for the preference of modern spelling over that of Gower and Chaucer. The man who admits that the change of *housbonde, mynde, ygone, moneth* into *husband, mind, gone, month* iz an improovment, must acknowledge also the riting of *helth, breth, rong, tung, munth* to be an improovment.[47]

Webster included few such spellings in his 1828 dictionary. *Tung* made it, as did *fether* for *feather* and *bridegoom* (as it was in Old English) instead of *bridegroom*. But those spellings died with Webster; his successors removed them from the dictionary. The Websterian spellings that stayed were mostly for words that had long been spelled in two ways in Britain. Webster hadn't invented those spellings; he'd opted for them.

Even those minor spelling reforms had a long, uphill struggle. Two years after Webster's 1828 dictionary, his former assistant Joseph Worcester published a competitor dictionary that gave many people what they wanted: English that looked and sounded more like London English. Worcester's dictionary immediately outsold Webster's, leading to a decades-long propaganda campaign that came to be known as the Dictionary Wars. After Webster's death, the war was vehemently fought by the savvy G. & C. Merriam Company, who had bought the dictionary rights from Webster's family. The battles were fought in the opinion pages, in advertising campaigns, and in commercial boycotts—with the Merriams refusing to do business with shops that carried Worcester. Each publisher was keen for the public to see their dictionary as the most authoritative, and so they published advertising tracts with testimonials from the ever-increasing number of American states—their judiciaries, their boards of education, their legislatures—claiming that their dictionary was the most informative and most trusted. They assured Americans that their dictionary was best loved in Britain—surely the greatest approbation and a canny move for the Americanizing Webster's.[48] Newspapers proudly came down on one side or the other of the war—usually Worcester's, spelling *favour* and *centre* long into the 19th century. Government bodies that used Worcester's spellings were held up as proof positive that "before many years the last remnant of the Websterian orthography [will be] extirpated, like a noxious weed, from the noble language it deforms and corrupts."[49] Merriam-Webster eventually won the Dictionary Wars, not because people liked Webster's dictionary or spellings better, but because Worcester died.

Books weren't the only way that Americans kept in touch with British English. Although schoolhouses were plentiful in the settled areas, opportunities for secondary and higher education were few. Those with money sent their children to England for their education. Those anglified young people returned to America, where their accents were imitated by family and friends. The characteristic "Boston Brahmin" accent associated with Harvard University and its environs came about through this kind of contact with later fashionable British English. Those who had come over on the *Mayflower* did not have the broad *a* in *grass* or the *r*-dropping in words like *father*, but the later East Coast establishment took the trouble to import those pronunciations. Keeping up that image of linguistic propriety, Harvard University trained its students in a "college pronunciation" that bore resemblance to the accent of the English upper classes, serving as "a breakwater against the tides [...] of misleading fashions" in American English.[50] Though the average 19th-century American had little direct contact with speakers of British English, many—if not most—still felt that the true home of English was in England. If they didn't have good access to what Old England sounded like, New England could offer an approximation.

The traffic in words, pronunciations, spelling, and grammar goes both ways across the Atlantic, so—barring any apocalyptic scenarios—we shouldn't expect the separation of American and British English to ever match the extent of the separation of Vulgar Latin into the modern Romance languages. At the same time, we should not underestimate the forces that still keep them apart.

4

AMERICA:
SAVING THE ENGLISH LANGUAGE SINCE 1607

The American of today is much more honestly English, in any
sense that Shakespeare would have understood, than the so-called
Standard English of England.

H. L. Mencken (1921)[1]

In 1613, only six years after the Jamestown colony was first settled,
Reverend Alexander Whitaker's *Good Newes from Virginia* was
published in London. In this sermon, Whitaker urged the English
to feel empathy for the Algonquin peoples, whom he saw as being
much like the English had been before Christianity. English cleric
William Crashaw wrote a preface for the publication, in which he
despaired at English badmouthing of the colonies:

amongſt the many diſcouragements that haue attended this
glorious buſineſſe of the Virginian plantation : none hath been
ſo frequent and ſo forcible as the calumnies and ſlanders raiſed
vpon our Colonies and the Countrey itſelfe. Theſe being deviſed
by the Diuell, and ſet abroach by idle and baſe companions, are
blowen abroad by Papiſts, Players, and ſuchlike, till they haue
filled the vulgar eares : And hauing once entred, then they run
(like wilde fire) from man to man : For as wilde fire hardly
finds a houſe which is not matter combuſtible; ſo theſe idle

96

tales hardly meete a man who giues (paſſage at the leaſt, if not) credit to them[2]

Four hundred years later, the notion of British calumnies and slanders upon America is still familiar, but some of the language is not. No one spells like that anymore. We've lost the ſ way of writing the letter *s*. We don't *give passage* to ideas or use the word *abroach* or put the adjective *combustible* after the noun it modifies. Both Brits and Americans have given up on *hath*, replacing the *th* verb suffix with *s*. English has moved along in remarkably similar ways in the two countries.

Still, it's not uncommon to hear claims that Americans today speak "like Shakespeare." Most of the time, these claims are about accents. Americans, they say, sound more authentically Elizabethan than all the sirs and dames who tread the boards at the Royal Shakespeare Company. In Shakespeare's day the *r* was more pronounced, *grass* always rhymed with *ass*, and there was no lip rounding in the vowel in *hot*. These pronunciations are found in most of America today, but they have suffered mightily in England.

The American linguist Albert Marckwardt coined a name for this situation: *colonial lag*. By his thinking, English in America had suffered the shock of transplantation:

Transplanting usually results in a time lag before the organism, be it a geranium or a brook trout, becomes adapted to its new environment. There is no reason why the same principle should not apply to a people, their language, and their culture.[3]

Unlike Marckwardt, I (and I suspect you too) can think of a few reasons why transplanted languages and cultures are rather different from transplanted geraniums. Their complexity, for one thing. The way they reproduce. The fact that no geraniums from the old pot are coming to visit the transplanted geranium in its new digs.

If we tried to modernize Crashaw's preface, we'd not see any colonial lag. The modern American translation would not be more like the original than the modern British translation. *Wilde fire* would become *wildfire* for both. We'd spell *Devil* with a *v*. We would turn *hath* into *has* and *blowen* into *blown*. Any American "lags" in the changes to Crashaw's language were short-lived. Rather than English getting stuck in one place and moving on in the other, most of English's evolution in the past four hundred years has been ticking along on both continents. But still, some British–American differences emerged because time provided different forks in the road, detours, and diversions.

For people (and there are so many of them) who argue that change corrupts English, any evidence that Americans preserve the language should surely be a redeeming fact. By pronouncing the *r*'s in *farmer* and the *a* in *secretary*, by keeping the words **closet** and **faucet** in active use, America has saved the English language! It has preserved those bits of English that the British have been careless with. Alas, linguistic complainers are rarely so consistent. Many of them assume that if there are differences in the two countries, then the way things are said in the new country must be the new way. Then when it's shown that the American way is the older way, the British complainers often lack "the magnanimity to acknowledge their mistake," as New Yorker Romeyn Beck complained about this very issue in 1829.[4] Old-fashioned American ways of talking are sometimes admired by traditionalists, but at least as often they are taken as a sign that Americans are a backward people who don't recognize that their ways of speaking are inelegant or illogical and in need of replacement.

A case in point is **I guess** meaning 'I suppose.' "There is no word, for which New-Englandmen are more teased," wrote Beck.[5] About seventy years later, in their style guide *The King's English*, the Fowler brothers Britishly admitted that "what we are often rude enough to call [Americans'] vulgarisms are in fact good old English," pointing out that Chaucer used *I gesse* in much the same way as Americans use *I guess*. But, they continue, "though it is good old English, it is not good new English." The Fowlers discount *I guess* as a viable part of the King's English because "we have it not from Chaucer, but from the Yankees."[6] Ew, the Americans touched it! Get it away! It's got *the lurgy*! (Or as the denizens of American playgrounds would say: *cooties!*)

Before I go much further on the topic of whose words are older, I've got to get this one off my chest. Britain, Americans call your football *soccer* because you taught them to. Just like *rugger* is a nickname for *rugby football*, *soccer* came from the full name of the game, *association football*. The word comes from England. You should be proud of it.

There, that feels better.

A case in point: punctuation

Punctuation was, it is sad to say, invented a very long time ago. Even more frustrating, it has remained with us ever since.

Anne Elizabeth Moore,
The Manifesti of Radical Literature (2007)

Words are like birds, and not just because they rhyme. Take the monarch flycatcher, for instance: a small, insectivorous bird of the Solomon Islands. On the big island of Makira, the birds are all black. Thirty-seven kilometers away on Ugi, a single gene mutation means that the monarch flycatchers have a chestnut breast. It's enough that Makira birds don't even recognize the Ugi birds as their own species.[7] Like Darwin's finches on the Galapagos, these birds just needed a little distance in order to start evolving in different ways. On other islands, an immigrant species moves in and replaces a local species, like the village weaver did in Mauritius, causing the cape canary population to crash. In the same way, sometimes a word changes in new environs and sometimes the habitat is changed by new words coming in. But then there's the feral pigeon. All over the world, pigeons look much the same, act much the same, pollute the cities much the same. Most English words are pigeon-like, infesting new places with little adaptation. Sometimes birds and words change through migration. Sometimes they don't.

Words for punctuation offer a neat little laboratory for viewing the possible fates of migrating words. The rules of punctuation, the forms of punctuation, and the names of those forms were all extremely volatile at the point when English people started settling in North America. The printing press had only been around for about 150 years, and standards for printed English were still developing. Different names for the same printed marks were competing for their own space in the linguistic ecosystem, and sometimes they found different niches in different places.

In some cases, British and American took the same path. Both opted for **comma** over the earlier term *virgule* (for the mark, that I just incorrectly put after the word *mark*). Both countries have also gladly adopted the latecomer **question mark** (1862) for ?, rather than earlier terms like *interrogative point* or *interrogation point*.

In other cases, punctuation terms that thrived in America succumbed in Britain. **Quotation marks** (1715) started in Britain and carried on in America, but then **inverted commas** (1839) took over Britain—for a time, at least. *Inverted comma* is not the most user-friendly name, since it takes the print compositor's perspective on the thing ("take a comma; turn it upside down"), rather than the perspective of readers or writers, who are more concerned with the significance of the mark in text. So in the 1970s and '80s, when creative writing became popular in British primary school curricula, educators championed a more transparent name: **speech marks**. These days, younger British adults increasingly call them *quotation marks*—a more grown-up version of *speech marks*.

Their parents and grandparents look on this as Americanization, replacing the very British *inverted commas*. But since *quotation marks* is older in Britain, we could instead consider it a revival, a restoration, a resurrection. Americans preserved the term *quotation marks*, took care of it, then released it back into the wild in its ancestral grounds.

And then there's the dot. At the turn of the 17th century, English writers and printers were increasingly separating sentences with a dot (replacing the colon that you can see in Crashaw's passage in the previous section). Around that time, **period** (1582) and **full point** (1587) were introduced as names for it. **Full stop** shows up a few years later (1600) to mean 'the end of a sentence.' ("Come, full stop," urges Salarino in *The Merchant of Venice*, wishing for the end to an overlong story.) Sixty-five more years pass before *full stop* is unambiguously used as a name for a punctuation mark. So by this time Britain has three ways of talking about the dot. Having several names for the one thing is not particularly economical, and the rise of grammar books and universal schooling increased the pressure to talk consistently about dots on pages. For a while, some used *full stop* to mean the dot at the end of a sentence, and *period* to mean the same dot in other contexts—for example in abbreviations. By the 20th century, Americans generally used *period* and didn't bother much with *full stop*, while Britons retained *full stop* and eventually lost *period*. (*Full point* is still occasionally found in printers' jargon.)

Then came the figurative use of *period*: *I won't go out with you. Period.* Americans had started using *period* in this way by 1914. The British found it useful and by 1920 started using it too. But the long-lost punctuation word *period* didn't sound quite right in Britain, so by 1923 Brits were using *full stop* for this kind of emphasis. With my linguist hat on, I'd call this a **calque**, or *loan translation*. In a calque, the image or idea comes from one place, and it's translated straightforwardly into another language. So, for example, English *flea market* comes from French *marché aux puce* ('market at the fleas'), borrowing the idea to name the market after insects, but not borrowing the French words for it. In the other direction, English *skyscraper* became French *gratte-ciel* ('scrapes sky'). *Full stop* provides a case of a calque between two varieties of the same language. Someone in America had the idea to say the name of final punctuation to emphasize a point, and that idea was borrowed. Period. But the words for conveying that idea were changed to fit with the local vocabulary. Full stop. And then something unexpected happened: the calque *full stop* popped over to America. A new version of the idiom in the US uses both: *Period. Full stop.*

- Barack Obama: "Voters who want to vote should be able to vote. **Period. Full stop.**"
- Marc Thiessen, of the American Enterprise Institute: "We do not interrogate terrorists any more. **Period. Full stop.**"[8]
- Music critic David Wild: "Bob Dylan is our greatest living writer. **Period. Full stop.**"[9]

Complaining about this latest Washington cliché, the *Christian Science Monitor* called it "a younger cousin to *at the end of the day*,"[10] another British turn of phrase that's had much success in American political and business talk. This isn't the only recent migration of British punctuation words to American shores. The optional comma before *and* in lists of three or more items had an American name first: ***serial comma*** (1922). Thanks to influential style guides, this comma is used more in the US. But Americans increasingly call it by its later British name: ***Oxford comma*** (1951). Why? Because calling it the *Oxford comma* "gives it a bit of class, a little snob appeal," according to *The New Yorker*'s "Comma Queen," Mary Norris.[11]

So names for punctuation marks have illustrated a few directions a language can take when it splits in two:

- The same old term can be used in both places, with no change. For instance, *colon* has kept the same name since the 16th century (though pronunciation of its second vowel has drifted: British "on" versus American "un").

- Different old terms can carry on in different places (*period* versus *full stop*).

- An old term can survive in one place, but be replaced by a new term in another place (*quotation marks* versus *inverted commas* and *speech marks*).

- The same new term can catch on in both places (*question mark*).

- Old words can get new meanings—and those new meanings may or may not be shared in both places. *Period. Full stop.*

After the Fall

UK: We call it Autumn, from the Old French word *autompne* and the Latin *autumnus*

USA: WE CALL IT FALL BECAUSE LEAF FALL DOWN

Circulated on Twitter

That gem would fit well into English comedian Michael McIntyre's bit about American English. McIntyre claims that Americans speak differently from Britons because Americans are a bit thick and need explicit instruction about the world. (This, from a man who lives in a country where paths are labeled *way in* and *way out* instead of *entrance* and *exit*.) *Pavement* is *sidewalk*, McIntyre says, because Americans need to be told what to do (walk) and where to do it (on the side of the road). You must say *horseback riding* (rather than *riding* or *horse riding*) to Americans, McIntyre warns, else Americans will try to ride on a different part of the horse. And *fall* tells us what happens to the leaves.

McIntyre's joke implies that Americans made up the word *sidewalk*. But no, the English invented that one in the early 17th century.

The "LEAF FALL DOWN" joke implies both that Americans came up with the name *fall* and that they don't call the season **autumn**. Neither of those implications stands up to scrutiny. (You may tell me that jokes aren't meant to be scrutinized, but some of us have nothing better to do.) *Fall*, for the season, sits in Johnson's 1755 dictionary, with an illustrative quotation from a 1693 John Dryden poem:

> What crowds of patients the town doctor kills,
> Or how last fall he raised the weekly bills.

Fall is not the original English way of referring to the season: that would be *hærfest*, 'harvest'. *Autumn* crept in from French in the 1300s, and then in the 1500s some started using *fall*, often in the longer form *fall of the leaf*. When America was settled, both these terms came—and stayed, each with its own jobs to do. Americans might plan to do things *in the fall* or take classes in the *fall semester*, but they use the phrase *autumn leaves* over three times more than *fall leaves*.[12] And who could forget *Autumn in New York*? (The jazz standard, that is. The 2000 film, which has Richard Gere romancing a terminally ill Winona Ryder, is best forgotten.)

While Americans didn't invent *fall*, it was far more successful in the US than it had been at home—so much so that it was among the earliest words to be complained about as an Americanism.[13] It was also at fault for one of the first recorded cases of British–American miscommunication. A Mary Muslin recalled an encounter in Scotland:

> A grave looking man who sat near me one day at dinner, said a good deal about the *fall* and the events that should have happened before and after the *fall*. As he spoke also about *Providence* and *Salem* and *Ebenezer*, and as great deference was shown to every thing he said, and being as I told you, a grave looking man in a

black coat, I was not sure but he might be some learned theologian, and imagined he was speaking about Oriental Antiquities and the fall of *Adam*. But I was soon undeceived. The gentleman had lived for some time in Virginia.[14]

He sounded impressive and intelligent until it was discovered that he was talking American. Typical.

Why did Americans take to *fall* while Brits forgot it? Maybe it's because Americans have more to be poetic about. Autumn in Britain is relatively drab. But for the occasional imported tree, the leaves fade to yellow and fall brown. Nothing to write home about, or use more descriptive language for. The early English colonists lived in parts of America where leaf-falling is truly spectacular, with red and sugar maples, red oaks, and sassafras exploding into fiery oranges and reds. It's so fantastic that billions of dollars in tourist money are generated each autumn in the six states of New England.[15] There's even an American word for those tourists: *leaf peepers*. Money really does grow on trees in America.

These days, *fall* has made its way back into Britain with the helpful clock-changing mnemonic **Spring forward, fall back**, apparently coined by the *Los Angeles Examiner* in the 1950s.[16] *Autumn back* just doesn't do the trick. On the Reddit "British Problems" website, the disgruntled were counseled: "Don't think of it as an Americanism, but as Elizabethan English." Better to be associated with people who only bathed twice a year than with the Americans.

Neither mad nor smart

Our greatest danger now is, that we shall continue to use anti-
quated words, which were brought to this country by our fore-
fathers nearly two centuries ago.

John Pickering (1816)

When John Pickering wrote *A Vocabulary, or collection of words and phrases which have been supposed to be peculiar to the United States of America*, he was well aware that many of these "peculiarities" had come over from England. The problem, as Pickering saw it, was less that Americans were making up new words and more that they were not keeping up with the fashionable standard of London, where **bank-notes** had replaced **bills** and no one said **brush** to refer to cut-down branches anymore. Though Noah Webster and others were arguing loudly for an American English separate from British, many Americans wanted to resist the words, like *folks* or *tavern*, that would make them sound like provincial hicks to the trendsetters back in England.

Adjectives seem particularly susceptible to these kinds of worries and criticisms. And they happen to be my favorite part of speech. I love their extremely malleable meanings. Adjective meanings are generally simpler than noun or verb meanings, telling us just one property of a thing. *Sharp* just tells us about the property 'able to cut.' Because adjective meanings are so minimal, they're relatively easy to apply to new situations—but then you have to interpret the adjective in a way that makes sense for that situation. A *sharp knife* has a honed edge. A *sharp stick* has a pointy point. A *sharp cactus* has lots of pointy points. When we take *sharp* out of the realm of touch and into other realms, we get new meanings: *a sharp musical note, a sharp look, a sharp cheese, a sharp wit, a sharp dresser*. (Americans added that last one.) We have a sense that all those kinds of *sharp* are somehow related to the 'able to cut' meaning, but they change and change.

To me, that is the mad beauty of adjectives. But not everyone sees that beauty, and so **mad** is one of those words that raise ire and make people crazy. (See what I did there?) Both the 'insane' sense and the 'angry' sense of *mad* go back to the Middle Ages; before that, it applied to animals and meant 'rabid.' Move it to talking about people, and the different aspects of the rabid animal come out: aggression (as if one is angry) versus loss of the senses and frenzied behavior (as if one is insane). By the 18th century, British English had mostly stopped using the 'angry' sense of *mad*, and so the use of 'angry' *mad* seemed a bit simple to English people—like you couldn't tell the difference between feeling angered and losing your senses altogether.

And so 'angry' *mad* stuck out as an Americanism early on, with the Reverend John Witherspoon allowing that it was also "perhaps an English vulgarism."[17] One wonders if Witherspoon had noticed this vulgarism in his Bible: "And being exceedingly mad against them, I persecuted them even unto strange cities" (Acts 26:11, King James Version). By 1909 Ambrose Bierce, in his "little blacklist of literary faults," thought the 'angry' sense was "an Americanism of lessening prevalence."[18] But that was just Bierce's wishful thinking; 'angry' *mad* has not gone away.

Smart is another adjective gone rambling—though it started as a verb. When something *smarts* it is painful, so the adjective *smart* first meant 'cutting' or 'painful.' *Smart words* were words that cut: hurtful, critical words. Cutting is often associated with intelligence—as we saw for *sharp wit,* but also in expressions like *incisive* and *rapier wit.* By the 16th century, *smart* was firmly associated with intelligence. Then it sailed off to America, put down roots, and became the thing to be in New York, according to the critic Luc Sante:

Unlike intelligence, which connotes disinterested speculation, smartness is practical and therefore democratic. It is the intelligence potentially available to all, not the province of a specialized elite. At its most populist, *smartness* becomes *smarts*.[19]

Meanwhile in Britain, **clever** took *smart*'s place, shifting in meaning from 'nimble-bodied' to 'nimble-minded.' In early America, *clever* meant 'having an agreeable disposition,' and so its return to meaning 'nimble-minded' provides evidence of the continuing British effect on American English. Meanwhile, British use of *smart* shifted to fashion: a *smart suit* or a *smart look,* or nowadays in the instruction to dress *smart casual*—not formal dress, but a well-put-together outfit. The now-American sense of *smart* has been grudgingly let back into Britain in *smart cards* and *smartphones* and other *smart technology.* These are allowable "terms of art," *The Economist Style Guide* tells us, while cautioning against the unnecessary Americanism of using *smart* to refer to human intelligence.[20]

The Vikings gave English the adjective **ill** meaning 'evil,' as in *ill will.* Its health-related meanings emerged in the 16th century, in plenty of time to be carried westward by English colonists. American *ill* tends to be just for the really evil conditions; I might say someone with cancer or schizophrenia is *ill*, but I wouldn't say it of someone with tonsillitis. But in Britain, you might be ill with a minor virus or infection. Americans mostly still use the Anglo-Saxon word **sick** to mean 'unwell,' whereas in Britain *feeling sick* has turned into a more specific description of stomach upset. *Sick* still prevails over *ill* in Britain when (as in the US) it is used before a noun: *sick day, sick leave, sick pay.* Both adjectives have also acquired positive meanings in American slangs that have travelled to Britain: *sick* via the surfing and skateboarding world and *ill* through hip-hop music.

The last adjective I'll mention (for now) is **regular**, meaning 'ordinary,' which took pride of place among the BBC's 50 "most noted" Americanisms in Britain. "I hate the fact I now have to order a *regular Americano*," wrote Marcus Edwards of Hurst Green. "What ever happened to a medium sized coffee?" The 'measured' or 'rule-based' meaning of *regular* (*we meet at regular intervals*) is shared by British and American English. The 'default size' sense was popularized in Britain by American fast-food chains whose fries or drinks come in *regular* and *large* sizes: the ordinary size and the more impressive size. I must pause to note that Marcus's good old days of *medium sized coffees* are probably a figment of Marcus's imagination. Before American fast-food and coffee chains invaded Britain, there just weren't enough coffee-size options to require such a phrase.

For Americans the 'ordinary' meaning of *regular* goes much further; there's *regular gas* (as opposed to the 'premium' kind), *regular Coke* (as opposed to the diet kind), and *regular guys* (as opposed to pretentious guys). That 'ordinary' sense of *regular* came over with the Pilgrims, and it flourished in the US. In Britain, it had dropped out of use by the mid-19th century. It *felt* like a new meaning when the fast-food companies brought it to Britain, but it had a British pedigree. Do you think that pedigree would make Marcus want to order a *regular Americano* rather than a *medium* one? No, I didn't think so either.

Is American provincial English?

The whole country was like some remote part of England that I had never seen before, the people like English provincial or colonial folk, in short, they were like queer English people.

Frances Kemble (1865)[21]

One of the problems with thinking that Americans talk like Elizabethans is that there was no single way that Elizabethans talked. They had no telecommunications, no combustion engines, no commuting, no voice recording, no dictionaries, and education was only for the privileged. Since they mostly heard people in their immediate vicinity, the Elizabethans sounded like the people near them and different from the people of other towns and counties. There were far more dialectal vocabulary differences and different grammatical rules, not to mention pronunciation differences. Listen to Americans today. You might find words or sounds they have in common with lowland Scots. And then you might find some things in common with Yorkshire speech or West Country speech. Maybe American English is what it is because it comes from all corners of the British Isles.

It's a romantic story, but often too good to be true. Take, for example, the verb *to mind*, in the sense that means 'heed': *Mind your parents! Mind the Scriptures!* This sense of *mind* isn't used in most British English, but it is found in Ireland and North America. It's fairly easy to conclude from those facts that Irish immigrants brought this meaning to the US. You must resist that conclusion! Resist, I say! The 'heed' meaning arose in England in the 1500s, then the English took that meaning to Ireland and America. In the 18th century, the English gave *mind* another meaning: 'be cautious about.' Like the 'heed' sense, this *mind* was used in commands: *Mind the gap! Mind your head!* At this point, the 'heed' meaning started to fall away in England. Not worrying (and perhaps not knowing) that it had become unfashionable in England, the Irish and the Americans went on using the 'heed' meaning happily, but separately. So in using *mind* to mean 'heed,' Americans aren't using an Irishism; they just have an old English meaning in common with the Irish.[22] General American English shares properties with the English of Ireland, Scotland, and northern and western England because distance and local identity meant that those regions were less likely (or at least slower) to be affected by the more recent "metropolitan" linguistic fashions of London–Cambridge–Oxford.

It works the same for accents. Speakers of General American English (the "standard" form of the language) can seem to have more in common with British northerners than with those who have southeastern accents that are closer to Received Pronunciation. In Scotland, for example, you can hear the *r* after vowels. In most of the North of England, there's a "flat" *a* vowel in *bath* and *grass* rather than the "broad" pronunciation *bahth, grahss*. These, like the case of *mind*, are instances of the British regions retaining older forms that the southeast has given up. That is, Received Pronunciation is a bit of a fashion-addled dandy. Its current pronunciations pop up anachronistically in any costume drama about upper-class English people because we tend to think of its clipped syllables and peculiar vowels as a "conservative" style of speaking. But the elites have never really been all *that* conservative when it comes to pronunciation. John Wells, author of the *Longman Pronunciation Dictionary*, has noted fifteen changes that RP underwent *during the twentieth century,* from the tendency of *Tuesday* to come out as *Chewzday* to the merger of the "aw" and "or" sounds.[23] Which reminds me of the (real) estate agent who said: "You're about to see a house without a flaw." "Gosh," said the amazed client, "what do you walk on?"

The earliest American English was fairly close to "metropolitan" English. The Puritans were mostly urban, literate folk and had Cambridge-educated leaders. Virginia was settled by gentry. English visitors to the colonies commented on "the English tongue being spoken by all ranks, in a degree of purity and perfection, surpassing any but the polite part of London."[24] "No Country or Colonial dialect is to be distinguished," except for the "whining cadence" of New Englanders, according to Nicholas Cresswell in the 1770s.[25]

Those with regional British dialects were often indentured servants, having promised between four and seven years' service to a master in exchange for the cost of the transatlantic passage. If they ran away, their masters posted advertisements listing their distinguishing features: "speaks West Country," "a Yorkshireman who speaks very broad," "born near Manchester in England and speaks with that dialect," "talks very broad Scotch," "has the Irish brogue on her tongue."[26] Old-country regional accents, while they lasted, stood out. Later settlements before the revolution were more diverse: the Quakers settled in the Mid-Atlantic colonies and the "Scots-Irish" in the backcountry of Appalachia. But the linguistic diversity did not last long. The conditions were right for **dialect leveling**: the tendency for mobile and changing populations to merge to the same standard of speech. Still more dialect leveling came as former indentured servants and new arrivals pushed the frontier westward. Old dialect ways loosened as people from different backgrounds mixed. A couple of generations in, few traces of the immigrant grandparents' dialects remained.

Some regional British words can be found in General American English, but they're not terribly numerous. One is *to pet*. Originally Scottish English, it's now the usual way to express the 'to smooth an animal's fur' meaning in the US, while the English generally *stroke* animals. *Finicky* is another regionalism that gained widespread usage in the US. It was first recorded in a glossary of northern English in 1829,[27] as one of many variants on the now mostly forgotten *finical*. The first American example, only slightly later, is from Edgar Allan Poe, who was raised by a Scottish foster father in Virginia. It's an immigrant success story: kid from the provinces strikes it rich in a new country where people aren't particularly aware of their unfashionable background. Only the kid is a Scottish word—and it's now taken over England too.

On a limited scale, some Old World regionalisms became New World regionalisms. Some western Pennsylvania dialect words, for example, have Scots-Irish roots, like the people who settled there. There's *jagger* (a sharp object, thorn), *neb* (nose, nosy person), and *whenever* to mean 'when.' One of the most telling markers of a western Pennsylvanian is using past participles after *like* or *need*, as in *this needs washed* (rather than *this needs washing*). They share this predilection with Scots English.

Constant change in the fashionable language of Britain and America has led to some reversals in status. What sounds posh in Britain might make you sound like a hick in the US. Saying *jug* instead of *pitcher*, for example. Or this sentence from then-Member of Parliament Gyles Brandreth, debating a 1994 proposal to ban French words from English, in retaliation for French attempts to ban English words like *hamburger* and *software*:

I reckon that, when it comes to the linguistic exchange rate mechanism, one cannot buck the market.[28]

An Oxford-educated Tory politician uttering *reckon* is just the thing to cause cognitive dissonance in a northern American listener like me. Till I moved to England, I believed *reckon* was something only cowboys and hillbillies said. People from the southern or western US might say *I reckon*, but if they move to a northern city, they will probably learn to use the more general American *I figure*. In the UK, *I reckon* still does that job, and no one but American visitors thinks it anything but a normal phrase to use.

Another such example is the pronunciation of *ate*. For an RP speaker, the word *ate* is pronounced "et." In General American, the "proper" pronunciation of *ate* is the same as *eight*. The "et" pronunciation in the American context is not proper at all. If an American writer wants readers to know that a character pronounced *ate* that way, they have to spell it specially, as in:

After we et dinner we set up there and went to talkin bout somethin or other.[29]

That sentence appears in an as-told-to autobiography of a black tenant farmer in Alabama. The author uses nonstandard spelling to indicate the clear nonstandardness of the farmer's speech. But in England, that just looks like bad spelling of the standard pronunciation.

My last example of reversal-of-status must include an apology to the students at my first teaching job—a remedial writing course in Illinois. Many of those students wrote *towards*. I took it upon myself to beat the *s* out of those students because I perceived **towards** as less literate than **toward**. Then I moved to England and discovered that people here prefer *towards* to *toward*. Most style guides these days say that it's fine to use either, but American copy editors often delete the *s* on the grounds that it sounds "sloppy" or "informal." In the UK, no one would think to think such a thing.

Original pronunciation?

Erbs? Really? You're French now are you, with your "erbal" tea and your "erbal" remedies?

David Mitchell, "Dear America" (2010)[30]

Any Briton in the United States or American in the United Kingdom has to make some crucial choices: which pronunciations to alter in their new country and which to keep as a matter of personal dignity. A complex calculation has to be made in weighing up the relative advantages of being understood, fitting in, and avoiding mockery versus the definite costs of losing one's linguistic identity by saying things that sound plainly ridiculous to you. I persist in my American rhyming of *sloth* with *cloth* because rhyming it with *growth* sounds un-slothful to me (even though the British pronunciation shows the word's ancient relation to *slow*). But I have given in to *tomahto* because repeating *tomaydo* two or three times was slowing down my lunch orders. And I pronounce the *h* in *herb* now because saying "erb" compels English people to comment, "You've dropped your aitch." When they do that, I feel compelled to give my whole "I haven't dropped it because it wasn't there in the first place" speech, and then nobody gets a timely lunch.

Americans pronounce **herb** as "erb" because that's always been its pronunciation among people who don't go about changing pronunciations. The word was borrowed from Old French, where it was spelled *erbe*. It was written *h*-lessly until the 15th century. At that point, scribes started tacking on an *h*, under the influence of their knowledge of Latin, where it's *herba*. For nearly four hundred years, the word was written with *h* but pronounced without. This was not a problem for English. We don't pronounce written *h* in *hour* or *honest* or *heir*, and our ancestors didn't pronounce it in *humo(u)r, hospital,* or *hotel.* It was only in mid-19th-century Britain that the *h* in *herb* came to be pronounced—because that's when dropping one's aitches became a real marker of social class in England. Saying "an ouse" instead of "a house" was social suicide—"the most vulgar and the least excusable" sin against English, according to one 1866 book that promised to teach Brits how to articulate an *h*.[31] The centuries-old pronunciation of *herb* was a casualty of these Victorian linguistic insecurities. (Pronouncing the name of the letter as *haitch* instead of *aitch* is another new thing that some Britons do—and Americans don't. Many Brits look down on that pronunciation, but it seems to be on the rise among young people.)

Other recent changes to British pronunciation are more mysterious. I've mentioned the southern English broad "ah" in *bath* and *grass* as opposed to the "flat" vowel used in other parts of Britain and most of America. Typically sound change in language affects all the occurrences of the sound in certain phonetic environments—for example all the London *r*'s softening into oblivion when they're after a vowel. The *a*-broadening change wasn't typical in this way, but instead spread through southern England rather unpredictably, word by word. *Grass* and *pass* have the new vowel, but *ass* (the animal) and *mass* usually have the old one. *Plants* has a broad *a*, but *pants* does not. *Path* has the new vowel, *maths* has the old one (we'll get to its *s* in chapter 6). And then there's *wrath*, which has gone from flat-*a* to broad-*a* to its current rounded vowel, rhyming with *cloth*. (Hearing Brits refer to Steinbeck's novel *The Grapes of Roth* always makes me wonder: Philip's or David Lee's grapes?) I asked phonetician John Wells how British *wrath* got its current vowel. He replied, "*Mystery* would be a good word to use." All we can say for sure is that the pronunciation changed in fashionable British accents, and Americans paid no attention. As for me, after nearly twenty years in the southeast of England, my /a/ floats somewhere in the Atlantic Ocean, tossed around by the Gulf Stream: not flat, not broad, not consistent.

What about that other niggling pronunciation difference: **schedule**? The internet-commenting classes in Britain are up in arms about increased use of the "sk" pronunciation, in place of the "sh" pronunciation that older Brits use. Can we comfort them with the notion that the invading American pronunciation is actually the original pronunciation? I'm afraid not, for two reasons. First, people aren't comforted when told that a word or pronunciation they don't like is "the original." I haven't written this chapter with the expectation that anyone will conclude, "We should all say *herb* without [h] because it's the original pronunciation!" No, I'm just here to undermine the notion that American English deviated from British English—when, in fact, British English just keeps deviating from itself. I also can't comfort anyone about their pronunciation being "the original," because both are mutated pronunciations.

Back around the turn of the 15th century, the word was *sedule* or *cedule*. The first consonant was a simple /s/. Then in the 16th century, overeducated Latin-lovers started writing it as *scedule* or *schedule*, mimicking the Latin spelling of the day. At the end of the 1700s, when advice books on "proper" and "logical" pronunciation became popular, people started debating what to do with that word now that its spelling didn't match its pronunciation.

The orthoepists, as these experts on "proper pronunciation" were called, debated whether to pronounce *sch* as it is pronounced in other English words, like *scheme* or *scholar*, or to pronounce it "sh," as it would be pronounced in French. (I don't think the French were flattered. They gave up on *schedule* entirely and turned to *programme* for many of the word's meanings.) Both pronunciations were promoted by different British orthoepists—but the French-style pronunciation won out in Britain, while the English-style pronunciation took root in America. Once you've read chapter 5, that outcome will seem entirely predictable.

Everyone loves a good revival

> To labour, as some [Americans] do, to raise old words from the dead, is [...] not tanti.*
>
> Letter from a friend to John Pickering[32]

Whether on Broadway, in architecture, at church, or in language, Americans do love a revival. The past few decades of linguistic research have cast doubt on several suspected cases of "colonial lag." Instead, these linguistic fossils seem to have been resurrected in or after the late 1800s.

We can find proof in **proven**. Originally Scottish English, *proven* (rather than *proved*) started appearing in England in the 16th century. Today, Americans tend to use *proven* as the participial form of *prove*: *research **has proven** this is true*.[33] British English has for some time preferred *proved* (except, strangely, in a phrase that is at the bedrock of British jurisprudence: *innocent until proven guilty*, which had once been *innocent until proved guilty*). Though Pickering reported that some writers in the southern US used *proven*, he noted that it was as "unknown in New England" as in

---

* I love the irony of Pickering's friend choosing his slang from Latin while criticizing Americans for raising English words from the dead. *Tanti* means 'worthwhile.'

England.[34] Indeed, *proven* doesn't show up in American writing in any meaningful numbers until the late 19th century.[35] For some reason, at that point Americans started thinking that *have proven* sounded better than *have proved*. Rather than a case of colonial lag, it was a revival of a near-dead form. (Meanwhile, *proven* remains an important word in Scottish law, which allows for three verdicts: *guilty, not guilty,* and *not proven. Not proven* is sometimes called *the Scottish verdict,* and has been jokingly translated as "not guilty, but don't do it again.")

Then there's **gotten**. Matthew Engel reported in 2010 that Britain is a nation "full of *gotten* haters—understandable because it is an extremely ugly word."[36] Over a hundred years earlier, Charles Whibley had protested:

America need not boast the use of *gotten.* The termination [*-ten*], which suggests either wilful archaism or useless slang, adds nothing of sense or sound to the word. It is like a piece of dead wood in a tree, and is better lopped off.[37]

Considering how horrid that *–ten* is, it's stunning that Engel and Whibley have logged no protests against *forgotten* or *misbegotten,* which the British continue to say. But were Americans being *wilfully* archaic in saying *gotten,* as Whibley claimed? Maybe. Until the mid-19th century, *gotten* was hardly ever written in American English.[38] In 1909, American journalist Ambrose Bierce declared that *gotten* had "gone out of good use."[39] *The New Yorker,* an American literary institution, still prefers **have got**. And yet, here in the 21st century, *I've got over it* sounds fairly ungrammatical to American ears. *Gotten* didn't just carry on in American English while it fell out of use in Britain—it was at least partially buried and then disinterred.[40]

The obvious question is: *Why resurrect these things?* If these old forms weren't preferred in America and were hardly used in Britain, why would they reassert themselves more than a hundred years after American independence? The answer: because that's when America's linguistic center of gravity really started to shift away from Britain.

Over the course of the 19th century, westward migration increased the distance between Americans and Britain. There wasn't just an ocean between them—there was an ocean and an ocean's length of land. The status of England-conscious New England as the cultural powerhouse of America started to wane as midwestern cities grew. Chicago, for one, sextupled in size between 1870 and 1900, thanks in large part to immigration from Ireland, Germany, and Scandinavia. This meant an ever-smaller proportion of Americans had ancestral links to England. American literature was coming into its own and moving away from New England, first with midwesterner Mark Twain, and later with writers from the South and the West. As more Americans started writing and being published, they felt less need to look to Britain for the written English standard. Archaisms like *gotten*, which had been considered "too vulgar" for formal publication, started sounding less bad to more people. The current fashions of British English stopped mattering so much because by this time there was enough American history—and enough America—for the language to really go it alone.

This could help explain another recent revival: the **subjunctive mood**, or more specifically the mandative subjunctive. The mandative subjunctive is a verb form that is used after other verbs like *suggest* or *request*, as in *I suggest that you be careful*. It indicates that the situation described (you being careful) is still a hypothetical situation: you're not necessarily being careful. Compared with other languages, the English subjunctive is hard to keep track of. In Spanish, it's clear-cut: "they speak" is *ellos hablan*, but put it in the subjunctive and it's *ellos hablen*—different suffix. English was once like that. In fact, one history of English grammar needed 156 pages to describe the many subjunctive forms and when to use them in Old English.[41]

119

But English has lost a lot of suffixes and verb inflections since Old English. Stripped of its suffixes, the mandative subjunctive form is now indistinguishable from the base form of the verb. That's obvious in the case of *I suggest you be careful*, where it's *you be* rather than the usual (indicative mood) form of the verb, *you are*. But for more regular verbs, the base form is the same as the indicative present-tense form in many situations. So if I say *I suggest you leave*, you can't actually tell if I've used the subjunctive or not, since we'd say *you leave* even if it weren't subjunctive. (I've just used the other kind of subjunctive in that sentence—*if it weren't* rather than *if it wasn't*. That's the conditional subjunctive, which has also suffered a decline and revitalization. I'm focusing on the mandative subjunctive because that's where the real British–American difference lies.)

So unless the verb is *be*, subjunctives are only noticeable if the subject of the verb is a third-person singular (a "she, he, or it"): *she leaves* is the indicative, but *she leave* is the subjunctive. Some people try to mark "subjunctiveness" with the modal verb *should*, and others just don't bother at all and use the indicative form. So we are left with these options:

> **Subjunctive:** *Lynne suggests that Phil **pick up** his socks.*
> **Modal verb *should*:** *Lynne suggests that Phil **should pick up** his socks.*
> **Indicative:** *Lynne suggests that Phil **picks up his socks**.*

By the 16th century, the subjunctive option (*I suggest he pick up his socks*) was in severe decline and the *should* modal-verb variant (*I suggest he should pick up his socks*) took over in all but the most formal circumstances, such as translations of the Bible or legal language. By 1906, the usage-guide-writing Fowlers had declared the subjunctive "almost meaningless to Englishmen."[42]

But over in American English, the subjunctive started to reappear in everyday writing in the mid-to-late 1800s. At the start of the 20th century, American writers used the *should* option in 67% of possible contexts; by the end of the century the rate was less than 1%. This took American English away from British, as the *I suggest that he should . . .* version continues to be used in British English. The indicative option (*suggest he picks up his socks*) remained a possibility, but the subjunctive moved into American English in a big way. One study found that by 1991 about 80% of mandative contexts in published American English had the subjunctive.[43] This return of the subjunctive is one of the most startling things to happen to English in centuries. Where did it come from? Why in America? Why then? There are a few hypotheses:

- Bible readers were familiar with the subjunctive in various uses. Perhaps religious Americans had particular awareness of those forms and were more apt to imitate them than the British were.

- Over time, the meaning of *should* in American English had become more and more restricted to 'ought to,' while in Britain it continued to have many uses. For example, Britons might say *I shouldn't be surprised if he comes,* whereas Americans use *wouldn't* or *won't* in that context. Perhaps because *should* was being used less in American English, it started to sound odd to Americans in the mandative context, and so they needed something else to fill the gap. They looked to the subjunctive.

- And then there were all those German and Italian immigrants to America whose languages had robust subjunctives. Perhaps these new speakers of American English had a preference for the subjunctive form, carried from their home languages.

- Or maybe spoken American dialects had kept the subjunctive alive through the centuries, though it wasn't fashionable in published writing. Then when published American English became less Britain-focused, the regional, spoken subjunctive started to show up in print and spread further.[44]

Those aren't mutually exclusive possibilities. A conspiracy of factors may have allowed the subjunctive's American resurrection. The truth of the matter is: we just don't know. And the American subjunctive revival has brought another mystery: Where did the new negative subjunctive come from? Look at the *not* in:

*Phil requests that Lynne **not mention** him in her book.*

Putting the *not* before the verb is new—a more archaic version would be *that Lynne mention not him* or *Lynne mention him not.* That *not*-before-the-verb supports the hypothesis that the Germanic languages of immigrants were a factor in the reintroduction of the subjunctive, since that's where the 'not' would go in their subjunctives.

We might not know where the revived subjunctive has come from or why, but we do know three things:

- The American literary establishment generally think the subjunctive is a good thing.
- The revived subjunctive has invaded Britain.
- People in Britain (well, those who know what a subjunctive is) don't know what to think about that.

American commentators often labor under the mistaken impression that the 20th century was the subjunctive's enemy, rather than its savior. Their discussions of the subjunctive often take a desperate, moralistic flavor. "Please promise me you will never lose your grip on the subjunctive," implores Roy Blount Jr.[45] Philip Corbett, Standards Editor of the *New York Times*, has repeatedly urged readers to "Save the subjunctive!," which he takes as a necessary part of "our goal of precise and literate usage."[46] Law columnist Patricia J. Williams even warns: "Without the deferential wistfulness of the subjunctive mood, speech becomes all-knowing, too powerful, as though fiction were but a nascent form of fact, one's every wish an abracadabra away."[47] If only scientists and politicians were better about using the subjunctive, she reasons, we'd have a more nuanced view of the world.

British writing guides, on the other hand, are all over the place. Should they admire subjunctive usage because it echoes classical languages and "can add elegance to your writing" (*Guardian and Observer Style Guide*)? Or is it to be avoided because it will make you sound "pedantic" (Gowers' *Plain Words*)? The *Economist Style Guide* advises, "If you are proposing a hypothesis contrary to fact, you must use the subjunctive," while Robert Burchfield, in *Fowler's Modern English Usage*, says the subjunctive is "seldom obligatory." Ernest Gowers' *Plain Words* claims that usually "the indicative would have been equally correct," but Simon Heffer's *Strictly English* warns that the indicative is "downright wrong." And, of course, for some, the subjunctive sounds a note that is wrong by virtue of its American timbre. Kingsley Amis frames the subjunctive as an indulgent Americanism, then commands: "Do not imitate them."[48]

One pedant's indulgence is another's necessity. In the main, British tolerance for the subjunctive revival has been much greater than for many of the other "archaisms" that have bounced back over the Atlantic. I suspect this may have something to do with the fact that much of the establishment in England had to learn the Latin subjunctive in their very posh boarding schools. If it's good enough for Latin, it must be "proper" English, not an "Americanism" like *gotten*. Triumphant headlines appeared in 2016 when a *British* (they emphasized) schoolboy in Cornwall wrote to Justin Bieber to inform him that he should sing *If I were your boyfriend* instead of *If I was your boyfriend*.[49] Nevertheless, the grammatical role model the schoolboy cited was the very non-British paragon of grammar Beyoncé, in her song "If I Were a Boy."

The subjunctive thus reminds me of the British Campaign for Real Ale. The drinkers appreciating those British ales see them as a retort to fizzy, amber, American-style beers. What they don't tend to know is that British brewers credit the American microbrewery movement for reviving those local brewing traditions in the UK.[50] Americans are helping the British rediscover their language and their ale. Celebrate the British boy who knows the subjunctive if you wish, but I'd also celebrate the Americans who made that possible. If I were you.

So what?

> It was our language first and, quite frankly, we don't care for your excuses about language evolving.
> Tom Stockwell, "How to Piss Off a Brit"[51]

I am not a sports fan, but I find them fascinating. The fans, not the sports. They say things like "We're up four points in the second half" or "Our defense needs work" or "We won the World Cup." As if (*as IF!*) they had *anything* to do with any of it. They share a delusion that they somehow belong to the team, that they own those points, that they had those injuries, that they ran or tackled or scored. And they don't just believe this of themselves—they transfer ownership of the other team's actions to the other team's fans: "You're going down!" they say. "We're going to kick your asses on Sunday," they (at least the American ones) threaten.

But my fan fascination quickly turns to fan frustration, and so I go about having conversations like this:

> "We scored three goals!" they say.
> "No you didn't," I say. "Those overpaid men on the television did. You were holding a beer, shouting at a television, and generally acting in a way that was unbecoming to a person your age."

Because I'm so confident that my friends and family appreciate that little correction, I'm going to apply it to Team British English and Team American English, who can be seen taking their roles in this joke . . .

An impatient American approaches a London hotel reception desk demanding to know where the elevator is. The receptionist replies "I think you mean *the lift*, which is just to your right there." The American doesn't take well to being corrected. "I'm from Chicago and we invented the damn things. They're *elevators*." The receptionist replies, "Yes, of course, sir, but *we* invented the language."

Today's Britons invented the language to an even lesser extent than the sports fans won the match last Sunday. The fans were at least *alive* when the match was won. If we can even talk of English being "invented" (which I'd advise against), who is this *we* (or *you*) who invented it? Sure, the history of the language is longest on a particular island, but that doesn't mean the people on that island today have any greater connection to the language than people speaking the language on another landmass. The adjectives aren't sprouting from ancient stone circles. The verbs aren't in the water supply. And the language isn't in anybody's genes. Growing up learning English involves exposure to the English of the immediate past—how your parents and grandparents talk—and making it into the language of our present. That makes anyone's English no more than four generations deep. The British of today are no more connected to the language of Chaucer than the people who grow up speaking English in the US or South Africa or Hong Kong. Our Englishes aren't parent and child—they're grown-up siblings.

When Brits accuse American English of changing "their" language, I enjoy pointing out some of the cases where the American form—the one that I use—is the original one. Happily, I get to do that rather often. The BBC's fifty "Most Noted" Americanisms included seventeen that the British had invented and forgotten about, including: *learn* meaning 'teach' as in *that'll learn you* (1382), *to wait on* (rather than *wait for*; possibly as early as 1390), *oftentimes* (1393), *half hour* (rather than *half an* hour; 1420), *transportation* (1540), *expiration* (1562; versus *expiry* 1790), *alphabetize* (1691), and possibly *zee* as a name for the letter (first written as such in a spelling book published in England, 1677). Some on the BBC list were invented after American independence—but not in America. The earliest citations of *to turn 60* (or another age; 1789), *physicality* (1827), *train station* (1856), and the figurative use of *leverage* (1858) are all British. These aren't cases of Americans holding on to words that the original settlers brought, but postcolonial British words that Britons have forgotten to say or that they notice only in American accents.

Of course, many Americanisms *are* newer forms, and the British hang on to some older forms. English is not a parade through time with one country marching in front and the other following. The linguist Mariane Hundt describes British and American English as partners in a dance.[52] Sometimes one leads, sometimes the other. They step together, they move apart, they cha-cha-cha to the side, they twirl back, they twirl forth. If you're old enough to remember the lambada, you'll know how entwined the dancers can become. I might take the dance metaphor a bit further. British and American English aren't dancers—they're troupes of dancers. Not all of them are wearing their assigned costumes, their choreographer has called in sick, and they don't all share the same sense of rhythm. One of the dancers has a crush on a dancer in the other troupe, and dancers from both troupes have started mimicking each other. Oh my god, some of them have started twerking!

5

MORE AMERICAN, MORE ÆNGLISC?

This abiding corruption of our language I believe to have been
the one result of the Norman Conquest which has been purely
evil. In every other respect, the evil of a few generations has been
turned into good in the long run. But the tongue of England [...]
has forever become the spoil of the enemy.

E. A. Freeman,
The History of the Norman Conquest of England (1876)

Frenemies. Is there a better word to describe the relationship
between England and France? Here are two countries that have
bullied each other so relentlessly that they measure their wars
in centuries.[1] But between the fights, they kiss (on both cheeks)
and make up, become allies, and, when they think the other isn't
looking, try to emulate each other. For the French, England (and
Britain more generally) has stood for nature and freedom; for the
British, France stands for civilization and order.[2] Having borrowed
ideas from British philosophy and politics in the run-up to their
revolution, the French still sometimes envy the wildness of English
gardens and the anarchy of British humor. Britain, meanwhile,
has long looked up to France as if it's the most grown-up and
sophisticated member of the school clique. Hey, the French are so
sophisticated, they even came up with the word *clique.*

And so English borrowed that word, and not just that one. For
almost a thousand years, English has been letting French into its

vocabulary, spelling system, and pronunciations. Given how the British have received "invading" Americanisms, you'd think there would be some protest against Frenchisms invading English. *Mais non.* In fact, the aspects of English that Britons want to protect against "Americanization" are often the Frenchest parts. Some seem to feel that English itself is not good enough, that it needs to be gussied up in the clothing of fancier languages—not just French but also the classical languages Latin and Greek. In contrast to their reputation as linguistic corrupters, Americans have done much to make English *more* English and *less* French.

Making English more English is arguably a good thing because it makes the language more accessible to those who speak it and those who are learning it. English becomes more opaque and less internally consistent when we borrow spellings and pronunciations from elsewhere. Tricky foreignisms become **shibboleths**: linguistic forms that mark people as members (or not) of the élite. (That accent mark on *élite* might've done that trick right there—though it's not my usual style.) Because of Latin, we have, for instance, *referendum* and *larva*. The English way to make a noun plural is to put an *s* at the end, but say *referendums* or *larvas* and some people out there will quietly (or maybe not so quietly) judge you for not knowing to say *referenda* and *larvae*. Such irregular foreign plurals in English serve little other purpose than to give a superior feeling to people who know their tricks. The same could be said of other spellings, pronunciations, and vocabulary that retain "foreignness" in English. They help well-educated people feel like they're accomplished, but they don't help us communicate with ease.

Now, I don't seriously want to take an anti-immigrant stance toward language. I'm not going to say the English should put all the Frenchisms on boats and send them back across the Channel. Vocabulary from other languages enriches English, giving us new things to talk about and new nuances of meaning. But there is an argument for allowing immigrant words to assimilate to English rules and patterns. Like many a wordy person, I enjoy the irregularities in language (or more precisely, I revel in my knowledge of them). But at the same time I worry that we devalue English when we consider the foreign forms "more correct," "more beautiful," or "classier." When we have a choice between a French option in English and an English one, shouldn't we opt for the English?

The case can be made (so I'll make it) that toning down the most egregious French, Latin, and Greek elements of English is a way of both making English *more English* and democratizing the language—making its standard forms more available to more people. Whose English is most English? Who is at the *vanguard* in efforts to de-frenchify and re-anglify English vocabulary, spelling, and pronunciation? Let's start with the British efforts.

Down with Romance (languages)

Our language, for almost a century, has, by the concurrence of many causes, been gradually departing from its original Teutonick character, and deviating towards a Gallick structure and phraseology, from which it ought to be our endeavour to recal it.

Samuel Johnson, Preface to *A Dictionary of the English Language* (1755)

It wasn't me who came up with the idea that English should give French and other foreignisms the heave-ho. For centuries English speakers have worried about the purity of the language—while at the same time stocking English with more and more non-native vocabulary.

After the Norman invasion of 1066, William the Conqueror set about unseating the English aristocracy and giving their land to his allies, many of them Norman French speakers. For the next three hundred years, the kings of England didn't speak English, and French continued to be an important language of government and the elite. Extensive borrowing of French words led Old English (a.k.a. *Anglo-Saxon*) to become Middle English. By the Early Modern period, French had waned as the language of the royal court. The Scientific Revolution (c.1550–1700) brought a new age of learning and exploration, for which English needed new words. Latin and Greek were pillaged to build new words for the new ideas, and even for a lot of the old ideas. Rhetorician Thomas Wilson (1524–1581) complained:

> Some seeke so far for outlandish English, that they forget altogether their mothers language. [. . . If] their mothers were alive, thei were not able to tell what they say.[3]

This "outlandish" (a good Anglo-Saxon word for 'foreign') vocabulary gave rise to the **inkhorn controversy**, a debate about whether English needed so many outlandish words. Some insisted that English was insufficient to serve as a language of science and learning, and so "classical" solutions were needed. Others objected to both the foreignness and the obscurity of these new words—the "inkhorn terms" typical of ink-carrying eggheads. Anti-inkhorner Sir John Cheke (1514–57) prepared a new translation of the Gospel of Matthew according to the principle that "our own tung should be written cleane and pure, unmixt and unmangeled with borowing of other tunges." And so Cheke used words like *byword*, *crossed*, and *gainrising* instead of *parable*, *crucified*, and *resurrection*.[4] Though some of the excesses of the inkhorn period died away, English writers continued to value verbiage from elsewhere over our simple English words. We say *fabricate*, *laboratory*, and *transcribe* (when we could have just kept saying *make*, *workshop*, and *write down*) because fancy Latinate words made educated English speakers feel knowledgeable and sophisticated.

"Purification" of English was back on the table for the Victorians. The Anglo-Saxonism of the 19th century was partly inspired by the burgeoning field of philology (what we'd now call *linguistics*), which ascertained English's family relationship to German. Perhaps it also helped that the French were long gone from the British throne, replaced by German stock. Around this time, Charles Dickens stressed that a writer should "not to seek abroad for sesquipedalian words. [...] Let him write Saxon and the Saxons understand him."[5] That jokey *sesquipedalian* aside, Dickens was fairly good at practicing what he preached: "It was the best of times, it was the worst of times." "Never close your lips to those to whom you have opened your heart." "No one is useless in this world who lightens the burdens of another." All memorable lines with almost no Romance vocabulary (just the *use* in *useless*).

My personal Victorian re-anglification hero is William Barnes (1801–86). Poet, priest, and philologist Barnes took Saxonism to its logical conclusion by publishing a list of words that he had "Englished" for the benefit of the public, including:

absorb	▷	forsoak
anniversary	▷	year-day
horizon	▷	sky-sill
laxative	▷	loosensome
literature	▷	book-lore
musician	▷	gleeman
punctuation	▷	bestopping

The spirit of Barnes lives on. For the 900th anniversary of the Norman invasion, the British humourist Paul Jennings tried to imagine a Frenchless English in a series of pieces for *Punch* magazine. ("To be or not to be? That is the ask-thing," he wrote.) Jennings' term for his linguistic creation, *Anglish*, has been adopted by promoters of a more Anglo-Saxon English—though you'd think that if they were really serious about it, they'd use the more Saxon spelling *Ænglisc*. In this vein, science-fiction writer Poul Anderson wrote a piece called "Uncleftish Beholding" ('Atomic Theory') to show how we might talk about nuclear physics if we hadn't let Latin and Greek into English:[6]

> Coming back to the uncleft itself, the heavier it is, the more neitherbits as well as firstbits in its kernel. Indeed soon the tale of neitherbits is the greater. Unclefts with the same tale of firstbits but unlike tales of neither bits are called *samesteads*.*

As much fun as these New-Old English words are, they haven't caught on. The modern anti-inkhornists have been more successful in encouraging a preference for existing native English words over fancy French and classical words. The Fowler brothers got things started in their granddaddy of modern style guides, *The King's English* (1908). Their Five Rules for vocabulary selection are, in order of importance:

1. Prefer the familiar word to the far-fetched.
2. Prefer the concrete word to the abstract.
3. Prefer the single word to the circumlocution.
4. Prefer the short word to the long.
5. Prefer the Saxon word to the Romance.

Though "prefer the Saxon" is the lowest on the list, you'll still end up with a fairly Saxon text if you only follow the rules above it. The Fowlers' cause was furthered by George Orwell's 1946 essay "Politics and the English Language," which urges: "never use a long word where a short one will do."[7] Long words are the refuge of the bad writer (possibly a Marxist, by Orwell's estimation). Such

---

* In case you need a translation: an atom is an *uncleft*, its nucleus is its *kernel*, protons are *firstbits*, neutrons are *neitherbits*, isotopes are *samesteads* and *tale* means 'number.'

ne'er-do-well writers use Latin- or Greek-derived words as "a kind of euphemism." Orwell's legacy is the Plain English movement, ~~dedicated to enhancing the comprehensibility of commercial and legal text~~—wait, sorry—urging businesspeople and lawmakers to use words and phrases that are easy for most people to understand.

The motivations of English purists have varied from nationalism to a desire for clarity, but an underlying theme is (as always) social class. French, Latin, and Greek are not the languages of the common person in Britain. Using more Englishy English, the thinking goes, makes your text more readily readable by a broader swath of society. While the Saxonist movement had supporters in the US, they were paid little attention—perhaps because Noah Webster was already liberating American English from French, at least in the spelling.

Saving English spelling

To Frenchify v.a. [from French.] To infect with the manner of France; to make a coxcomb ['dandy'].

Johnson's *Dictionary* (1755)

English earns its reputation as the most difficult alphabetic language to read. Every English sound can be spelled in more than one way and no alphabet letter consistently has the same pronunciation. Take one of the simplest cases: *b*. The sound /b/ can be written *b* as in *trouble*, *bb* as in *stubble*, or *bh* as in *Bhutan* or *bhangra* (an Asian-British musical style). So, we have at least three spellings of /b/. Conversely, the letter *b* sometimes symbolizes the sound /b/ and sometimes it's silent, as in the digraphs (two-letter combinations) *bt* in *debt* and *mb* in *plumber*. When we look for rules in the system, we find exceptions: don't pronounce *b* in *plumber*, but do pronounce it in *slumber*. By one count, there are over a thousand ways of spelling the forty-plus basic sounds (or *phonemes*, to use the linguistic term) of English. In other words, the average English phoneme can be written in more than twenty ways.[8]

The longevity of the system is largely to blame for this madness. English has been written for almost as long as it has existed. Way back in the beginning there was no authority to tell people how to spell, so people spelled words the way they thought they sounded (which might mean different spellings in different places). Over centuries, the sounds changed, while spelling became increasingly fixed. This left us with silent letters that used to be spoken and lots of letters (and letter combinations) with multiple pronunciations: *the tough coughs as he ploughs the dough.*

Immigration and imperialism have also left English with more ways of spelling than strictly needed, since they've brought English into contact with other ways of pronouncing and spelling. The *h* in *Bhutan*, for instance, comes from how the name of the kingdom was represented in Sanskrit and then transliterated into the Roman alphabet. English shrugs at that *h* and keeps it, even though we don't pronounce it. What's another silent letter to us? Languages with more phonetic spelling systems are less forgiving of such foreign spellings; the country is *Bután* in Spanish and *Butan* in Maltese. If we went down that route, we might spell it *Bootan*. Down that route, English speakers might eat *keesh* and *keenwa* and cut things with *mashetties.*

The way I see it, we might as well blame French for *all* the irregularities of our spelling system. Sure, words like *Bhutan* and *quinoa* didn't come to us from French, but French messed up English spelling so much that English speakers were left feeling blasé about introducing more inconsistencies in the system. More specifically, Norman French scribes mucked up English spelling.

After 1066 the Normans essentially took over the business of writing in England, leaving indelible marks on the English spelling system: killing off letters and introducing less fit-for-purpose alternatives. French never had the Old English letters thorn (þ) and eth (ð), nor the sounds they represented, so Norman scribes rooted them out and introduced a less efficient digraph in their place: *th*. We also lost the letter whin (þ) for the /w/ sound, replaced by a "double u," and the letter ash (æ), which signaled something like the vowel in *mat*. (In fact, it signaled the first sound in *English*—that is, *Ænglisc*—until the Normans came along and slapped on the *E*.) Norman scribes introduced more digraphs, like the *gh* and *ch*, in order to make English spelling more consistent with their ideas of what sounds should look like and what letters should sound like. Essentially, Norman scribes got us spelling English as if it were French.

The Normans also gave English a lot of words, with spellings that reflected original French pronunciations. Since at that point spellings were not expected to stay fixed, they easily changed over time and place; for instance English took the Old French *boef* (Modern French *boeuf*) and made it into *beef*, with *bouf, bege, byffe, beoff, buif, beff, beafe, biefe, beffe, beefe, bœfe, bief*, and *beife* along the way. It wasn't until after the printing press, after dictionaries, and after widespread primary education that English spellings settled down into "correct" and "incorrect" versions. While by that time French scribes were no longer dictating English spelling, they'd established in English-speaking culture some ideas of what "looks proper" in English spelling. "Proper" thus often means French-like. In the age of spelling standardization, English folk got the idea that spelling was a complicated thing, and so learnéd spellings—the ones with extra letters and nods to other languages—came to be preferred over phonetic ones.[9] So English acquired spellings like *labour* with a *u* and *machine* with a *ch*, which both have more to do with French pronunciation and spelling sensibilities than with how English works.

Spelling standardization really got going in the 17th century, just as the English were colonizing the New World. This created the opportunity for different standards to arise in America and

Britain. Samuel Johnson's *Dictionary of the English Language* (1755) became the most influential force in solidifying English spelling. Johnson's dictionary is sometimes praised as being one of the first descriptive dictionaries—describing how the language *is* used, rather than prescribing how it *should* be used. But this liberal, descriptive approach did not extend to spelling. Take, for example, *ambassadour*, the spelling Johnson preferred over *ambassador*. His entry for the word quotes William Shakespeare, John Dryden, and Joseph Addison, who all seem to agree with him that the word needs a *u*. But if you look at the original publications that Johnson quoted from, it's the *u*-less *ambassador* you'll find; *ambassadour* was Johnson having his way with the spelling system. The example of *ambassadour* shows that the power of Johnson's dictionary was not absolute. We spell it *ambassador* now, and so did people in Johnson's time.

Just over twenty years after the London publication of Johnson's dictionary, the United States declared its political independence and started declaring its orthographic independence, with Noah Webster's "Blue-Back Speller" (1783) and later his *American Dictionary of the English Language* (1828). Webster's desire to simplify spelling had been influenced by Benjamin Franklin, who had proposed a complete rejigging of the alphabet on phonetic principles. Had Webster tried to go that far, Americans might well still be spelling like the British. It was hard enough getting people to drop the *u* from *labour*—American arguments about that lasted for most of the 1800s. Getting everyone to spell it *leebyr*, in Franklin's style, would have been a step too far—cutting Americans off from the literature of the past and the rest of the Anglophone world. Webster's spelling reform successes were mostly limited to spellings that already existed in the language. He didn't make up *color* or *center*—they had been around for a long time. Webster's eventual contribution was to make those spellings respectable.

The early arguments for American spelling reform were often political in nature. For linguistic patriots of the early United States, British English standards reeked of the corrupt aristocracy. American spelling reforms relieve English of some of its many homages to French—long the language of the British aristocracy—and its nods to the classical languages of learning, Latin and Greek. Rather than looking to the elites and the past, the reforms looked at the English of the present, bringing some spellings more into line with their pronunciation: *skeptic* instead of *sceptic*, *check* instead of *cheque*. As acceptance of Webster's spellings grew, other spelling reform movements developed—again with varying levels of success. Around the turn of the 20th century, newspapers and professional bodies in education, linguistics, medicine, and science were taking decisions on the future of American spelling. Not all of their experiments worked; for instance, though the National Education Association (NEA) proposed *tho, altho, thru, thoro, thoroly*, and *thorofare* in 1898, none of these are the standard American spellings today. More successful was the NEA's proposal to remove unpronounced letters that came by way of French: *program* (not *programme*) and *catalog* and *prolog* (losing their *-ue* endings—though it must be noted that Americans usually use the *-ue* in all *-ogue* words except *catalog*).[10]

By 1906, the prospects for further spelling reform were good enough that the industrialist Andrew Carnegie founded and funded the American Committee for Spelling Reform—more commonly known as the Simplified Spelling Board—peopled by lexicographers, academics, and the likes of Mark Twain and Melvil (born *Melville*) Dewey of the Dewey decimal system. The movement was probably undone by President Theodore Roosevelt's enthusiasm for it. Once the Simplified Spelling Board had published its list of three hundred spelling suggestions, Roosevelt ordered its instant adoption by the Government Printing Office. This was met with instant and international derision. In the UK, *The Sun* summed it up:

Mr Andru Karnegi (or should it be Karnege?) and President Rusvelt (or is it Ruzvelt?) are doing their (or ther) best to ad to the gaiety of nations (or nashuns) by attempting to reform the spelling of the English langwidge. No dowt their (or ther) intentions (or intenshuns) are orl rite, but their (or ther) objekt is orl rong, not to say silly (or sily).[11]

Congress soon reversed Roosevelt's efforts. The Simplified Spelling Board hobbled on for a few more years, but that was pretty much the end of concerted efforts to legislate American spelling. The American linguistic landscape—and, really, English as a whole—is moved more by the forces of the linguistic marketplace than by the proclamations of committees.

American spelling reform generally takes the spelling system in the direction of "more English" and "more democratic": more English because the spelling rules are more logical for our language as it is spoken (rather than for French or Latin) and more democratic in that accessibility and learnability are selected over curtseying to the French-derived aristocracy and their apologists. A spelling system with a better match between sounds and letters is better for educating the masses and thus building responsible citizens. This is not to say that the US has arrived at any sort of spelling utopia. But it is a little further down that road ...

Cheating at Scrabble

[You Americans] spell through T-H-R-U, and I'm with you on that, 'cause we spell it "thruff." And that's trying to cheat at Scrabble.
Eddie Izzard (1999)[12]

In a list of 1,737 American–British spelling differences,[13] the British column has 558 more letters than the leaner American column. Is that why expert Scrabble players score about 5% more points when playing with the official British Scrabble dictionary than with the American one?[14] Probably not, but let's not let that spoil Eddie Izzard's joke. Where did all those extra letters come from? Where have they gone? Are they historically justified? Helpful to pronunciation? Consistent?

Words that come from Latin or classical Greek (often via French) can look more "classical" in British English because of their use of the ligatures (joined-up letters) æ and œ, now usually written as the digraphs *ae*[15] and *oe*. To name a few examples:

American	*British*
e	*ae*
encyclopedia	*encyclopaedia*
feces	*faeces*
pediatric	*paediatric*
e	*oe*
ameba	*amoeba*
diarrhea	*diarrhoea*
estrogen	*oestrogen*

You find these spellings in words with ancient Greek roots: æ and œ are the Roman-alphabet versions of the original Greek *αι* and *οι*. But for the most part, these words are not ones the ancient Greeks or Romans would have known. Instead, they are the product of "post-classical" Latin, the academic Latin used long after native Latin speakers had died off. For instance the English word *haematology*, 'the study of blood and blood diseases,' was cobbled together in the 19th century from the Greek word for 'blood' and the Greek-derived suffix -*ology*, from the classical Greek word for 'speech.' English speakers seem to love these Greeky, Latin-sounding words and so have made tons of them and borrowed another ton from the French, who also swoon for classical-sounding words. Had English speakers been a bit more like the Germans, we might have shaken off the spell of complicated Greek-ish spellings. Germans reserve the Latin–Greek words like *Diarrhö,* 'diarrhoea,' for medical contexts. The everyday German word for it is *Durchfall* ('falling through'). German children don't go to *paediatricians,* but to *Kinderärzte* ('children's doctors'). Unlucky English kids have to contend with a mouthful of Greek syllables.

The *ae* and *oe* spellings don't do much for English, since the sounds they represent could as easily be spelled *e.* The digraphs in *aeon* and *foetus* make the same sound as the first *e* in *even.* The ones in *anaesthetic* and *foetid* sound like the *e* in *etch.*[16] American spelling reformers reasoned that if the *ae* and *oe* sounds can be expressed just as well by the letter *e,* then *e* is all we need. And so Americans spell *eon, fetus, anesthetic,* and *fetid.* Where *ae* and *oe* represent sounds other than "ee" and "eh," Americans use the digraph, as in *Gaelic, maelstrom, alumnae,* and *oeuvre.* So words starting with the prefix *aer(o)-,* like *aerate, aerobics, aerosol,* keep the *ae* because it is pronounced like the vowel in *air,* not like *err* or *ear.* Following the pronunciation, American English has gone all the way in anglicizing **airplane** and **airport**, while the French **aeroplane** still hangs on in British.

But even where *ae* and *oe* are pronounced in an *e*-like way, the American drive for simplification has not been absolute. Proper names and mythological terms, like *Caesar, Oedipus,* and *phoenix* tend to keep their digraph spellings in America and Britain, out of respect for their bearers. With the over-voweled exception of *aeon/eon,* words beginning with *ae* have been resistant to change in American. *Esthetic* and *egis* are possible spellings in American English, for instance, but Americans tend to prefer *aesthetic* and *aegis.* *Aesthetic's* relatives *kinesthetic* and *anesthetic,* on the other hand, lose the extra *a* in American. Why do Americans think *aesthetic* and *aegis* look naked without their *a*'s, while they're happy to lop the *o* off *(o)edema, (o)esophagus,* and *(o)estrogen?* It's all quite inconsistent—though consistency is supposed to be a selling point of American spelling. My best guess is that it's about who uses the words. The scientists go for the shorter, more straightforward spellings, while the aestheticians and oenophiles hang on to the extra letters as a badge of (European) culture and learning.

The British aren't altogether consistent about *ae* and *oe* either. Latinate words that came into English before the Renaissance generally have just an *e* in British. Thus *ether* is much more common in the UK than *aether* and *demon* wins out over *daemon*. British spelling is also guilty of some overenthusiastic insertion of classical-looking letter combinations into classical-looking words, such as Latin *fetus* (not *foetus*), and Latin *sulfur* (via French *sulfre*, rather than the Greek *ph* in British *sulphur*). These faux-classicisms were enough to embarrass parts of the British medical establishment, as shown in this doctor's letter to *The Lancet* in 1952:

> I shall resist to the last ditch any movement for the general replacement of diphthongs [he means *digraphs*—LM] by single vowels—the American practice. But when, etymologically, the foreigner is correct and we are wrong, it would seem that by adhering obstinately to a false diphthong we are weakening our case for maintaining our justifiable diphthongs in the face of contrary "common usage" by far more than half the English-writing world.[17]

The Lancet and the *British Medical Journal* now consider *fetus* and *fetal* the "correct" spellings, but most Brits still use *foetus*. In a survey I conducted in 2015, only 27% of UK medical personnel preferred *fetus* over *foetus*, often expressing the assumption that the *fetus* spelling signals encroaching Americanism, rather than respect for Latin.[18] Even though the editor of the British National Health Service (NHS) website *knows* the history and debate about the word, his Editorial Style Guide for the NHS marks *fetus* as an

Americanism to be avoided.[19] It doesn't matter that the *o* is not pronounced. It doesn't matter if it differs from the Latin word. What matters is that no one will mistake you for an American if you spell it *foetus*. It's better to be wrong than to seem American.

French letters

The late Archdeacon Hare [...] some years ago, expressed a hope that "such abominations as *honor* and *favor* would henceforth be confined to the cards of the great vulgar." There we still see them, and in books printed in America; and while we are quite contented to leave our fashionable friends in such company, I hope we may none of us be tempted to join it.

Henry Alford, *The Queen's English* (1888)

When the British redcoats surrendered after the Battle of Yorktown, it was to at least as many French troops as American ones. When the new nation was born, France was the second country (after Morocco) to formally recognize the United States of America. And yet, one of the first projects of American patriots was to eradicate vestiges of French in the spelling system. What bad manners! (But good spelling.)

Noah Webster, in his speller and dictionaries, encouraged Americans away from some French-inspired spellings that do not reflect English pronunciation. The **re-** to **-er** change in words like **centre** and **theatre** is one. Some of these words go back to Latin, where the *r* was pronounced at the beginning of the final syllable, rather than the end of a word: *centrum, theatrum*. In French, a final *e* replaced the original Latin *-um* suffix: *centre, theatre*. Others, like **litre** and **manoeuvre**, were invented in French and reflect French pronunciation. For English the *-er* spelling is more in keeping with our pronunciation: it is not "ruh," but "urr" or "uh," depending on whether you're an *r*-pronouncer or not. So Americans gave *liter* an *-er* like the words it rhymes with: *eat-er, neat-er*. Though *-re* to *-er* has been one of the most successful spelling changes in American English, it's not entirely consistent. *Acre* and *ogre* did not become *acer* and *oger*. You can see why: putting the *c* and *g* next to the *e* makes the spelling less like the sound: *acer* and *oger* look like they should be pronounced *aser and oadger*. Webster had tried to fix this, but his *aker* (for *acre*) was a step too far for the American people.

I've come to think of the *-or/-our* divide as the mascot for American–British linguistic differences—especially in the word *colo(u)r*, for which Americans and Brits roundly abuse each other. On Twitter, @BritishLogic proclaims "People who spell *colour* without the 'U' don't deserve to live," while on *Urban Dictionary* an American defines *colour* as "British douchebag-tense for the word COLOR." When the US band Foo Fighters named an album *The Colour and the Shape* (a quote from their British manager), a *Time* magazine reviewer took them to task: "If you're going to spell *colour with a u* in your album title, shouldn't you at least try for pretentiousness?"[20] That said, a good number of American Anglophiles swoon over the *u*.

The *-our* ending gives a picture of French influence on English. Though plenty of "good old Anglo-Saxon" words are today spelled with an *ou*, no one in England had thought to put those letters together till the Normans came along. The *ou* that the Normans initially brought was pronounced in French as it is written: a diphthong formed of an /o/ rounded off with a /u/. Because of sound changes in English, the *ou* combination now stands for a number of different sounds (as in *double, sound, shoulder*). In general, any English *ou* that's been around since before American colonization is one of the following:

1. A spelling that Norman scribes introduced when trying to transcribe how English vowels sounded to their ears.

2. A French word borrowed into English, or
3. A more recent spelling introduced because we've become accustomed to seeing *o* and *u* together in certain contexts.

As an example of the first case, French scribes turned the Old English words **mold, molt, sholder**, and **smolder** to **mould, moult, shoulder**, and **smoulder**. Americans dropped the interloping *u* (missing the one in *shoulder*, alas) and in doing so made the spellings more true to the words' English history and pronunciation. The second and third situations are illustrated by words with the *-our* endings.

The *-o(u)r* variation in American and British spelling is represented by thirty-odd words and their derivatives. Not a lot of words, but ones you're likely to run into, like **colo(u)r, favo(u)rite**, and **neighbo(u)r**. We can divide the words into three groups, according to how French they are and therefore how "honestly" (which is to say, *etymologically*) they came by their spellings.

The first and biggest group are French words that the Normans brought to English. While in Modern French these mostly end in *-eur* (*couleur, odeur, honneur*, etc.), the Norman French of 950 years ago used *-our*:

ardo(u)r, cando(u)r, clamo(u)r, clango(u)r, colo(u)r, enamo(u)r, favo(u)r, fervo(u)r, hono(u)r, humo(u)r, labo(u)r, odo(u)r, parlo(u)r, ranco(u)r, rigo(u)r, rumo(u)r, savio(u)r, savo(u)r, splendo(u)r, succo(u)r, tumo(u)r, valo(u)r, vapo(u)r, vigo(u)r

When these words were first used in English, they were spelled all kinds of ways, with *-our*, *-or*, and even *-ur*, as in *colur* and *odur*. While the Normans spelled them with *-our*, all except *succo(u)r* had come to French from Latin, where they had been spelled (and pronounced) with *-or*.[21] So both *-or* and *-our* are historically motivated spellings, depending on how far back in history you wish to go. By Shakespeare's time, -our was generally the preferred spelling for the words that still have it today, but his works still had at least as much *honor* as *honour*.[22]

While the case for -*our* is historically compelling, it is undone by English's inconsistency in honoring that history. Words like *factor, liquor, author,* and *tremor* started out with -*our* spellings in English (because they had had them in French), but they quickly settled into the more phonetic, Latin-like -*or* spellings. Those became the standard spellings in Britain even before Americans started removing *u*. Thus, this first group of -*our* spellings fails all the tests for a logical or historical spelling system:

- The -*our* spelling does not reflect pronunciation (*valour* doesn't rhyme with *devour* or even with *velour*).
- Its historical basis is not as historical as it could be (French, rather than Latin).
- -*our* spellings are not consistently used (*tumour* has a *u, tremor* doesn't).

Since the -*or* spellings were more consistent and closer to English pronunciation, they served Webster's simplification agenda. Since they were more Latin-like, they also suited his preference for staying true to etymology. The loss of the *u* also served Webster's desire to distinguish an American standard from the British one. Not that the matter was settled in Britain. Twenty years after Johnson's dictionary (while Webster was a student at Yale), English writers were still arguing about the *u*. English minister John Ash presented *color, honor, labor,* and *vigor* in his 1775 dictionary as the "modern and correct spelling from the Lat[in]." The -*our* alternatives were presented as "the old spelling" or "the more common spelling" from French. Ash extended *u*-lessness to all the derivatives of these words in his dictionary, including *honorificabilitudinity,* a synonym for *honorableness* that surely deserves a place in your next conversation. His fellow clergyman John Wesley, however, advised English clergy to "avoid the fashionable impropriety of leaving out the *u*" since "this is mere childish affectation."[23]

The second group of *-o(u)r* words came to English from French, but their *-our* spellings are *English* inventions in order to make the words look French*ish*, while allowing English speakers to ignore the French vowels of the original forms. The French-derived words whose *-our* spellings are not French are:

arbo(u)r—from French *herbier* (later influenced by Latin *arbor*)
armo(u)r—from French *armure*
behavio(u)r—ultimately from French *avoir*
demeano(u)r—derived in English from the verb *demean*
endeavo(u)r—from French *en devoir*
flavo(u)r—from an Old French word spelled *flaur, fleiur*, or *fraor*

Except for *arbor*,[24] these words have no Latin version with an *-or* spelling. Ash's dictionary kept the *u* for these words, but Webster saw no reason to persist in these French-ish *u*-spellings. His change to *-or* made the spellings truer to modern English pronunciation.

In the last category are words with no French history at all:

glamo(u)r—from 17th-century Scots
harbo(u)r—Middle English *herberwe*
neighbo(u)r—Old English *neahgebur*

Harbour and *neighbour* probably acquired *-our* spellings because their endings sounded *u*-like to the Norman scribes. The words are English, but the modern spellings have been sieved through French spelling sensibilities. *Glamour* is the oddest of the *-our* bunch because it tends to keep its *u* in American as well as British, despite the best efforts of the Simplified Spelling Board to change it. *Glamour* originally meant 'magical spell'—the kind woven by

Scottish witches, not Parisian fashion. It had not yet made it into English dictionaries by Ash and Webster's day. Other early spellings were *glamer* and *glamor*, indicating that it was never pronounced with a *u*. Perhaps a certain magazine (founded in Hollywood) has something to do with *glamour's* resistance to *u*-lessness. Because we think of French as fashionable, we maintain the vestiges of its spelling system in English to indicate style and sophistication. That *u* in *glamour* is precisely a matter of fashion.

This is all to say that whether or not any *-our* word is French in origin, the *u* wafts Frenchness all over our spelling system. It started with the influence of French scribes and continued due to its French–aristocratic associations. Webster was making English more Englishy when he struck the *-our* from words that didn't rhyme with *tour* or *sour*. (With the exception of *four*, which would have been confusing as *for*.) But the British won't take those words in the Englishy direction because to drop the *u* would be seen as (*horrors!*) Americanization.

The success of *-our* in Britain comes at a price. Not just the price of printing the extra letters[25] but the psychological and educational price of orthographic irregularity. British spellers have to learn when to include the unpronounced *u* as well as when **not** to include it. Yes in *clamour*, no in *tremor*. Yes in *labour*, no in *laborious*. Yes in *vapour*, no in *vaporize*. Yes in *honour, honourable,* and *honouree* but no in *honorary* and *honorific*. English is terrible to spell, and British English isn't trying to make it any easier.

Zee problem

When I see American spelling, I cloze my ize.

Donagh Marnane[26]

In 2012 a British learning-disability charity quizzed over two thousand adults on their spelling and found that about a third could not spell *definitely*. The headlines that followed proclaimed that the population had become too dependent on spell-checkers, which had ruined our ability to spell. Those headlines made me more concerned for the population's critical reasoning faculties than for their spelling. The fact that a lot of people in 2012 couldn't spell tells us only that a lot of people in 2012 couldn't spell. Unless we know how well people in 1972 spelled, we cannot know that spelling skills have worsened. And unless we've ruled out other possible explanations (changes in how spelling is taught, in how much reading people do, etc.), we should have no particular reason to blame spell-checkers. In fact, we should be open to the possibility that spell-checkers help us to learn spelling. If not for the gentle insistence of spell-checkers, I am sure I'd still be spelling *accommodation* with one *m*. Technology can teach.

But people like to blame technology. And so Britain worries about American "spelling imperialism," which broadcaster John Humphrys says "now stretches via your desk-top through spellcheck," resulting in "a deep sense of grievance at what the Americans are doing to us."[27] I've had to listen to this grievance (a *lot*), but I haven't seen the damage. Awareness that Americans spell things differently seems to have ignited a newfound sense of orthographic patriotism in many Brits. Sure, you'd probably find more *color* in Britain today than fifty years ago because there are people who have not figured out how to change the dictionary in their spell-checker or auto-complete feature. But British English has not succumbed to *color*; it is still considered to be a misspelling.

The case of *-ise* and *-ize*, on the other hand, indicates that technology may be moving "correct" spelling in the US and UK away from each other rather than merging them. It's a complicated situation with a complicated history. The *-ize* spelling, like *ae*, *oe*, and *ph*, is a way of representing a Greek spelling in English using the Latin alphabet. But the French spell the same suffix as *-ise*. Some of these words came into English from postclassical Latin, which used the Greek *z* (*characterize* from *characterizare*), some from French with an *s* (*specialise* from *spécialiser*), and some were invented in English by using *-ise* or *-ize* as a suffix. For instance, *apology* gave rise to *apologise* (and later *apologize*) and *personal* got the verb form *personalize* (and later *personalise*).

Then in the 19th century, use of the suffix exploded. The *Oxford English Dictionary* records about nine hundred new *-ize* words from the 1800s. That's as many *-ize* words as had been added to English in the previous six centuries and three times as many as they record for the 20th century.[28] The year 1825 gave us *lionize, minimize,* and *objectivize.* The 1850s were good for *euphemize, externalize,* and *serialize.* Most of these new words were British before they were American.[29] This verbifying suffix-fest coincided with—maybe even spurred on—the mid-1800s British shift towards preferring the *-ise* spelling for both new and old verbs. This shift may have been inspired by the large number of 19th-century *-ise* words that were borrowed directly from French, including *galvanise, mobilise,* and *polarise.*

The 19th-century rise of the *-ise* spelling in Britain coincided with its downfall in America. Noah Webster's shift to *-ize* makes the spelling correspond unambiguously to the /z/-ful pronunciation (*-ise* can also be pronounced with /s/, as in *promise, anise,* and *vise*[30]). But while the shift to *-ize* is one of Webster's most successful interventions, it's also terrifically incomplete. Americans don't use a *z* in the verbs *advertise, merchandise, surprise,* or *compromise,* though they're all pronounced with /z/. There are historical explanations for some of the exceptions, but the facts of the matter are: Webster's change made American spelling more stable, in that it reduced the number of spelling options, but it didn't make the spelling completely regular.

While Americans had made a firm decision about how

to spell the suffix, the British didn't feel a particular need to conform. The preference for *-ise* in the 1800s was reversed (at least for some words) after the publication of the *Oxford English Dictionary*, starting in 1884. Faced with many words with complicated spelling histories and usage, the OED editors decided to treat all the words the same and to present the *-ize* spelling before the *-ise* one for each verb. They chose *-ize* on the grounds that the suffix goes back to Greek, even if not all the words containing the suffix do. The *z* spelling became more popular with British publishers after the OED, but the *s* spelling was still considered an acceptable alternative. (As we'll see in chapters 6 and 8, the British can be rather tolerant of variation in the standard language, feeling less of a need for strict uniformity.)

Things went wrong for the British *z* (and that British tolerance) in the 1990s. The graph below shows the proportion of *-ize* spellings from 1990 to 2005.[31] The graph could be used as a dictionary illustration for the word *nosedive*.[32]

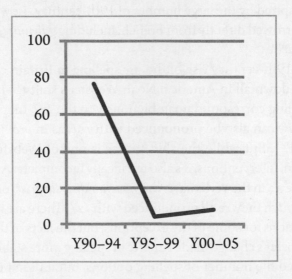

British *-ize* spellings used in the *Collins Bank of English* (Ishikawa 2011)

In the 1990s, *The Times* in London and Cambridge University Press suddenly switched allegiance to *-ise* after preferring *-ize* for the seventy years prior. At this point, spell-checkers had been readily available for about a decade, but since they allowed both *-ise* and *-ize* in British English, documents could pass muster while confusingly spelling the same word in two ways. The internet had recently been rolled out to the public, giving people more opportunity to read other countries' spelling than ever before. These developments led to two lines of thinking:

1. Spellings should be consistent within a document—no more mixing *-ize* and *-ise*, and
2. If Americans are spelling it *-ize*, then *-ise* must be "the" British spelling.

And so people started believing that *-ize* is American (perhaps even believing that the spelling was invented in America) and that it is simply wrong in Britain. A spoof "message from the Queen" that does the rounds after US elections declares that Her Majesty is retaking the colonies and "the suffix *-ize* will be replaced by the suffix *-ise*," as if *-ize* is not British. There's even reluctance to use *-ize* among those who know that the fashion for *-ise* is recent. A 2011 letter in the *British Medical Journal* quotes *Fowler's Modern English Usage*:

> The primary rule is that all words of the type *authorize/authorise*, *civilize/civilise*, *legalize/legalise* may legitimately be spelt with either *-ize* or *-ise* throughout the English-speaking world except in America, where *-ize* is compulsory.

But then the letter writer concludes:

> Speaking purely personally, I think that anything that is compulsory in America should be avoided.

Our globalized communication culture hasn't killed off -ise; it has strengthened it. -Ise is not just a suffix; it is a badge of honor, declaring to all and sundry, I AM NOT AMERICAN. True to form, when wanting to look not-American, British English looks more French.

Foreign accent syndrome

In Paris they just simply opened their eyes and stared when we spoke to them in French! We never did succeed in making those idiots understand their own language.

Mark Twain, *The Innocents Abroad* (1869)

The United States and Britain are both thoroughly multilingual societies. Over three hundred languages are spoken in London, and as many as eight hundred have been claimed for New York. But American and British *people*? Not so multilingual. Only 18% of Americans and 39% of Brits claim to be able to hold a conversation in more than one language—compared to 66% in Germany and 94% in the Netherlands, for instance. In a pot-kettle-black situation, Americans and Brits each claim the other does terrible things to foreign languages. Americans have a British reputation for doing bad things to French and pronouncing foreign words "in a pretentious way,"[33] and Britons, some Americans believe, "go out of their way to pronounce certain foreign words incorrectly."[34]

In most cases, the finger-pointing about incorrect pronunciation is pointless. Americans stress the second syllable of two-syllable French loanwords: *beRET, balLET, baTON, bourGEOIS*. The British stress the first: *BEret, BALLet, BAton, BOURgeois*. The French do neither of these things. French does not have the very English rule that words must have one most stressed syllable, and so the French syllables are more evenly pronounced. Americans have a broad *a* in *pasta*; Brits, a flat *a* (as in *pat*). Similarly, Americans tend to say "oh" in the middle of *risotto*, while Brits say "aw." The Italian *a* and *o*? Well, they're somewhere in between. All words borrowed into English are anglicized, but since that anglification happens in different national contexts, it can go in different directions.

Thanks to immigration, Americans have more Spanish and Italian borrowings and perhaps more of a feel for them, while the British stay closer to their neighbors the French. In pronunciation, American *oREGano* rather than British *oreGAno* is a long-standing example of American staying closer to Spanish. Americans are more likely than Brits to pronounce Spanish *ll* as "y," whereas you are more likely to hear the English *l* sound in a British *paella* or *mantilla*.[35] (Both Englishes tend to use "y" in newer imports like *tortilla* and *quesadilla*, but not in older borrowings like *guerrilla* and *armadillo*.)

Things get weird when we stereotype how the other language sounds, rather than actually listening to it. *Ibiza*, an island off the Valencian coast with weather that is conducive to British hedonism, becomes a hyperEnglish-hyperSpanish mess in the common British pronunciation "eyeBEEtha." The *z* is diligently pronounced as "th" in the Castilian Spanish style, but the first vowel loses its connection to Spanish entirely. On the other side, Americans, wanting to make *lingerie* sound like other French words they knew, made the final syllable "ray," in complete contravention of the word's French pronunciation, not to mention its spelling.

At the same time, pronouncing foreign words in English ways can be a badge of patriotic or social-class pride. George Orwell observed that "nearly every Englishman of working-class origin considers it effeminate to pronounce a foreign word correctly."[36] At the other end of the class spectrum, a British etiquette book from 1836 advises: "In speaking of French cities and towns, it is a mark of refinement in education to pronounce them rigidly according to English rules of speech."[37] To this day, *Debrett's Everyday Etiquette* recommends that you "restrain any desire to show off your skills by over-pronouncing foreign words."[38] In upper-class Britain, attempting French pronunciation of French words in English signals too much earnestness or too little self-confidence—both objectionable qualities of the aspirational middle classes. Some French names in England are pronounced as if they've never met either language. English villages that grew out of the estates of the Norman gentry have names like **Beaulieu,** pronounced "byoo-lee," and **Belvoir,** "beaver."

In the US, attention to the "correct" pronunciation of foreign names seems polite to some, but to others it's seen as aligning one-self with the "educated elite" rather than with "middle America." Politicians who pronounce *Iraq* or *Pakistan* with more anglicized vowels may be signaling an "America-first" mind-set or may be attempting to woo voters who are wary of the "educated elite" and their more "worldly" pronunciations.[39] But somehow that doesn't apply to *Paris* or *France,* which in American rhymes with *pants.*

French à la carte

The British Empire was created as a by-product of generations of desperate Englishmen roaming the world in search of a decent meal.

American food writer Bill Marsano (2004)

The way to a language's vocabulary is through its stomach, and French continues to feed food words to English. The past hundred years have brought in *chèvre, clafoutis, clementine, coq au vin, cru-dités*—just to mention a few that start with *c*. British English ingests a lot of French, like **rocket** (or **roquette**), **courgette**, and **coriander** (with a pre-Websterian spelling change from *coriandre*), while the American words for those foods show a more varied linguistic diet, with its **arugula** (Italian dialect), **zucchini** (Italian), and **cilantro**

(Spanish). The history of American immigration is written all over the American vegetable vocabulary. There must be more to it, though, because British English doesn't just use more French loanwords than American does. It uses fewer English words, throwing them over for French imports. For instance, British English replaced the nice English compounds *eggplant* (1767), *sugar pea* (1707), and *kidney bean* (1548) with the French *aubergine* (1796), *mange-tout* (1823), and *haricot bean* (1653)—though the Brits later borrowed *kidney bean* back from Americans and now use *haricot* for what Americans call *navy bean*.

When Americans use French foodie words, it's sometimes in non-French ways. That really gets some British goats. Take *entrée*, for example, which in American English means 'main course,' and which today's Britons hardly use at all, except when enthusing about how Americans misuse it. American use of *entrée* is "completely nonsensical," "has riled me up for years," "makes my skin crawl," "blows my mind," needs "a grassroots revolution to make it stop"[40]—and that's just from the first of the seven million hits I got when I searched the internet for "American entree stupid."

Why do Americans use *entrée* differently from the French? Could it be because the French changed? It could, actually. Dan Jurafsky, in his book *The Language of Food*, traces *entrée*'s nearly 500-year history in French, then English. The word entered English in the 1700s, at which point entrées were hot meat dishes laid on the table at the same time as other dishes, in a banquet arrangement. Entrées were distinguished from roasts, which took center stage. In the 1800s, it became stylish to serve meals in successive courses, and *entrée* named the third course of a meal—after the soup and the fish, but before the roast. When people stopped serving roasts and other hot meat dishes, Americans kept talking about the prepared meat dishes as *entrées*, even though they were now the main course. The great French chef Escoffier used the word in much the same way: steaks, casseroles, stews, leg of lamb, ham—all classified as *entrées* in his 1921 *Le Guide Culinaire*. As our ideas of 'main courses' moved away from meat-meat-meat, so the meaning of *entrée* spread to include fish and vegetarian dishes. Interpreting *entrée* as 'first course' is a mid-20th-century change in French—and in Francophilic British.

The other bit of Menu French that Americans are said to get wrong is *à la mode*. The French means 'in the current style,' and in New York in the 1890s the style of the moment was ice cream. Ever since, American *à la mode* has meant 'with ice cream.' Ice cream may not feel as stylish now, but *à la mode*'s new meaning has a practical side effect: you know what you're getting when you order pie *à la mode*. Had we left it meaning 'in the current style,' we'd be held at the whim of the chefs, and the *mode* could be desiccated pea puree this week and cardamom foam next week. "But you could just call it 'with ice cream'; that would be clearer!" the little British voices in my head say. To which I reply: "Yes, and you could say *with spinach* instead of **Florentine** or *with ham and pineapple* instead of **Hawaiian**." Menu English respects no boundaries, no etymologies, and (ironically) little good taste. We might as well stop thinking of the French-origin words as French. They're English now. They can develop in whichever direction English takes them.

Academy schmacademy

I'm reminded of how much my generation has lost by adopting a cheapened version of French, peppered with English words. [...] I'm not yet ready to be devoured by the language of capitalism, even if I know that growing pains are inevitable. Just like the British will never consent to saying "y'all" until their dying day.

French author Jessica Reed[41]

If you find it disrespectful to the French to remove their letters, pronunciations, and meanings from English, just remember: the

French have an entire institution dedicated to un-Englishing their language.

It started in 1634 when King Louis XIII of France granted a royal patent to the Académie Française, the pet project of his chief minister, Cardinal Richelieu. This royal support transformed a mere Paris literary salon into the utmost authority on the national language, and later a model for similar language regulators around the world. Apart from a twenty-year hiatus after the French Revolution, the Académie has been responsible for ensuring that French is "pure, elegant and capable of representing all of the arts and sciences."[42] But before the Académie could guarantee the purity of French, it had to invent it. Modern French, as a national language, was relatively new, developing from the dialect used by the Parisian elite, as distinguished from the many vernacular languages used in most homes and in the provinces. The Académie was charged with recasting Parisian French as *le latin des modernes*[43]—the Latin of modern people.

For more than a century, however, the Académie has mostly concerned itself with linguistic immigrants.[44] The purity of French must be guarded against *les anglicismes,* including *le weekend, un briefing,* and *shooter un mail.* For the Académie's 350th anniversary, 2014 was declared *l'année de la reconquête de la langue française*—or, to put it in our crude tongue, the year of winning back French from "the English peril."[45] The Immortals of the Académie (as they call themselves) don't discriminate between the American and the British, instead taking a strong stance against "*la montée en puissance de l'anglo-saxon*"—the rise of the Anglo-Saxon.[46] That French intellectual use of *Anglo-Saxon* speaks volumes— throwing us back a thousand years to Old English, ignoring the fact that today's English gets (by some counts) the majority of its vocabulary *from French.* Many of the anglicisms that the Académie protests, such as *vintage* (in the sense of 'antique') and *dedicacer,* 'to dedicate,' are only English words because they were imposed on

English by the Norman French invaders. (In the case of *dedicacer*, the English haven't even changed the meaning from the original French—the French had just stopped using it.) If the Académie is going to refer to English as *Anglo-Saxon,* as if it's a relic of the Dark Ages, they shouldn't be surprised if we get medieval on their *derrières.*

6

LOGICAL NONSENSE

Americans have such a curiously un-English way of being strictly consistent and logical in their doings.

Grant Allen (1890)

"You may be right on a technicality." That is how a copy editor—let's call him C—tried to end an argument with me the other day. I was right. And it was technical. It started when C claimed that *hung over* must be spelled as two words: we put spaces between verbs and adverbial particles like *over*, so we must put a space in *hung over*, as we do in other verb + *over* combinations like *flew over*. That seems like a logical argument. But a logical argument is only as good as the premises it rests on, and the premise that *hung over* is a verb phrase is just plain wrong. I threw the evidence at him: if it were a verb, it could change its tense marking. But it can't: the champagne I'm drinking tonight isn't going to hang me over tomorrow. *Hungover* is an adjective, and so C's argument could not hang together.

C was open to a logical argument when it supported the outcome he wanted: a space in *hung over*. Once new facts undermined his logic, they were "technicalities" that could be ignored. It reminded me of when people try to end arguments with the accusation "That's just semantics!" I have news for them: semantics is the most important part of any argument. And technicalities are the essence of grammar.

I tell this story because it illustrates how very attached people are to the notion that their way of using English is more logical than other ways of using English—until the logic is tested. If you show that a grammar stickler's premise is incorrect or if you offer an exception to their "logical" rule, you cannot expect to be thanked for that favor. At that point, logic is shoved aside and tradition, precedent, or aesthetics becomes the weapon of choice: "Write it this way because we always have." "Write it this way because that's how it works in Latin." "Write it this way because it looks better." Though their arguments for their preferred phrasing often end with appeals to its alleged age or beauty, language pedants do seem to like to start their arguments with appeals to logic.

The idea that English should be logical really got going with the popular grammarians of the late eighteenth century: Englishman Robert Lowth (1710–87) and American-in-England Lindley Murray (1745–1826) in particular. Rather than following the great writers and speakers as his model for good English, Bishop Robert Lowth's *A short introduction to English grammar* (1762) dismissed the grammatical ken of everyone from John Milton to the King James Bible. Lowth argued that a double negative makes a positive and that one must say *this is she* rather than *this is her*. In other words, he started treating English as if it were mathematics. Negating a negative makes a positive. Two pronouns on either side of *is* must have the same (nominative) case, just like two numbers on either side of an equals sign must be equivalent.

Lowth's grammar was popular in Britain, but also influential in America, where it was first reprinted in 1775. But Lowth's rules became even more influential because they were imitated by the most successful grammar writer of the early 19th century: Lindley Murray. An American Quaker trained in law, Murray relocated to England after the revolution, hoping (don't ask me why) that the weather in Yorkshire would improve his poor health. He published his *English Grammar* (1797) for the neighboring girls' school, not intending to publish it further. But it proved too successful to hold back. Republished in the US in 1800, it went through ten editions in that first year alone. Murray repeated Lowth's rules against double negatives, mismatched pronoun case, and prepositions at the ends of sentences, and added more rules, including the ban on singular *they*. These kinds of regulations, and the ill-applied logics used to argue for them, have plagued English ever since.

English isn't arithmetic, but many people want it to have clear rules like $2 + 2 = 4$. Rules themselves are not a problem. The problems come when so-called grammar fans conclude that if one rule is right, then anything else is illogical. That's just not a logical way of thinking. It's like saying that if $1 + 4 = 5$, then $1 + 1 + 3$ cannot also equal 5. Nevertheless if there are two ways to spell a word or construct a sentence, then people will conclude that one way must be the better way. And our natural egotism means that we're particularly good at coming up with reasons why our own familiar ways of saying or writing things make more sense than less familiar things. That's *logic* in the sense of Ambrose Bierce's *Devil's Dictionary*: "the art of thinking and reasoning in strict accordance with the limitations and incapacities of the human misunderstanding."[1]

But wouldn't it be great if language were logical and maximally efficient? If sentences had only as many syllables as strictly needed? If each word had a single, unique meaning? If there were no homophones, so we'd not be able to mix up *dear* and *deer* or *two* and *too*? No, absolutely not. No way. Quit even thinking that. What are you, some kind of philistine? If Shakespeare hadn't played with the number of syllables in his sentences, he would not have been able to communicate in iambic pentameter. If words could only have one meaning, we would have to invent a completely new vocabulary every time a new technology came along. Instead of clicking on an icon to open a computer file, you might have to kilk on a zinwang to nepo a wordcomp dak. And if we didn't have homophones, we couldn't have puns. A world without puns! That would be a world without steak puns! And a steak pun is a rare medium well done![2]

Not only would a logical language be an unpoetic, humorless hassle, it wouldn't be a human language. It wouldn't vary across people and borders like human languages do. British and American English may follow basically the same rules and have the same basic structures, but sometimes the rules are vague and the structures are sketchy, and so they can be applied in different ways. We don't differ on the big things—there isn't a dialect of English that says *cat the* instead of *the cat* or one in which *cats* is the singular and *cat* is plural. But where the language leaves options open, dialects can differ. Some nouns for places need a *the* before them and some do not. Which kind of place noun is *hospital*? The suffix *-ed* marks a regular past tense, but is *learn* a regular verb or not? There are rules and patterns, but there are also choices to be made. The fact that we don't make them all the same way is not a crisis of logicality—it's a fascinating aspect of the human condition.

We make the choices we make on these matters because people around us made those choices and we heard them. A dialect is essentially a collection of social habits. We become so used to hearing particular forms that the choices behind them don't feel like choices. When people ask me questions like

- *Why do the British (often) say* goatee beard *when a goatee can't be anything but a beard?*
- *Why do Americans emphasize the* new *in* New Year *(rather than the British style of stressing both words)?*

... the answer I most often give is: "Because that's how the people around them say it." Whatever historical or linguistic reasons there are for these differences, that's what the answer comes down to.

I don't say *tarp* instead of *tarpaulin* because (in the words of a charming man on Yahoo Answers) "Americans shorten our language . . . because they only have half a brain."[3] I say it because that's what my dad calls the thing that he uses as a dust sheet when painting. (And excuse me, Mr. Yahoo Answers: it was not Americans who shortened *cardigan, spaghetti bolognese, café,* and *the BBC* into *cardie, spag bol, caff,* and *the Beeb.* Plenty of Brits are shortening "your" language.)

We in Anglophone countries may be particularly prone to misunderstandings about how language works; few of us study other languages enough to have any sensible basis of comparison. What grammar we learn in school is often oversimplified to the point of self-contradiction. ("Verbs are action words!" they tell us. "*Was* is a verb!" they tell us. Can you see the problem?) And so our "logical" justifications for saying things in a particular way are often based on faulty premises. And the faultiest premise of all is: "If it's logical to say it my way, then it must be illogical to say it your way." Objectively speaking, your way of saying something is probably just as weird as anyone else's. It certainly deserves no less explanation than theirs.

The logic of the herd

Unfortunately, or luckily, no language is tyrannically consistent. All grammars leak.

Edward Sapir, *Language* (1921)

A sure cure for American Verbal Inferiority Complex is a trip to England. British English sounds much finer when it's filtered through *Masterpiece Theatre* and BBC America. When Americans are immersed in the full-strength stuff, it smarts. And so it was for this correspondent (let's call her J), who wrote to me after spending some time in London.

American usage is bad enough, but I found British English atrocious, [including] a strong tendency to use singular nouns with the plural form of verbs, e.g., *The gang are going to have a tough time protecting their patch* and *MI5 are looking into terrorist links.*

The issue at hand here is what linguists call **subject–verb concord**: how the number (singular or plural) of the subject of the sentence influences the verb form. In most sentences, **a singular subject** (←like this one) **goes** with a singular verb (←like *goes* back there), and **plural subjects** (←like this one) **go** with plural verbs (←like *go* back there). That seems straightforward, but J's examples have tricky subjects; they refer to singular things (a gang and the British security agency MI5) that are made up of multiple people (gang members, agents). We can think of a gang as being a singular whole, or as being a collection of individuals. That makes *gang* a **collective noun**, meaning that it has a singular form but potentially plural meaning.

Now, if you want logic in your language, there are two completely logical approaches to subject–verb concord. The difference between them becomes evident with collective nouns. The first uses **grammar logic**—it looks at the forms of the words:

- If the subject is in the plural form, use the plural verb form.
- If the subject is in the singular form, use the singular verb form.

The second uses **meaning logic**, asking what the words represent in the real world:

- If the sentence is about something the group has done as a unit, use a singular verb: *The company has gone bankrupt.*
- If the sentence describes the individuals in the group doing something as individuals, make a plural verb: *The company are giving up their Saturdays for charity work.*

In the meaning-logic approach, sometimes both verbs are equally "logical," since things that a group does as a unit can also be things that the individuals in that group do. So if a band (unit) *is playing*, then the band (individuals) *are playing*. The logic thus allows for subtle distinctions, as between *My family is big* ('my family has a lot of people') and *My family are big* ('the members of my family are large'). In the grammar-logic approach, you'd have to say *the members of my family* or *everybody in my family* in the second case.

Which of these logics is "better" is a complete matter of taste. As an American, J is accustomed to the grammar-logic approach. In fact, she probably had it drilled into her at school—I know I did. And so she's super judgemental when others don't follow the rule she was taught. What we rarely admit to ourselves is that we don't always follow the logical path we've chosen. Despite American devotion to grammar logic, sometimes Americans peek at the meaning of a singular noun and decide to use a plural verb. A *Houston Chronicle* article about rappers with *Lil* in their stage names tells us:

> *A surprising number are from Houston.*

Number is singular; we can tell from that *a* at the start of the sentence. But if we write *A surprising number is from Houston*, the wrong meaning comes through. (Which Houston number is surprising? Their area code?) We've peeked at the meaning of *number* and chosen to make the verb suit the noun's meaning rather than its singular grammatical status. In American, like British, you're also likely to find a plural verb when the subject is at odds with itself, as in *the gang hate each other* (not *the gang hates each other*). We also sometimes use singular verbs with plural things. An *and* should make a noun phrase agree with a plural verb. So we say *Clark and Lois **are** coming to dinner*. But then we say *Gin and tonic **is** what they like to drink*—treating two nouns as one thing. Despite the best grammar-logic intentions, Americans peek at the meaning and sometimes throw grammar logic out the window.

It's tempting to look at the British use of plural verbs with singular collective nouns and conclude that they're using meaning logic. But they're not, exactly. British grammar guides are pretty honest about it. "No firm rule," says *The Economist Style Guide*. "There is no rule," says Gowers' *Plain Words*. In this chaos, they advise writers to do their best to approach the matter with sense and a good ear. Even a good ear will have a hard time with British subject–verb concord. The echoes of constant linguistic change make it hard to follow the tune.

The plural verbs struck my American correspondent so forcefully not because they're all she heard in England, but because she only noticed the verbs that were unusual to her. And plural verbs with collective nouns are definitely unusual to Americans. One study showed that Americans use plural verbs after *army*, *association*, and *public* less than 1% of the time in written and spoken English. The respective numbers for written British English were 21%, 10%, and 38%, and for spoken British they were 21%, 50%, and 72%.[4] Singular verbs with collective nouns have been on the rise since the 18th century. Americans moved faster in that direction (no colonial lag there!), but Britons were headed that way too.[5] Until recently.

New research indicates that the British path toward singular verbs (grammar logic) may have reversed in the late 20th century.[6] Perhaps relatedly, whether Britons choose singular or plural verbs seems to have less to do with meaning logic (whether the members of the group are acting independently) and more to do with whether the particular collective noun is one that often occurs with plural verbs.[7] *Team* is one that seems to attract plural verbs. During the 2016 Olympics, news sources talked about *Team GB* equally with singular and plural verbs, regardless of whether the team was acting as a single unit or a set of individuals in the particular sentence.[8] For instance, in an article about women's basketball, I read: *Team GB are ranked 49th in the world.*[9] Grammar logic says that the verb should be singular—and so does meaning logic: the individuals within the team are not each ranked 49th; the team as a whole is. But since British English speakers are now accustomed to hearing about teams with plural verbs, *Team GB are* just flows off the tongue and into the brain—rankling only those Americans who want grammar logic. The music press is similar: "The The **have** recently released the soundtrack to Hyena," *The Big Issue* tells us, knowing that *The The* is a band that consists of one musician.[10] Politics gives another set of collective nouns. A British civil servant recalled to me that when he started at the Foreign Office in the 1980s, he was instructed to write *Her Majesty's government is*, but any foreign government *are*. In the past decade, though, members of Parliament used *are* about nine times more than *is* after the word *government*. Whether domestic or foreign, the government are plural.

The British reversal of centuries' progress toward singular verbs with collective nouns raises the question: Is this another case like -ize, where British English might be changing course in reaction to American English? Certainly, if any such reaction is happening, it's at a subconscious level. But that's where all the interesting things happen—and logic doesn't live there.

What counts?

E pluribus unum.—'From many, one.'
                    Motto of the United States of America

Singular and *plural* sound like simple, logical concepts: *singular* means 'one'; *plural* means 'more than one.' If only it were so simple. As we've just seen, a team is one singular thing, but sometimes it acts like several plural individuals. If I have a table *and* a chair, that's two things. Why do we call them *furniture* rather than *furnitures*? If a man has had a testicle removed, why can't we say he's lost *a genital*? Many attempts have been made to find the logic in these things, but they rarely get very far before the rule hits an exception. Some nouns can be easily used as singular or plural, depending on how many things they refer to: *chair/chairs, letter/letters, child/children*. Other nouns, like *furniture, sludge,* and *joy*, tend to stay singular. And others still, like *genitals, scissors,* and *leftovers*, tend to stay in the plural. Happily, British and American mostly agree on these. Where we don't agree, the odd singulars or plurals can be jarring.

British has a few always-plurals that American doesn't. In the UK, if you can't get your **flies** closed, you might need to step on the bathroom **scales**. In the US, if you can't get your **fly** closed, you might need to step on the bathroom **scale**. The British plural *scales* harks back to the old-fashioned kind, on which two things are balanced on a pair of suspended bowls or plates. A *scale* was one of those suspended bowls; if you put something on a scale, you were putting it on one side of the apparatus. The whole thing was made of two scales. The singular American *scale* has changed with the times: the bathroom scales of today are self-contained objects with only one surface to put a weight on. *Fly* went the other way, starting out singular in Britain (mid-1800s) because it referred to a single flap of cloth that concealed a clothing fastener. In the 1950s the British started saying *flies*—perhaps thinking of the two sides of a **zip** (or as Americans would say, **zipper**), rather than the flap of cloth. American English talks of scales and flies as single wholes; British speaks of them as matched pairs. We're counting up the world differently.

English uses its singular form for both individual objects that can be counted (*one shark, two sharks*) and for masses that can't be counted (*water, salt*). We can count the sharks in the sea, but we can't calculate how many waters are in the sea. Sharks have nice boundaries. If you have a swimming pool containing five sharks, and you add another shark, the sixth shark remains a distinct shark. Water doesn't work like that; add more water to the pool and it disappears into the water, uncountably. So even when there's lots of water around, it's still singular: *water*. The basic distinction between countable and non-countable nouns is much fuzzier than those examples make it look. For instance, English treats *pasta* as a mass noun and *noodles* as a countable noun, though they're basically the same thing. We eat **peas** in the plural, but **sweetcorn** (or as Americans say, *corn*) in the singular. You can fit about the same number of peas or corn kernels on a plate, but we talk about one as if there are many individual pieces on the plate and the other as if it's just one mass. Most linguists think these things are just arbitrary matters of habit: we learn to treat one as countable and the other as non-countable and we don't think much about it. Others look for deep explanations. At least British and American treat pasta, noodles, peas, and corn grammatically the same. We vary more in how we eat them than in how we say them. (To give one example, Americans are often surprised at the British use of sweetcorn as a pizza topping or sandwich filling.)

Then along come **mashed potatoes**. Or along comes **mashed potato**. Americans say it in the plural—the potatoes were countable before they were mashed, and so they stay countable afterwards. Brits look at the mass of finished product and call it *mashed potato*. This is part of a small pattern: Americans talk of **scrambled eggs**, which Brits often call **scrambled egg**. Americans ask if *there are* **onions** in the stew; Brits can ask if *there's* **onion** in the stew. The British tendency is to think of the inseparable mass in the pot; the American tendency is to think in terms of the countable food before it gets to the pot. Why? Who knows? The situation is easy to describe, but hard to explain.

Lego is an example that drives fans of the building toy bonkers. Americans play with **Legos**, after which their parents will inevitably step on *a Lego* then scream bloody murder. Brits play with

Lego, then step on *a piece of Lego* or *a Lego brick*, then scream blue murder. Proponents of the British singular mass noun often claim that their version is what the Lego company prefers. That's not quite true. Whether mass or count, nouns are a nightmare for companies trying to avoid **genericide**: the loss of a trademark because it has become an everyday name for a type of product. If you can talk of buying *store-brand Legos* or *own-brand Lego* then the Lego company has lost the battle to claim that their name represents only their product. Companies in this predicament insist that these words are not nouns, but proper adjectives. It's not *Legos*. It's not *some Lego*. It's *the Lego building system*. Genericide is not a particularly British or American affliction, but we differ in which companies and products have succumbed. Brits refer to *Tannoys*, *Biros*, and *Hoovers*, which Americans call *public address systems*, *ballpoints*, and *vacuum cleaners*. Americans talk of *Kleenex*, *Band-Aids*, and *Styrofoam*, which the British generically call *tissues*, *plasters*, and *polystyrene*. The British *Lego brick* is a fine adjective use, in keeping with the corporation's wishes, but British mass-noun use, as in *I play with Lego*, is no nobler (for intellectual property purposes) than *I play with Legos*.

Most often, where one country has a singular mass noun and the other has a count noun, it's the British who don't count. Britons play **sport**, pay **tax**, provide **accommodation**, launder bed **linen**, get **toothache**. Americans play **sports**, pay **taxes**, provide **accommodations**, launder bed **linens**, get **toothaches**. But watch out for one type of count noun that Britons alone use. If an English person says they could *murder a Chinese*, there is (probably) no reason to call the police. What they mean is that they could devour an order of chow mein or General Tso's chicken. Americans might use *Chinese* as a mass noun referring to a type of food (*Wanna get some Chinese?*), but are more likely to use it as an adjective in the phrase *Chinese food*. And despite their American origins, only the British *go for a McDonald's* or *a Burger King*. This fast-food count-noun pattern echoes the established British hot-drink pattern. Americans meet other Americans *for coffee*. If they want to count how many coffees, they generally add a countable noun, like *cup*: *two cups of coffee*. Brits might meet *for a coffee*. But we all meet for *a beer or two* after work. The patterns of difference are incomplete and illogical. At the end of the day, when the beer is flowing, we're mostly the same.

Doing the math(s)

[For a Briton to say math] is seen as crossing a red line and going over to the other side. It is an even greater red line than becoming a US citizen.

William Thomson (2012)[11]

I was taking my very English daughter through the very American experience of Judy Blume books. The books had been bought online in the UK, but as we read *Otherwise Known as Sheila the Great*, I became certain that our copy had been imported from the US. It was full of words like **Mom**, **apartment**, **elevator**, **can** (of dog food), **quart of milk**, **closet**, **junior high**, and **string beans**. More usual in a British children's book would be: **Mum**, **flat**, **lift**, **tin**, **two pints of milk**, **wardrobe**, **secondary school** (which covers US junior and senior high), and **runner beans**. Although my daughter lives with an American and spends plenty of time in the US, I had to explain some of the basic vocabulary.

But then came **maths**. Uttered by an eleven-year-old character from New York, that *s* at the end of *maths* confirmed beyond doubt the British provenance of the edition. The publishers had been willing to assume that young British readers could make their way past foreign unknowables like **cooties** (on UK playgrounds, **lurgy**) and **dresser** (**chest of drawers**). But expose youngsters to the Americanism **math**? God, no. Save the children!

The British stiff upper lip is jolted into a trembling fury by *math*. Here's a typical online comment on the subject:

> It's *maths*, not *math*. Look at the long version: *mathematics*. *Math* doesn't roll off the toungue [*sic*] as well with the hard sound at the end.
>
> Please pay respect to this fine ancient subject that is as relevant today as it was with the divine Pythagorean brotherhood and pronounce it nicely.
>
> Maths.
>
> Maths.
>
> Maths.[12]

It's got almost everything you could want in an internet rant. There's bad spelling, appeals to some faraway ideal time, and gaping gaps in common sense. It's just missing the traditional internet-ranting reference to Nazis. "Hey!" I want to yell at this guy. "If we want to pay respect to Pythagoras, shouldn't we say it in Greek? In whose world is 'ths' is easier to say than 'th'? And why would anyone think that the *s* on the end of *mathematics* is needed after you abbreviate the word?"

Maybe I should answer that last question. *Math.* (1847) and *maths.* (1911) started out as written abbreviations, each with a dot at the end. People originally would have said *mathematics* when they read them aloud (just as you say "mister" when you read *Mr.*). But it wasn't long before the very pronounceable abbreviations became words in their own right. **Clipping** is the linguist's term for making new words by shortening old ones, and English doesn't mind clipping at all. It's how we got *lab* from *laboratory*, *pub* from *public house*, *memo* from *memorandum*, and *exam* from *examination*. The American *math* is a proper clipping—just the beginning of the word. Just as we have *lab* and not *laby* and *exam* not *examn*, Americans clip *mathematics* to *math*, not *maths*. The

British version is more of a **contraction** than a clipping, since it includes both the start and end of the word. That's something we do in written language, abbreviating *attention* as *attn.* or *doctor* as *Dr.* When we read those abbreviations we pronounce the whole word, not the contraction. It's unusual to make new *spoken* words by using the beginning of a long word plus its last sound. So why keep an *-s* on *maths*? Push British English speakers on the matter and you get explanations like this:

> **Math** is an Americanism. In British English, if we seek to abbreviate *mathematics*, we maintain the plural of the original word and shorten it to *maths*.[13]

This comes from the well-populated genre of writing guides by people who don't know a lot about language—this one by Simon Heffer. I won't call him a journalist, because he mostly writes opinion, rather than investigation. His two books bemoaning the "corruption" of English are cases in point. If Heffer has the opinion that *maths* sounds nicer than *math*, I'm happy to respect that opinion. But whether *maths* is singular or plural is a matter of grammatical fact, and Heffer has the facts absolutely wrong. *Mathematics* and *maths* are not plural in English. I can tell this by reading none other than Simon Heffer, in a column he wrote in 2016:

> If one intends to study science at university then **maths is invaluable**.[14]

Does Heffer think that maths **are** invaluable? No. Deep down, below his made-up "facts" about language, he knows that *maths* is singular. Maths *is* interesting. Maths *is* sometimes hard. Maths *is* essential for modern life. Maths *is* these things. It is a mass noun that happens to have an *s* on the end. It is not a plural. If it were plural, I'd do two mathematics each day. After my morning mathematic, I might take a walk. In the afternoon, I might choose to do a more difficult mathematic. And when I had finished both my mathematics, I might say: *Mathematics are some of my favorite things; I love them.* But they aren't. *Maths* is one of my favorite things. Just one. Singular. I love *it*.

Elsewhere in the opinion pages, Matthew Engel complains about the cliché ***do the maths***. "I only half-cringe," he writes, "because it still retains its British 's.'" But no s was retained. It was added. The original expression is American: ***do the math***.

Though it does seem to confuse some Brits who think it's plural (while using it as a singular), saying *maths* causes no problems to the language. It certainly does no harm to mathematics. Six British mathematicians have even managed to win the Fields Medal (the "Nobel prize" of mathematics) despite their extra esses. The s is a harmless flourish. But the insistence that Americans are wrong for saying *math*: that has to go.

Who wore it shorter?

A great deal of the long-windedness and ambiguity which is creeping into our usage originates in America. Unfortunately, there are many uncritical folk here who think it clever to copy American usage.

Roxbee Cox, Baron Kings Norton (1979)[15]

Americans are often stereotyped as overdoing things. Guns, teeth whitening, cinnamon—all American habits that British people have asked me to explain "why so much." (Some are easier to explain than others.) And then there's the linguistic version of the "why so much?" question: "Why do Americans insist on putting extra syllables in words?"

The Economist Style Guide warns, "many Americanisms are unnecessarily long." To help you avoid these long Americanisms, they give thirteen examples and their preferable British equivalents. The list includes *normalcy* and *specialty*, to be replaced with *normality* and *speciality*. Have you noticed? These British "shorter" forms are one syllable longer than their excoriated American counterparts.

And so it goes. We've already seen that American spellings are shorter than British ones, that British English keeps more of *mathematics* in its abbreviation, that instead of a short, no-nonsense subjunctive verb form, Brits add a *should* to give the same meaning. And now some are worried about extra syllables? I'll show you some extra syllables. And I'll include the dates of their first recorded usage so we can see who's adding and who's subtracting.

British	American	
to burgle [1872]	to burglarize [1871]	*America the Long-winded*
expiry [1752]	expiration [1562]	
to be obliged [1340]	to be obligated+ [1533]	
transport+ [1712]	transportation [1540]	
zip [1925]	zipper [1925]	
to acclimatize [1802]	to acclimate+ [1792]	*Verbose Britannia*
aeroplane [1868]	airplane [1906]	
aluminium [1812]	aluminum [1812]	
normality [1848]	normalcy+ [1857]	
to orientate+ [1848]	to orient [1728]	
to pressurize (someone) [1945]	to pressure (someone)+ [1911]	
soya [1771]	soy [1696]	
speciality+ [1834, in 'specialism' sense]	specialty [1852, = 'specialism']	

These are the only examples I've found of "same-ish word, different syllable count" in standard use in the two countries. Rather than America bulking out words with extra syllables, we can see some blatant British syllable addition (**acclimatize, aluminium, orientate, pressurize, soya**) and American syllable removal: inventing *airplane* and *normalcy* and using *specialty*, a shorter form that had existed in the language (though not with the 'specialism' meaning) since the 1300s.

Sometimes a nationlect has both words in regular use—these are marked in the table with +. Some of these exist as variants within the nationlect with no meaning difference (*orient/orientate* in the UK, *normalcy/normality* in the US). But often where there are two forms, there are two meanings. Britain now uses *transport* for everyday travel because *transportation* had strong connotations of criminal exile, especially to Australia, in the term *penal transportation*. *Specialty* without the *i* is the correct British word for a medical specialization, but not for a chef's signature dish. Americans may *pressure* people to do things, but they *pressurize* their tires. They may *obligate* you to do things, but are *much obliged* when you comply.

The two that raise the most hackles are *burgl(ariz)e* and *alumin(i)um*. A BBC America article on "Ten American words you'll never hear a British person say" claims that:

> While Americans say *burglarize*, Brits say *burgle* because it's a crime committed by burglars, not burglarizers.[16]

And that oft-heard reasoning is just as faulty as the oft-heard reasoning on *maths*. If *burglar* had come from *burgle*, then we would spell it *burgler*, with an *e*, not an *a*. The verb *burgle* is a **back-formation** from *burglar*: that is, a word made by removing perceived prefixes or suffixes from another word. (*Orientate*, from *orientation*, is another example.) Using *burgle* for what a burglar does is like saying that vicars like to vic and caterpillars are known to caterpill. *Burgle* was clearly a joke word when it started out. But faced with *burglarize* as an American intruder, the British lost their sense of humor and started taking *burgle* seriously. In the US, *burgle* still sounds jokey.

Alumin(i)um is known to induce expatriate crises. If I say the

American *aluminum* in Britain, I'm mocked, but I feel silly saying it in the five-syllable British way. So I avoid it altogether: *Pass the tinfoil, please.* If we want the oldest name, it's the *n*-less *alumium*, proposed by Sir Humphrey Davy in 1808. Not satisfied with the sound of it, Sir Humphrey replaced it with *aluminum* in 1812. Almost immediately, scientists complained that it didn't sound "classical" enough because other element names tended to end in *-ium*, and so *aluminium* was born. From then, the *-ium* version was used in the international scientific community—until 1925, when the American Chemical Society set its standards. As well as dumping the etymologically incorrect *sulphur* in favor of *sulfur*, they chose the shorter, older form *aluminum*. About this event, physicist James Calvert wryly commented: "It is usually the English who have trouble pronouncing more than three syllables in a word, not the colonials."[17] Looking at how the British pronounce names like *Leicester* ("Lester") and how many Brits pronounce words like *inventory* ("inventry"), it's not a bad observation. At least in the case of *alumin(i)um* both countries pronounce the word as they spell it.

What the . . . ?

The reader is mystified for a moment by *the*, but soon sees that all he has to do is neglect it.

H. W. Fowler,
A Dictionary of Modern English Usage (1926)

In one of the great Monty Python sketches, the question "What's on the television, then?" is answered with "Looks like a penguin." The joke plays on an ambiguity—the question is about broadcast programming, but the answer is about a stuffed penguin perched on the television set. It is a British ambiguity (though Americans can get it). Americans are much more likely to say *on television* for the programming meaning than *on the television* (and nowadays

Brits can too). Is this why British humor is so admired? Not the dry wit or the surrealism, but the ambiguous definite articles?

Oh, probably not. But British English does do well on the *the* front. British women go through *the menopause*; American women just go through *menopause*. I have been told that the *the* is needed because you only do it once. *The* is a *definite* article, after all; it's supposed to indicate some kind of uniqueness. But that reasoning is contradicted by *puberty*: not even the British call it *the puberty*, even though, like menopause, you only go through it once.

In general, *the* shows up more in British English than in American. Despite America's greater tendency to use *the* with some diseases (*the flu, the measles, the mumps*), British English has more *the* in other places:

- In time phrases: *all the afternoon, on the Tuesday, June the sixth*.
- In ways of talking about unusual things: *He's the odd type who doesn't like the occasional drink* (both instances of *the* might be *an* in American).
- In referring to roads, such as in *the King's Road* or *the London Road*. *The High Street* (always with *the* when talking about it, but not necessarily on the road sign) is the British equivalent of *Main Street*—a central street with shops.
- In talking about sporting events: one listens to *the cricket* or watches *the tennis*.

Americans notice a British lack of *the* before *hospital*. In Linguistese, the British *in hospital* is **anarthrous** (without an article) and the American *in the hospital* is **arthrous**. (I only mention this because *anarthrous* is one of my favorite words.) Saying it the British way (*He is in hospital*) makes sense if you consider other anarthrous places like *school, prison,* and *church*. The lack of *the* indicates that we're talking about someone taking a particular role with respect to an institution. If you're *in hospital*, you're a patient. If you're *in school,* you're a pupil or student. If you're *in prison,* you're an inmate. If you go *to church,* you're a congregant. Nurses, doctors, cleaners, and technicians work *in **the** hospital*—only the patients get the *the*-less phrase.

While *school, prison,* and *church* show that the British distinction between *in hospital* (having a patient role) and *in the hospital* (being there for any other reason) is part of a pattern, you're far enough into this chapter to guess that it's an irregular pattern. The pattern works for *prison, school, church, college,* (in the US) *summer camp,* and (in the UK) *university,* but not for other institutions. If it were a perfect pattern, then Muslims would *go to mosque* (which they seem to do in Pakistani English, but not in British or American), the pampered would *go to spa,* and drinkers would *go to pub* (which is currently a more robust institution in Britain than any church).

The influence of Gaelic, which has the equivalent of *the hospital* in such phrases, is probably why it's a bit more common to hear of patients *in the hospital* in Scotland or Ireland than in England. Some linguists think Gaelic influence is why Americans say *the hospital.*[18] I am not convinced. Instead, I suspect that *hospital* is another case like clothing and car parts: Britons and Americans had to devise their own ways of talking about these things because they came pretty late in the development of the language. The first modern hospitals in England (as in, places where people were trying to actually *cure* disease) were founded in the 1710s, followed by the first American hospital in 1752. The first cases of *in hospital* don't show up until the mid-19th century, so rather than Americans saying things less like the English, it was the English who were now talking about hospitals in a new way.

The moral of the *the* story: sometimes *the* is just a syllable. At other points in English's history, people have studied *the Latin* and *the mathematics,* practiced *the millinery* and *the dressmaking,* saved things for *the posterity,* and played *the chess.* English lost those *the*'s, and it will no doubt lose and gain others.

Why noun when you can verb?

America, with the true instinct of democracy, is determined to give all parts of speech an equal chance.

Charles Whibley (1908)

Prince Charles has a lot invested in words. As I write this chapter, we still have the Queen's English. But pretty soon it'll be the King's English again. King Charles's English. Taking his inheritance seriously, Charles has asserted that American English is bad because Americans "invent all sorts of new nouns and verbs and make words that shouldn't be." When he's in charge, it seems, Charles will exercise his divine right to decree which words should be. Lexicographers across the land will scurry to effect His Majesty's wishes, lest they be imprisoned in the Tower of London or exiled to the antipodes.

OK, maybe I'm reading too much into his "words that shouldn't be" line. But which words was he talking about? Hardly any words are invented from scratch, so I suspect that Charles meant new words made from old words: the verbed nouns, the nouned verbs, the compounds, the prefixed and the suffixed, the clipped and the blended. Maybe especially those verbed nouns. They're all the rage—that is to say, people rage at them. Simon Heffer urges his fellow Britons to resist "this American habit" of *sourcing* ingredients and *authoring* books.[19] During each 21st-century Olympics, the British air has filled with complaints about the "new verbs" *medalling* (in the US, *medaling*) and *podiuming*. Everyone seems to forget that they heard the same complaints four years earlier. If you'll allow me to adjective a noun, the *funnest* part of these complaints is the unwittingly hypocritical use of verbed nouns. An executive promised that if he ruled the world, he "would **outlaw** the use of nouns as verbs."[20] A blogger worries about the "**butchering** of our language." Maybe they're in on their own jokes using those noun-derived verbs. But they don't seem to laugh much.

According to Heffer, it's clear "from even a cursory encounter with one of that country's television programmes" that Americans are responsible for the verbed nouns.[21] That's his evidence. Was his cursory encounter with an episode of *How I Met Your Mother*? Maybe *Baywatch*? I'm going to go out on an academic limb here and say: that's not enough evidence. It's also not hard to get more evidence. To do that, I chose two sections of the *Oxford English Dictionary*: words starting with *ca-* and *mo-*.[22] There I found 464 verbs (not counting those marked obsolete), 220 of which had first been nouns. That's not even counting the verbs, like *cannibalize*, that were built from a noun and a suffix. In other words, if you want to do away with verbed nouns, you'll have to give up nearly half your verbs.

More than half (112) of those noun-verbs come from before 1800, with peak verbing in the 1500s and 1600s. That's when we got *to cake, to carpet, to cane, to camp, to caution, to moan, to mob, to mortgage, to mouth*, and many more. My favorite verbed noun from the period is *to cater*. Originally, a *cater* was a person who *cated*, or dressed food. So modern-day *caterer* is a noun from a verb (*to cater*) from a noun (*cater*) from a verb (*to cate*). *Impact*, a perennial horror for anti-verbers, is another case like that: a verb meaning 'to press in' became noun meaning 'impression' became verb meaning 'to make an impression.' So verbing nouns is nothing new—and neither is nouning verbs (*a long walk, a light drizzle, a good read, when push comes to shove*) or making adjectives into verbs (*to best, to cool, to short*).

Those who complain about "new, American" verbings often concede that the verbs existed before America did (as Heffer had to for *to source* and *to author*). But has the flavor or rate of verbing changed in the American era? Benjamin Franklin certainly worried about it. He wrote to Noah Webster in 1789, urging him to speak out against the "awkward and abominable" verbs *to notice*, *to advocate*, and *to progress*.[23] (All of which had been in use in Britain before America was colonized.) Nineteenth-century travelers commented on the American propensity to *mail* letters, to *room* with others, and to *interview* people.[24] All that time, though, the British were making verbs out of nouns too. Of the fifty-two 19th-century verbs in my OED sample, thirty-six are British, including *to cab* (*it somewhere*), *to catapult*, and *to motor*. The sixteen American ones include *to cable* ('telegraph') and *to can* ('tin').

In the 20th century, 40% of all new verbs in the OED started out as another part of speech.[25] American verbing does speed up in the "American century"—but only to the point that UK and US come to a draw: twenty-eight new verbs each in my OED sample. These include British *to caddy* and *to MOT* (pronounced "em-oh-tee": 'to have or pass the government-required vehicle inspection') and American *to camouflage* and *to monitor*. Australians contributed two more: *to motorbike* and *to mozz*, 'to jinx,' from the Australian (via Yiddish, I was surprised to learn) phrase *to put the mozz on*.

Why do Americans get the blame for verbing, then, if the British have been doing it all along? My hypothesis is that verbings cause a bit more mental distress than other new word usages. Our minds are creatures of habit when it comes to processing incoming sentences. If you hear *I think we should . . .* your brain knows that a verb will soon follow, and so it waits in expectation of that verb. It dims the lights on the mental pathway to nouns and gets the verbs ready for action. If a known noun then shows up, your mind has to scramble to get back on track and find a way to interpret that noun as a verb. After hearing the new noun-verb a few times, you'll get used to it, but for a while you might hang on to the resentment that "somebody else changed my familiar old word and made me work a little harder to understand it." It's an old person's problem. The next generation will live with the new verb all their lives, and so it won't "clang" in their ears and brains. In the 1930s, people were up in arms about the new verb *to contact*. By the 2000s, we're so used to *contacting* people that only the nerdiest of language nerds noticed when it was anachronistically uttered on *Downton Abbey*.[26]

English is susceptible to **conversion** (the linguistic term for changing a word's part of speech) because our nouns, verbs, and adjectives can look and sound a lot alike. Most English nouns don't bother to wear their nouniness on their sleeves. For a word like *camp*, anything goes. It sounds like other adjectives (*damp*), other nouns (*lamp*), and other verbs (*stamp*). And so the language doesn't mind if you *camp at a camp camp*: verb, adjective, noun. But for nouns with suffixes like *-tion* or *-age* that say, "I'm a noun," verbing can seem to go against the grain of the word itself. Though some suffixed nouns end up as verbs (like *caution, motion,* and *position*), usually we try to avoid such nouny-sounding verbs. Instead we make back-formations like *televise* from *television* and *tase* from *Taser*. When the noun suffix stays on, as in the case of *leverage*, it strikes many people as a very strange verb indeed. Nevertheless it's a fool's errand to take the *-age* off in order to avoid "verbing." *Lever* spent nearly six hundred years as a noun before it too became a verb.

The verbed nouns that blend most easily into the linguistic landscape are those that express a concrete meaning that newly needs expressing: *to skateboard, to google, to pepper-spray*. The ones that have most annoyed are those that express more abstract actions: *to leverage, to action, to broker*. Being abstract means that more of an argument can be had about what the verbs mean and whether their meanings could be expressed with old verbs. These verbs are associated with the hated business-speak, which also gives verbing an American sheen (as we saw in chapter 2), whether deserved or not. The businessy verbed nouns that British newspapers complain about are as likely to be British as American. "This will anniversary as we move into the first quarter of 2011," reads one British department store's market report, while another says, "better-balanced autumn ranges should allow M&S

to anniversary tougher comparisons."[27] Um, it has something to do with years . . . I'm not sure. They haven't verbed that noun yet where I come from.

People like Simon Heffer who complain about verbing are often concerned that the new verbs "shunt perfectly serviceable ones out of the way and into desuetude."[28] That misses the point of why those nouns became verbs in the first place: not to replace another verb, but to replace a more long-winded expression containing the noun. *To interview* wasn't dreamed up to replace *to talk with*, but to be more efficient than *to have an interview with*. People are *tasked with doing things* because that's shorter than *giving someone the task of doing something*. *Caddy* is shorter than *serve as a caddy for*, *motorbike* is shorter than *travel by motorbike*. No existing words were harmed in creating this efficiency.

It's not just noun-to-verb conversion that bothers people. "The American obsession with the prepositional verb is notorious," gossips the first BBC News style guide (1967). I have to say, *obsession* seems a much better word for the British reactions to these American forms. **Visit with** "should be made unwelcome," says *The Complete Plain Words*.[29] To **head up a committee** is "vulgar," declares Simon Heffer,[30] and for John Humphrys **meet with** embodies "the obesity of our language."[31] These British complainers quickly conclude that since *they* don't use those prepositions, the prepositions must be unnecessary. Their diagnosis of redundancy reveals a dispiriting shortfall in curiosity about the language. They have not made any effort to notice that the prepositions clarify and add nuance in American English.

In the case of **meet**, American English is fighting ambiguity. Usually, language tolerates words with multiple meanings pretty well. The context will sort out for us that *broke* means something different in I *broke my toe* and I *broke a world record*. But for *meet*, the context often leaves a lot of possibilities open. *I met the mayor before the ceremony* could mean:

a. I made the mayor's acquaintance before the ceremony started.

b. I encountered the mayor on the way to the ceremony (and perhaps we exchanged pleasantries).

c. I went to a place at a predetermined time in order to see the mayor.

d. The mayor and I sat down and had a meeting prior to the ceremony.

American English rebels against this ambiguity, and it does so with prepositions. The 'encounter' meaning (b) has mostly been replaced by *run into*. (That one has proved so useful that Brits are saying it too.) The 'rendezvous' meaning (c) gets an *up*: *The mayor and I met up* or *I met up with the mayor*. The 'have a meeting' sense (d) has been taken over by *meet with*. Now that all of those meanings have their own expressions, the default way for Americans to interpret *I met the mayor* is the (a) sense, 'make the acquaintance of.' For British English speakers who don't use these prepositions, the listener (or reader) has to do more work (if they can be bothered) to determine which kind of meeting activity went on.

Other phrasal verbs add other nuances. *Visit with* involves sitting down with someone and having a conversation. That's different from visiting. I could visit an unconscious person in (the) hospital, but I couldn't visit with them. Add *up* (an adverbial particle, really, rather than a preposition) after a verb and the action becomes more active and complete. He could *head* the committee as a matter of ceremony, but if he *heads it up*, he's invested in the process.

When British usage gurus aren't complaining about added prepositions in American English, they find time to complain about missing ones. They say that **protest** is "incorrect for **protest against**" and that one should not (Americanly) **appeal** a verdict but instead should **appeal against** it. Here I have to note that not every preposition adds more meaning—some are just a matter of linguistic habit. We *listen to* music, but if we were to decide tomorrow to drop the *to* and *listen music*, we'd have little choice but to interpret it the same way. The same is arguably true of *appeal against*—if there's no meaning difference between *appeal against the verdict* and *appeal the verdict*, then the preposition is a matter of tradition and window dressing, not meaning.

More British pedantic consternation is inspired by the American ability to say things like *I wrote the company to complain*, where Brits must *write **to** the company* (and Americans can as well). American English lets *write* follow the same pattern as *read* or *tell*, but British English makes *write* follow only the same pattern as *read*. (The bold one is normal in American English only.)

read pattern	*tell* pattern	*write* pattern
read poetry to the kids	*told a story to the kids*	*wrote a letter to the kids*
read poetry	*told a story*	*wrote a letter*
read to the kids	~~*told to the kids*~~	*wrote to the kids*
~~*read the kids*~~	*told the kids (about it)*	***wrote the kids*** *(to say "hi")*
read them poetry	*told them a story*	*wrote them a letter*

There's no *logical* reason why *write* shouldn't follow the *tell* pattern. They are both verbs about transferring information through language, which means they both need to be arranged with other phrases that describe a communicator, a recipient of the communication, and something that's communicated. The people who object to *write the kids* do so because it's not what they're used to hearing. It's not an approved convention for using the verb *write* in their nationlect. Fair enough. If it's not part of your nationlect, you don't need to say it. That doesn't make it wrong to say. It's just not yours to say.

Can I get some logic here?

It infuriates me. It's not New York. It's not the 90s. You're not in Central Perk with the rest of the Friends. Really.

Steve of Rossdale, Lancashire[32]

Can I get a coffee? This simple question tops many a British list of annoying Americanisms. When it does, it's not long before someone (like Steve) claims it's "straight out of an old *Friends* episode."[33] Is it possible that one sitcom is responsible for one of Britain's most common and complained-about ways of ordering food and drink? Let's look at the evidence. *Can I* (or *we*) *get* is used in 30 requests in the 236 episodes of *Friends*.[34] Considering that *Friends* was on UK televisions nearly nonstop during the '00s, often with four episodes per day, that means the phrase probably showed up on British televisions every other day for about seven years. Maybe that, paired with the simultaneous boom in American coffee chains in the UK, was enough to do it. But to blame an American sitcom for *Can I get a coffee?* is to ignore the glaring Britishism in the question: referring to a cup of coffee as *a coffee*. Except for one instance each of *a coffee to go* and *a decaf,* the Friends ask for *some coffee* or *some cappuccino* or *a cup of coffee.* The Britishism *a coffee* was just making its way into American English at about the same time as *can I get* was entering Britain.[35]

After blaming *Friends*, British *can-I-get* grumblers launch their logic against the question. No, you cannot *get a cup of coffee,* says a Louisa C. in the *Mail on Sunday,* "unless you are planning to clamber over the counter and start fiddling with the steam spouts."[36] But interpreting *get* as only meaning 'work to obtain' is just pure stubbornness. Louisa and her compatriots use *get* to mean 'receive' in all sorts of contexts, so it's not a long jump to understand it as meaning 'receive' in the ordering-coffee context. In fact, one of the most frequent (and pre-*Friends*) uses of *can I get* in Britain is *Can I get a copy of this?* The askers of that question are rarely asking 'Can I take over your copy machine?' or 'Can I write out this text?' They mean 'Would you give me a copy of this?' or 'Can I receive a copy of this from you?' The British *get refunds* and *get birthday presents,* so the 'receive' sense of *get* is alive and well. All that's changed is that it's now heard in coffee-shop questions.

The appeal to logic is a distraction tactic. The real reason *can I get* sounds bad in Britain is because it's not the way British folk have been taught to make a polite request. Being polite (especially in Britain)[37] is largely a matter of saying words that are routinely associated with being polite. For Brits, *Can I have a coffee?* works as a polite request. It works less well for Americans, for whom it can sound like asking permission to have coffee, rather than asking to be given coffee. For people without *can I get* in their repertoire of polite-request forms, the *get* can sound a bit rude. They then want to explain to other people why they shouldn't say *can I get*, and they get tripped up by trying to apply logic to the situation.

I can't help but think, though, that *can I get* was doomed to complaint from the start because *get* is the runt of the English verb litter. People hate this useful 12th-century Viking gift to English. Kingsley Amis recalled that at his school *get* and *got*

> were suspect words, not exactly erroneous in themselves but vulgar. *I'll get it* or *he's got it* were said to be expressions lazy/stupid people fell back on because they were too stupid/lazy to think of or to know genteel words like *obtain* or *possess*. Even today both *get* and *got* retain a whiff of informality, so they should be avoided in solemn contexts or when trying to impress an octogenarian.[38]

Robert Burchfield's teachers similarly left him "wondering if *get* could ever be used in an acceptable manner." Even after growing up to write the third edition of *Fowler's Modern English Usage*, Burchfield seemed no more confident on this point. Other style guides, from Gowers' *Plain Words* (1954) to *Garner's Modern English Usage* (2016), reassure us that *get* and *got* are perfectly good English and that we should not fear using them. But those style guides have to keep repeating that message because we English speakers are just not so sure.

Get avoidance is probably why Americans started preferring to say *I have (a job* or *a husband* or *a pineapple)* and why Britons did not complain when that particular Americanism started taking over the more traditional British English *I've got.*[39] Whatever matters of taste keep people from wanting to say *get* and *got* (not to mention *gotten*), it remains one of the most useful words in English—with dozens of different applications, including many that were invented in the US and have since spread to the UK, like:

- 'to answer': *Get the door, would you?*
- 'to bother': *What gets me is the price.*
- 'to best in an argument': *You've got me there.*

No need to fret about *get*. As Anthony Burgess once demonstrated, you can just relax and use it all day:

I get up in the morning, get a bath and a shave, get dressed, get my breakfast, get into the car, get to the office, get down to work, get some coffee at eleven, get lunch at one, get back, get angry, get tired, get home, get into a fight with my wife, get to bed.[40]

Let the logic go

When dealing with people, remember you are not dealing with creatures of logic, but with creatures bristling with prejudice and motivated by pride and vanity.

Dale Carnegie, *How to Win Friends and Influence People* (1936)

Logical languages are good for computer coding, but they stymie human communication. We're not robots. We're poets. Every day we have new things to talk about. Every day we're building relationships with other people. And every day we find new ways to do these things using the raw materials of English. And English lets us, because it is a fantastically flexible medium in which to create things.

The extent of English's flexibility was brought home to me early in my linguistics training. The professor assigned our class to find ten examples of a particular word out in the world and then try to find the meaning of each instance of the word in a dictionary. Anyone who could find all the meanings probably hadn't looked carefully enough at how the words were used. It's impossible for a dictionary to represent the full extent of how we use words because they change—or rather we change them—constantly. Think of the word *table*. In *I put a table in my painting,* it doesn't mean 'table'; it means 'image of a table rendered in paint.' In *The whole table wants beer* it means 'group of people sitting at a table.' When a priest says *Everyone is welcome at our table,* he might well mean 'our church' or 'our community.' Often when we say *table* we only mean the 'upward-facing surface of the table,' as in *Clear the table* or *Put flowers on the table.* We rarely bat an eye (or an ear) at such specific uses of the word. On a daily basis, we wring new meanings (some that might only be used once) out of the words we know. On a daily basis, we combine words into phrases that have never before been said. And yet we (mostly) communicate well. There is no need for alarm. There's need for wonder. We are fantastic communicators, and so is English.

So if someone tells you that a word cannot mean X because it already means Y or that we should all stop saying Z because it is logically inconsistent, just say to yourself: here is a person who doesn't have a very good sense of how English works. If you want to entertain yourself, you can point out the inconsistencies of their argument. If you want an easy life, you can just ignore them—up to a point. If you see that person spinning their illogical yarns in front of a classroom or a government education department, you have a moral duty to step in.

7

LOST IN TRANSLATION

For as long as they mean what they mean to mean, we don't care if they make sense or nonsense.

Norton Juster,
The Phantom Tollbooth[1]

During his time as prime minister, David Cameron was desperate to seem hip and relevant, despite his boarding-school-and-private-clubs background. But, of course, white-bread, middle-aged men trying to be hip are the most unhip things out there. Cameron was mocked for singing along to Ed Sheeran, for bragging that President Obama called him *bro*, and for liking to *chillax*.[2] LOLgate was his "the Emperor has no hoodie" moment. It happened when former *News of the World* editor Rebekah Brooks described texts between herself and Cameron at a legal inquiry:

Robert Jay, Counsel to the Inquiry: How were these texts signed off? Everyone wants to know.

Justice Leveson: Do I?

Brooks: He would sign them off "DC" in the main.

Jay: Anything else?

Brooks: Occasionally he would sign them off *LOL*, 'lots of love,' until I told him it meant 'laugh out loud' and he didn't sign them that anymore.

Cameron wasn't alone in using *LOL* to mean 'lots of love.' We've survived a period of grandmotherly Facebook statuses like "Uncle Morton has passed away. LOL to his family." How many laughing LOLs had they seen and misunderstood before realizing their mistake? How can any of us ever be sure that we know what other people mean when they use words?

Communication involves a million little acts of faith. I have to believe that what I mean by words is the same as what you mean by them. That faith is tested on a regular basis—when we learn, like Cameron did, that our meanings aren't shared. Though these things happen to us repeatedly, we don't think of them as happening often. LOLgate probably didn't send Cameron into an existential crisis along the lines of "What if all my communications are failing, without me even knowing it? What if I am more alone and misunderstood than I ever imagined?" I too brushed these things off rather innocently, until one experience changed everything. This is the story of how my world was turned upside down by a *frown*.

It happened when I read a 2010 blog post in which Michael Wagner, a native German speaker, described an interaction with a Canadian-English-speaking friend at an art gallery.[3] Looking at an image of a face, his friend asked:

Do you think this is a frown or a moustache?

Wagner was puzzled:

Whatever "this" was, it was clearly below the eyes, and also, the facial expression was sad—so how could it be a frown?

For Wagner, as for most speakers of British English, a frown is an expression of displeasure that involves contracting the brow. But for me, and many speakers of American English, frowning involves turning down the corners of the mouth to indicate unhappiness, and more particularly sadness. That meaning is a 20th-century invention, and most American dictionaries have not yet noticed it. Some (mostly older) Americans still have the 'brow'-only meaning. But the new meaning is widespread, and more American than British, as our emoji names show. The ☹ is most commonly called *sadface* in British English, whereas it's *frown* or *frowny face* in many American contexts—including the standards document for Unicode, the international (but Americentric) body that approves new computer symbols.[4]

I blogged about Wagner's discovery, and a series of eureka moments followed. "So *that's* why Americans say *turn that frown upside-down* to mean 'cheer up,'" said the Brits. "So *that's* why people in books are always *frowning in concentration*," said I. Until that point, I'd assumed that concentrating made them sad. I had lived outside the US for twenty years before I discovered that others might be calling my scowls *frowns*. I had probably all my life known older Americans who used *frown* with the brow meaning. Had it not been for Wagner's blog, I might have gone my whole life without discovering this communication gap, despite my professional interest in words. The discovery brought home to me a lesson I'd already learned: that differences in meaning are rife and hard to notice.

For instance, I'd spent years being put off by English people's description of my accent as "an American **twang**." To me, people from Kentucky or Texas have twangs, with vowels plucked from a guitar or a banjo. I have an accent (of course; we all do), but I'd describe it as mumbly. In my world, you can't be mumbly and twangy at the same time. I had concluded that the *twang* accusations were another case of the out-group homogeneity effect: that the English think all Americans sound alike.

But then I read a reference to Peter Capaldi's "Scottish twang" and another about Sir Ian McKellen having a "slight German twang" when he plays Magneto in *X-Men*. I had to think again.

Surely, the English can't be so bad at accents that Scottish, German, and Texan all sound alike? And so that's when I discovered that *twang* in British English has two meanings. It can mean the kind of plucked-guitar sound that I think of as a *twang*, but it also means 'a trace of an accent.' Once again, most dictionaries don't include both meanings, but the variation came out in a survey.[5] When asked if *twang* meant 'a definite regional accent (of a particular type)' or 'a slight accent (of any type),' 85% of American respondents said that it's a definite accent, whereas British respondents were fairly evenly split between the 'definite' and 'slight' accent meanings. The British have two meanings for *twang*; I only had one. When they said I had an American twang, they might have been saying that they considered me to have a "soft" accent. I had been insulted by what they probably intended as a compliment. I'll never know how many times I've taken a British compliment as an insult or a British insult as a compliment. My optimistic solution is to just assume that any negative comments are surely just a translation problem. (Try it; it's good for the ego and keeps you out of arguments.)

Adventures in bacon

That's not bacon! That's ham!

My American niece Maddy,
refusing to eat British bacon

Not all dictionaries have caught the differences between the mostly-American and mostly-British meanings of *frown* and *twang*, but when they do catch them, they'll have to represent each of them as having two meanings. In linguistic terms, *frown* and *twang* are **ambiguous**: they have more than one distinct sense. Many meaning differences are more subtle than that. To take one example, there's *bacon*. The US and UK share a dictionary-type definition for *bacon*: 'meat cut from the back or sides of a pig, salt-cured and usually sliced thin.' But if you order bacon with your breakfast in Britain, you will get a different kind of bacon than you would get in America. In either case, if the bacon that showed up was not the kind of bacon that you had expected, you could grumble to yourself that you like the other kind of bacon better, but you couldn't complain (unlike my inexperienced niece) that they hadn't given you bacon. So you might want to say that the *thing* bacon differs in the two countries, and the word *bacon* is the same.

You might want to say that, but I don't. If different people use the same word to habitually refer to different things, then that tells us that there's something different about what that word signifies for different people in different places. Our verbal behavior varies when it comes to *bacon* because word meaning is not as stable and definite as dictionary definitions lead us to believe.

When lexicographers set out to record meanings, they are looking to describe the boundaries of the meaning: What can be called *bacon* and what cannot be called *bacon*? For the US and UK, the boundaries of *bacon*hood may be the same. As far as I know, there are no meats that can be called *bacon* in Britain that cannot be called *bacon* in the US and vice versa. But the outer boundaries of a word's meaning are only part of what determines how we use the word. The other part of the story is what's at the center of the meaning. The category of *bacon* isn't just defined by what is and isn't bacon; it also matters what we think "typical" bacon is. Linguists and psychologists talk about this in terms of **prototypes**. "Prototypical bacon" is our ideal concept of bacon—not necessarily which bacon we like best, but the set of properties that makes something supremely bacony. In the US and UK, the prototypes differ, and that has linguistic consequences. The foods that are closest to that bacony ideal get called *bacon*. The things that are within the bacon boundaries but not close to that ideal can be called *bacon* too. But we're not very comfortable with just calling them *bacon*.

Prototypical British bacon is cut from the back of the pig. It is shaped like a pork chop (but boneless and much thinner) and has a rim of fat around its edge. Because that's the prototype, Canadian bacon, which is fairly similar (but for the fat), could easily be called *bacon* in British English. But prototypical American bacon is fat-streaked strips cut from the side of the pig. That's too far from the British prototype. Brits *can* call the strips *bacon*, but they tend to call them **streaky bacon**. The distance from the prototype forces a linguistic intervention. And it works in reverse: I've heard Americans say, "In England they eat Canadian bacon." Those with more gastro-geographic sensitivity might call it *British bacon*. Those with a greater bacon vocabulary might call it *back bacon*. But Americans have to call it something more than *bacon* if they want to bring up the specific image of the pork-chop-shaped slice. The typically American long strips are just *bacon* in the US (the term *streaky bacon* is not known there) because that's the American *bacon* prototype.

While dictionaries of American–British linguistic differences have lots of examples of words with different meanings, they tend to be along the lines of "*First floor* means 'ground floor' in American and 'floor above the ground floor' (US *second floor*) in British." The examples in this chapter are more along the lines of "These words mean the same thing, except they don't."

The soup and sandwich gulf

Man to waiter: "Would it be possible to get baked beans on toast? I'm not British—I'm just crazy."

J. C. Duffy cartoon in *The New Yorker*

Britain offers many culinary delights (how impoverished my life was before crumpets!), but as an American ordering from British menus, I have experienced a fair amount of confusion and disappointment. When my food arrives it's often not what I expected. Once I realized the problem was rooted in different meaning prototypes, I could use that knowledge as a coping mechanism. Instead of crying into my soup, I could look at British *soup* as an intellectual problem to be solved.

I discovered this when I was virally indisposed, and my English (and vegetarian) spouse kindly offered to procure for me the American's ultimate cure-all: chicken soup. When he returned with what appeared to be a pureed chicken in cream (had it been deboned first? I couldn't tell), I could only feel more under the weather. He tried again and brought me something curry flavored. After some internet research, I sent him off again in search of cock-a-leekie, a Scottish broth with chicken and vegetables. It did the trick, and inspired my ongoing analysis of soup disappointments. It wasn't just that different soups are popular in the two places: American chicken noodle, British carrot and coriander, and so forth. The soups we had in common were different too. If I ordered "vegetable soup" at the university refectory, I received a green sludge or an orange sludge, depending on the season. What I'd expected (and hoped for) was a broth with some vegetables floating in it. A café I frequent offered a "Chinese five-spice pork soup" that was just what I wanted—a clear broth with meat and vegetables to scoop out. But it was just what I wanted only the first time I ordered it—after that they started Englishly pureeing it (still tasty, but sludgy). While both countries have pureed soups and chunky soups, the soup prototype differs:

American *soup* prototype: a savory food consisting of small pieces of meat, vegetables, and/or starchy things (e.g. noodles, barley, rice, matzo balls) in a warm broth.
English *soup* prototype: a warm savory food made from vegetables and possibly meat that have been well cooked and liquidized.

These are not our definitions of *soup*, but our prototypes for it. All sorts of other things can be called *soup* in the two countries, but the prototypes indicate what the "soupiest" soups are. The American prototype is more like chicken noodle soup. The English prototype is more like a typical tomato soup. (I say *English* rather than *British* because the prototype seems to vary within the UK. Many popular Scottish soups are broths with bits.)

The difference in *soup* prototypes has various linguistic consequences. For instance, when I've made chicken-and-dumpling soup, English friends have complimented me on my **stew**. American *soup* includes things that might be called *stew* in Britain because the British prototype for soup is concentrated at the smoother end of the scale than the American prototype.

The prototypical soupiness of a 'liquid with things in it' in American English means that Americans don't need a separate word for that type of soup. But British English does need a word for it, and uses **broth**. *Scotch broth*, for example, is a meat broth with barley, vegetables, and mutton. Now, before I order the Chinese five-spice pork soup I ask: Is it a broth or a puree? In American English, *broth* is just the clear liquid part of the soup—what Brits (and sometimes Americans) would call **stock**. We don't need a special word for soups with bits in, because that's what *soup* usually means in American.

These cultural differences show up subtly in dictionaries. Most define *soup* as "a liquid food." But the American dictionaries specify "often containing pieces of solid food" in their *soup* definitions. British dictionaries don't mention solid pieces. The only qualifier in a British definition of *soup* is "usually served hot at the beginning of a meal."[6] This might offer us another insight into the prototypes. If British soup tends to be a starter and American soup is often a meal, then it's no wonder that one is heartier than the other.

Bacon and soup are my particular mealtime obsessions. I may be a typical American in that regard: the words *bacon* and *soup* (as well as *bisque, bouillon, broth, chowder,* and *consommé*) all occur more often in American English than in British.[7] A more British obsession is the sandwich—so much so that you can get potato crisps (US *potato chips*) in flavors like ham and mustard or bacon and ketchup, in case you want to feel like you're having a sandwich with your sandwich. It all started when James Montagu, the fourth Earl of Sandwich, got a reputation for having cold beef between two slices of toast, so that he could eat without interrupting his card playing. (That is, the word *sandwich* got started then. Eating things between bread had been going on for over two thousand years.) But the British are so particular about sandwiches that they use the word *less* than Americans do. In Britain, a **sandwich** is some filling between two *slices of bread*. Not a roll. Not a bagel. Not a baguette. Without sliced bread, it's not a sandwich.

The American *sandwich* prototype is much like the British: savory fillings within two slices of bread. But American sandwiches are allowed to wander further from the prototype, because they interpret the 'bread' requirement more loosely. An American sandwich can be on a roll, on a bagel, on a bun, on a croissant, and at breakfast time, on an English muffin (an American speciality which is only vaguely related to the muffins of England).

Two linguistic effects of the *sandwich* divide are an American preposition and new meanings for bread terms in British. Americans, as I did in the last paragraph, use **on** to indicate the relationship between a sandwich and the type of bread it uses: *tuna on rye, ham and cheese on a bagel, bacon on toast.* The last of these causes me some trouble when I try to order the kind of bacon sandwiches I like. "Can I have my bacon sandwich on toast?" I ask. My lunch companions then tease me for wanting a sandwich served on top of a piece of toast. The phrase *on toast* in British English is reserved for what Americans might call *open-face sandwiches,* except that the toppings are often foreign to us: beans on toast, mushrooms on toast, even spaghetti on toast. I've stopped asking for my bacon sandwich on toast and have developed a guilty appreciation for the prototypical British hangover cure, the **bacon butty**: a bit of bacon in grease-sodden white bread with ketchup or brown sauce, a British concoction that bears some relation to American steak sauce (but not enough resemblance, in my book).

For Britain, the result of the narrow definition of *sandwich* is a richer sandwich vocabulary. Any other bread-product name gains an extra meaning. *Baguette* can mean 'a long loaf of French bread,' or it can mean 'a sandwich-type food consisting of a filling in a cut-open baguette,' as in *a ham baguette*. And the same is true for *roll*, *bagel*, and **bap** (a regional term for a kind of soft bread roll). In American English, *a cheese bagel* is 'a bagel with cheese baked into it,' but in British English it could also mean 'any bagel cut horizontally and filled with cheese.'

The importance of the bread in British bread-and-filling concoctions is further emphasized by the US–UK differences in meaning for **burger** and **hot dog**. In both countries, a cooked patty of ground beef in a bun with some garnishes and condiments is a prototypical *burger*. But how the category stretches away from the prototype differs. In Britain, the hamburger-style bun is central to the prototype. Put a breast of chicken on a bun, and it'll go on the menu as a **chicken burger**. The menu at a burger chain near us has mushroom burgers, goat's cheese burgers, and halloumi burgers—that is to say a burger bun with a large mushroom or a slab of cooked cheese inside.

Meanwhile in America, "burgerness" is defined as a ground food shaped into a patty. The surrounding bread is less relevant. **Turkey burgers** are ground turkey shaped into a patty. The chicken breast in a bun is on the menu as a **grilled chicken sandwich**. A **mushroom burger** in the US is probably a hamburger with mushrooms on top, rather than a mushroom served in a bun, which would be a *grilled portabella sandwich*. Because the word *hamburger* is so focused on the meat in American English, its meaning has stretched to make it a synonym for **ground beef** (= UK *beef mince*). For instance, the American product *Hamburger Helper* is a box of seasonings and pasta to which one adds loose ground beef. There is no bun, and it's not made into a patty, but it is *hamburger.*

So, American *burgers* are chopped things that can be put into buns. British burgers are bun-surrounded things. Those things may have been chopped (but maybe not).

Similarly, a ***hot dog*** in Britain is a sausage in a long roll. The type of sausage is anyone's guess. I've been served British "hot dogs" that were American-style frankfurters, but I've been served more that have been something else: a piece of Cumberland sausage or some gourmet lamb-and-garlic concoction. For Americans, a *hot dog* has to be a frankfurter-type sausage; it's the meat that tells you it's a *hot dog.* But for the bread-conscious British, the type of sausage is less important than the fact that it's in a roll.

Burger and *hot dog* are, of course, imports from America. Their meanings changed in British English because its speakers used the British way of conceptualizing other bread-and-filling foods as a means to interpret these words and extend their meanings. And with that, I think I ought to move away from food words. This chapter has involved too many calories already.

A different class of people

A wise American reporter based in London once told me that every British news story is, deep down, about class. Every American story, he said, is about race.

Simon Hoggart (2008)[8]

In America, the traditional English social-class structure was bleached by the realities of building new colonies, expanding westward, and integrating with other immigrant cultures. Racial divisions in society, on the other hand, have been more obvious throughout American history. Given the different histories of social class and race in the two countries, the words that label groups of people have evolved in different ways.

Immigrant is an early Americanism, noted in Pickering's 1816 dictionary. It later emigrated to Britain. But how we interpret *immigrant* has varied with the immigration stories our countries tell. Mid-20th-century America took pride in being a "nation of immigrants." There, *immigrant* raised images of European people: the British, the Germans, the Irish, and the Italians all coming together in the American melting pot. Even if they were born elsewhere, black people were not counted in immigrant numbers until after the Civil War.[9] American stereotypes of immigrants changed after 1965, when immigration quotas stopped favoring Europeans. Since then, terms like *illegal immigrant* and *undocumented alien* have been on the rise, but there remains a sense that immigrants are, as John F. Kennedy wrote, "the secret of America: a nation of people with the fresh memory of old traditions who dared to explore new frontiers."[10]

The UK, on the other hand, doesn't tell a story of itself as an immigrant nation—though the Angles, the Saxons, the Vikings, and the Normans (not to mention a good number of the royals over the ages) came from someplace else. Though this changed somewhat after the opening of European borders, *immigrant* in 20th-century Britain worked as a code word for 'nonwhite'—quite the opposite of the American connotation. British right-wing politician Enoch Powell, for instance, made racial opposites of the "immigrant-descended population" and white English people in his "Rivers of Blood" anti-immigration speech in 1968.[11]

So although dictionary definitions of *immigrant* are much the same in the US and UK, in practice the word conjures different images in the two countries. Sarah Lawson, writing in 1970, pointed out that white Americans had trouble using the word *immigrant* of black people because the American story of immigration involves assimilation, something (especially southern) whites didn't think black people capable of. The opposite was true of *immigrant* in England: no assimilation was expected, so the word was used of black people because they "fit in" less.[12] This has changed as the nation's 20th-century immigration stories fade from memory. But the word *immigrant* still sounds a different dog whistle in the political rhetoric of each country.

Similarly, "racial"[13] labels in the US and UK reflect different national demographics. In both countries, the basic racial sense of *black* is 'person of sub-Saharan origin.' But both countries have more specific political senses of *black* too, which can be seen in their approaches to Black History Month.

In the US, Black History Month has been marked every February since 1976, growing out of the then-fifty-year-old Negro History Week. The month is for celebrating the contributions of African-Americans to the United States, but more particularly the contributions of slaves and descendants of slaves. We get that more restricted sense of *black* in contexts like an article by Debra J. Dickerson with the tagline "Barack Obama would be the great black hope in the next presidential race—if he were actually black":

> *Black*, in our political and social reality, means those descended from West African slaves. Voluntary immigrants of African descent (even those descended from West Indian slaves) are just that, voluntary immigrants of African descent. . .[14]

In American English *black* can mean 'having sub-Saharan ancestry,' or it can refer specifically to the cultural and historical experience of the majority of black people in the US.

In 1987, Britain imported the idea of Black History Month and put it in October. But in the UK, the month focuses on "the history of Asian, African and African Caribbean peoples."[15] Today, that inclusive 'nonwhite' sense of *black* is sometimes used in British political contexts, but it feels old-fashioned. Newer bureaucratic terms show *black* in contrast with other "nonwhite" ethnicities: *BME* (*Black and Minority Ethnic*) or *BAME* (*Black, Asian, and Minority Ethnic*). The possibility of adopting the American term *people of colo(u)r* has been debated, but is somehow considered a linguistic step too far.

British journalist Joseph Harker's description of the 'nonwhite' meaning of *black* highlights that *black* is not the only "racial" term that has different secondary meanings in the US and UK:

In the late 1980s Asians started calling for a distinct, non-black identity. And then east Asians [...] began raising their voices too.[16]

Where Harker says *Asians*, he means 'from the Indian subcontinent,' and so when he wants to talk about people from China, Korea, or Japan, he has to say *east Asians*. In America, the situation is just the opposite: say *Asian* and people assume 'east Asian.' When people mean 'south Asian,' they'll probably say *Indian* or maybe *South Asian*.

Social-class vocabulary is almost impossible to translate because of the very different stories the two countries tell themselves about class and social mobility. Nowhere is this more evident than in the middle.

Reference to **middle class** is about twice as common in American English as in British, and the phrase **the middle class** occurs about five times more in American English than British.[17] The phrase comes up more in the US because "most Americans see themselves as members of an egalitarian middle class."[18] The requirements for American middle-class membership are attainable and desirable. According to a 2015 survey, American *middle class* entails a secure job and the ability to save money. Less than half of Americans think the middle requires home ownership or a college degree.[19] That means that in the mid-to-late 20th century *middle class* could encompass everyone from the fast-food burger flippers to the franchise owners making the profits from the burger flipping. Until recently Americans rarely used the term *working class* to refer to the class below "middle," because *working* (rather than inheriting or claiming benefits) is one of the defining qualities of the American middle class. American *middle class* thus puts the majority of people on the same level. It's not that Americans are blind to the social, cultural, and financial distinctions between us, but they are expressed in more subtle ways—by what we *do* (for example, **blue collar** or **white collar** work) rather than what we *are*. Ample use of *middle class* allows Americans to express, "We may be different, but no one's better than anyone else." This may be changing since the economic crisis of 2008, but in the 20th century, Americans were mostly one big middle class.

The British, on the other hand, talk about **the middle classes** (plural) about five times more than Americans do. While the singular *middle class* brings people together, the plural divides them: *lower, middle,* and *upper* middle classes and further variations on and divisions within those. A 2013 UK survey identified *the established middle class,* the *new affluent workers* (young professionals who fit middle-class social stereotypes), and the *technical middle class* (as in: *technically,* they have enough financial security to be middle class, but they don't meet the middle-class stereotypes).[20] In practice, the "technical middle class" are the least likely to be referred to as *middle class* in Britain. *Middle class* isn't really about financial security. (Even **upper class** indicates family position more than actual wealth.) Home-owning, university-educated British professionals have told me they're *working class*. In fact, 60% of the British population in 2012 identified as working class—the same as in 1983.[21] Their class identity has little to do with their current situation; they focus on where and how they were raised—which has contributed to their class-based way of speaking (as we'll see more in chapter 8).

British class terms, especially *middle class*, are "a minefield for foreigners, especially on account of all the denying and evading," according to former *New York Times* London correspondent Sarah Lyall.[22] When some of my students surveyed a group of southern English people recently, the subjects were taken aback by the "How would you identify your social class?" question, with one of them exclaiming, "I thought we didn't talk about class anymore!" And yet 89% of the British population feel they are judged on the basis of their class membership.[23] British "Are you middle class?" quizzes abound online. They don't bother asking your income, but do ask, "Where do you do your food shopping?" "Do you own a barbecue?" "Have you ever worried about the pronunciation of *quinoa*?" *Middle class* implies a certain kind of aspirational consumerism: "synonymous with prosperity, not yet wealth, but with carefree liberality in all things costing money."[24]

Aspiration has long been a marker of middle-classness, and the middle have been mocked from above and below for it. The English journalist Decca Aitkenhead recalls middle-class students "faking a proletarian accent for the entirety of their university education" out of sheer embarrassment at their class status.[25] The middle-class quizzes congratulate failure. One quiz (unbelievably) told me: "You're not middle class at all. **Good on you**."[26] So when English folk call others *middle class*, it's often a put-down. When they use it of themselves, it's often with an affected self-derision that provides "a way to distance yourself" from the shame of aspirationalism "while still enjoying its comforts."[27]

To sum up, while Americans see "I'm middle class" as meaning 'I'm average, like other people,' in Britain it feels more like you're asserting that you're above other people, or that you aspire to be above other people.

All manners of differences

Americans are intrigued by good manners, in part because they don't have any. [. . .] They] manage to combine an overall public rudeness with heartfelt concern for others' welfare.

Stephanie Faul, *Xenophobe's Guide to the Americans*

Supplication, gratitude, and, most important of all, apology are central to English social intercourse, which is why English people seem to express them endlessly, as if to the hard of hearing.

Antony Miall, *Xenophobe's Guide to the English*[28]

The British (especially the English) have a reputation for politeness because they say *please* and *sorry* a lot, and because too many Americans have watched too many Hugh Grant films. The truth is: Americans and Britons are both *polite*, once you acknowledge that *polite* doesn't mean quite the same thing in the two places. And once we do that, we also have to acknowledge that *please, thank you*, and *sorry* don't mean the same things either.

Politeness theory (yes, that's something we linguists do) thinks of polite behaviors in terms of how they help us to "save face." *Face* is the self-image that we want to project, how we want to be perceived and treated. It's complicated because we want two contrary kinds of face at the same time. We want to feel valued and feel like we belong: that's **positive face**. We also have a **negative face**: we want to be free to do what we want to do without regard for others and how they see us. If I ask for your opinion on something, it might build your positive face to know that I care what you think. But it also threatens your negative face because now you feel you have to do something for me (tell me your opinion). And once you tell me your opinion, perhaps I won't like it, and then you'll lose positive face. But if you refused to tell me, you'd lose face for being unhelpful. Maintaining face is one big catch-22.

How we handle these contrasting human needs for belonging and independence can vary, giving us different cultures of politeness.[29] Mainstream American culture is very positive-face oriented. Americans generally want to feel like they are appreciated, like they belong, and like everyone is equal in an interaction. (Hence the large middle class.) Those desires affect how we interact. For instance, Americans give compliments and personal information very easily in order to build a sense of familiarity. Some traditional "good manners" fall by the wayside because they don't aid the cause of making people feel close and equal. Friendliness, not just formality, counts as politeness.

Meanwhile in Britain, the politeness style is traditionally more negative-face oriented, carrying on from the days of stricter social hierarchies and reflecting a greater desire for privacy. The rules and phrasings of politeness are more consistently applied. As de Tocqueville wrote in 1840, American manners are "neither so tutored nor so uniform" as the British. But "they are frequently more sincere."[30]

What happens, then, when we talk with each other? Americans congratulate Brits on their formal manners, but sometimes find them a bit stiff or standoffish. Americans in Britain, on the other hand, sometimes find themselves in situations like this one from American writer in Britain Ellen Hawley:

> [We] were in the outdoor section of a café once—a cramped, eat-your-lunch-and-get-out kind of place—and as a couple who'd been sitting nearby wove past our table to leave, one of them said, "In this country, we say *please* and *thank you.*"
>
> Sadly, by the time we'd processed the words, they were too far away for a snappy comeback, but "In our country, we're polite to strangers," did come to mind.[31]

Just to show you this isn't a one-off experience, here's Lisa, an American exchange student in Cambridge:

> One day, after I'd been eating [at a particular place] for a week or so, I ordered my usual as I always did: "May I have a baked potato with cheese and broccoli?" The server responded with, "No, not unless you start saying *please*."
>
> I was gobsmacked. Wasn't the *may I* an implicit *please*? Wasn't it supplication enough? I hadn't demanded a potato for God's sake. I refrained from pointing out that correcting someone else's manners is the worst possible offense, because I have been raised with manners. I did not go back there again.[32]

Americans add *please* to requests about half as much as Britons do[33]—not because they're less polite, but often because they're trying to be polite. Adding *please* to something that's already a request doubly marks it as a request: *Could you move?* is already a request with the softening "could you" formulation (rather than an unsoftened *Move!*). Since it's already softened and clearly a request, the *please* seems redundant. Americans thus often interpret *Could you move, please?* as a marker of urgency ('This request is really a request!'), and that sense of urgency makes the request sound either bossy or desperate, rather than considerate.

As an American commented on my blog: "*Please* winds up feeling impolite with people that you don't have the right to order around, i.e. anyone other than your children."[34] It's in that very hierarchical parent–child relationship that we learn to use *please*: adults model use of *please* to children, and require that children say *please* when making requests of adults. Adults get to boss children around, and children get to plead with adults. That just doesn't seem like the right way to behave in many grown-up American contexts, where egalitarian behavior is expected. Two American studies on the effect of *please* found that adding *please* when taking orders for a charity cookie sale *decreased* the chance that the cookie would be ordered. The *please* seemed inappropriate in the small-request situation, and so Americans balked at it. But with a more desperate request, a plea to not report a student's cheating, using *please* doubled the chances that the request would be granted.[35] In that case, pleading was more socially acceptable and raised more sympathy.

Americans find it odd to use *please* in situations where the request will necessarily be fulfilled, as when ordering at a restaurant. Ordering a pizza is not seen as a request, so much as giving the waiter the information they need to do their job. The American etiquette columnist Miss Manners echoes this when she writes:

> Miss Manners has no wish to discourage you from saying *please* [but] ordering food in a restaurant is a business transaction, not a petition for a favor. It is not customary to say, in a store, for example, "May I please buy this?"[36]

Not customary in America, Miss Manners, but expected in Britain. Britons say that ordering at a restaurant without a *please* sounds like "an army officer to a private" or "a lord giving an order to his butler."[37] British customer service relations are more fraught with the echoes of class differentiation—in many ways, the shop assistant or waiter is expected to resent having to serve others. Therefore requests are delicately phrased so as not to raise that resentment. And so rather than marking a plea or a bossy order, British *please* is a routine part of making minor requests—part of what linguist Richard Watts calls *politic*, rather than polite, behavior.[38] No Brit is going to comment on your politeness if you say *please*—it's just part of the linguistic wallpaper. But boy, will they notice it if you don't say *please*, as Ellen and Lisa discovered.

The routineness of *please* in Britain is reflected in the fact that the British use more set phrases containing *please*. When Rachele

De Felice and I analysed *please* in US and UK corporate emails, we found that *can you please* started 11% of British requests (versus 2% of American ones).[39] The British data included more formulaic examples like *please accept our congratulations*, where, despite the imperative form, no actual request is being made. The phrase *please find attached* occurred ten times more in the British emails. In American business discourse, this is considered bad form. The snail-mail equivalent *please find enclosed* has been dismissed in American style guides as "worn-out formula" (1928) and "borrowed from an earlier generation" (1989). "A more ridiculous use of words, it seems to me, there could not be," wrote Richard Grant White way back in 1880.[40] Instead Americans tend to give the same information as a statement rather than a request. Instead of *please find attached*, American emails say things like *I've attached the document.*

Americans use *please* more than the British in one type of request: the ones that are intended to be rude. In internet forums people write things like "Please don't quote from the scriptures if you don't know what you are talking about" or "Oh please, quit embarrassing yourself with mindless, imbecilic posts like that." The implicit bossiness in American *please* means it fits well in overtly aggressive situations.[41]

We have to remember I'm talking about national tendencies. Individuals and regions may differ in how they express politeness. But the fact that the number of *please*s is so very different in the two cultures tells us that individual differences sit within a larger cultural trend. And it's not just for *please*.

I was shocked by my own newfound Britishness recently when someone held a door for me and instead of saying an American *thanks*, I said a British **sorry**. The British use *sorry* at four times the rate that Americans do.[42] By saying *sorry* to the door-holder I made it sound as if I had some shame at having troubled him (though I hadn't asked him to hold that door). If I had Americanly said *thanks*, I would have stroked (in a manner of speaking) the door-holder's positive face by showing appreciation.

The English have a reputation for apologizing for things that aren't their fault. To some extent, this is just reflexive—the first word that comes to the mouth, no particular polite intention required. But sometimes the English *sorry* seems like an act of passive-aggression. Hang around the English long enough and you'll hear some complain: "I apologized to that woman when she knocked into me, and she didn't say *sorry* back!" The point of saying *sorry* was to get a *sorry*. I experimented with this while volunteering in a British charity shop. When I shelved books, shoppers often bumped into me. If I said nothing, they'd pretend it hadn't happened. If I said *sorry* after they bumped me, they'd apologize. It reminded me of politicians' apologies. Not so much 'I regret what I've done,' but 'I regret that you've caught me doing it'. *Sorry* is anything but the hardest word.

Excuse me creates its own diplomatic crises. Americans can use it to mean either 'Excuse me for what I've just done' or 'Will you excuse me for what I'm about to do?' Brits tend to use it only for the latter meaning, and so when Americans push past them with a late *excuse me*, it is seen as the worst type of forwardness.

Thanking is where American politeness comes into its own. The British have more synonyms for **thanks**, including **cheers** and **ta**, but Americans do more actual thanking—twice as much as the British in one study of speech, and about a third more in our email study.[43] Showing appreciation fits with the American positive-face orientation: 'I value you and what you do.'

If you were only to study customer-service encounters, though, you'd have a different impression. There British *thanks* abound. Godfrey Smith translates customer-service *thank-you* in his book *The English Companion*:

It takes four *thank-you*s for a ticket to be bought on an English bus.

1. First the bus conductor heaves in sight and calls out *thank-you* (I have arrived).
2. The passenger then hands over his 30p with an answering call of *thank-you* (I note that you have arrived and here is my fare).
3. The conductor then hands over the ticket with another *thank-you* (I acknowledge receipt of your fare and here is your ticket in return).
4. Whereupon the passenger replies *thank-you* (thank you).[44]

The example is out-of-date: buses no longer have conductors and tickets are much more expensive. Still, the *thank-yous* are familiar. An equivalent American interaction would most likely have two *thanks* exchanged at the very end. Instead of the other *thank-yous*, Americans might say *hello* or *here you go* or *OK*. The sociolinguist Dell Hymes noted that:

> British *thank you* seems on its way to marking formally the segments of certain interactions, with only residual attachment to 'thanking' in some cases.[45]

The conductor is not really thankful for having spotted the passenger and the passenger is not really grateful to the conductor for taking his money. They're just saying, 'I've done my bit of this interaction—now it's your turn.'

American children are not only taught to thank, they are drilled on the American polite way to respond to thanks: **you're welcome**. Henry Hitchings notes the lack of British attention to such responses in his book *Sorry! The English and Their Manners*: "although *you're welcome* is gaining ground, it is still viewed as an Americanism and even a sham."[46] In many cases, the British response to *thank you* is *thank you*, just as the response to *sorry* is often *sorry*.

A quite nervy slut

A piece of advice for any American guys who are planning a
first date with an English girl. Don't be like one of my American
friends and tell her you think she is *quite pretty*. He was lucky to
get a second date.

Vicki Hollett (2010)[47]

Janus words are the worst. Named after the two-faced Roman
god, these words look in two directions, meaning opposite things:
temper, meaning 'to harden' (metal) and 'to soften' (a criticism);
or *dust,* meaning 'remove dust from' or 'apply dust to.' Those Janus
words give little trouble because we know both meanings and the
context tells us which meaning to go for. But what if you had no
clue that a word had an opposite meaning? What if both opposite
meanings could be used in the same context? That's the problem
of transatlantic Janus words. People in the US might have no idea
that the word means the opposite thing in the UK and vice versa.

To give a starter example, I read with interest an article for which
a British reporter tried to guess which shoppers were British in a
New York department store (back in 2007 when the exchange rate
made UK-to-New York shopping jaunts profitable). The British, he
figured, would be men with sideburns wearing too much Diesel-
brand clothing and "slightly scruffy" women with "the rabid Buy
Now look in their eyes."[48] The first couple the reporter approached
were indeed British. The second were Danish. Then, he writes:

The third attempt gets another strike.

I thought I understood that—until I read that the third couple were
the MacFarlanes from Edinburgh. My American mind understood
strike as in baseball: a failure. The *strike* in the British reporter's
mind was like striking oil. A success. Not too different is *bomb*. If

an American performance is *a bomb*, it has failed spectacularly. If a British performance *goes down a bomb*, it is a wild success.

My transition from American to British academia involved a period of complete bafflement in meetings. In Britain, if something is *moot* it is up for debate. In American, *moot* means 'not worth debating' because the issue has already been deemed irrelevant. Winston Churchill relates a story in which leaders of the British and American armed forces misunderstood each other's use of *table*:

> The British Staff prepared a paper which they wished to raise as a matter of urgency, and informed their American colleagues that they wished to "table it." To the American Staff "tabling" a paper meant putting it away in a drawer and forgetting it. A long and even acrimonious argument ensued before both parties realized that they were agreed on the merits and wanted the same thing.[49]

The British metaphorical meeting table is in front of the committee—*on the table* is where a matter can be seen. In American meetings, the table is a metaphorical storage unit—it's where the matter sits when no one's doing anything to it. To *table* a motion in that case is to suspend the discussion of it, to shelve it. When it's time to discuss the matter again, Americans take it off the table and put it on *the floor*, where the speakers are.

And then there are the transatlantic Janus words that can accidentally insult. The first time someone told me that I'd made my abode very *homely*, I very nearly slapped him. He Britishly meant 'cozy and comfortable' (Americans would say *homey*), but I Americanly heard 'plain and ugly.' A homely face, in the American way of meaning, is one that is best suited to staying at home. If someone calls you *nervy* in American English, they're saying you've got a lot of nerve—you're overconfident. In British English, you'd be a bundle of nerves—timid and apprehensive. And, to add an example that is not exactly about opposite meanings, my American friends once got a shock from my English spouse. While walking to our car after dinner in New York, it was pointed out that their fifteen-year-old had a fair amount of her dinner on her clothes. My husband teasingly shouted, "We don't want that **slutty** teenager in our car!" I don't think he'd finished the sentence before I rushed to inform everyone in earshot: "That means 'slovenly' in British English!" (Though, it must be said, the 'slovenly' meaning is now nearly dead in the UK. Call a woman who doesn't dust a *slut* and you can expect to be clobbered.)

There are many more ways for us to embarrass ourselves with contrary meanings, but I'll end this section with one of the trickiest transatlantic Janus words: the intensifier *quite*, as in *quite happy* or *quite tall* or *quite boring*.[50] *The Economist Style Guide* takes the standard line:

> In America, *quite* is usually an intensifying adverb, similar to *altogether, entirely* or *very*; in Britain, depending on the emphasis, the tone of voice and the adjective that follows, it usually means *fairly, moderately* or *reasonably*, and often damns with faint praise.[51]

The difference is illustrated in a survey posted through my English letterbox by a local politician:

How concerned are you about the proposed NHS [National Health Service] changes and their effects on the Royal Sussex County Hospital?

Very ☐   Quite ☐   Not at all ☐

Reading that, I could see no choice; *very concerned* and *quite concerned* signal much the same thing to me. Another American who read it thought the choices were in the wrong order: that *quite concerned* is more concerned than *very concerned*. The English people I showed the survey to were more comfortable with the *quite* as a middle-ground choice—though they thought it cheeky of the politician to offer these choices; since the interpretation of *quite* is context-dependent, the choices are difficult to interpret. I cynically suspect that the politician (a member of a party that's been working hard to dismantle the National Health Service) chose *quite* rather than *somewhat* in order to be able to use the results in any way that suited him. But still, it is a more reasonable survey in British English than in American.

The other problem with *quite* (and quite a lot of British vocabulary, actually) is the everlasting possibility that it is being used ironically. British people often express frustration with Americans "not getting irony." That's a bit unfair. Americans get irony—they just don't always get *British* irony because it's used in places where irony isn't the expected response. As British comedian Simon Pegg put it, irony is

> like the kettle to us: it's always on, whistling slyly in the corner of our daily interactions. To Americans, however, it's more like a nice teapot, something to be used when the occasion demands it.

The British need for irony emanates from a social demand for modesty and what anthropologist Kate Fox calls "the importance of not being earnest" in English culture.[52] It often takes the form of self-deprecation. Sarah Millican explains her entry into stand-up comedy: "People were laughing at me anyway, so I thought I might as well start charging them." Richard Ayoade describes his acting career with "I certainly couldn't be an actor. That would be terrible. For everyone."[53] Americans are fine with earnestness and have a reasonable expectation that if they say something good about themselves, others will celebrate it with them rather than thinking them unforgivably self-centered. Since Americans are

217

not looking for irony in those situations, they don't always see it coming when Brits use it.

The good news is: if you interpret someone else's *quite good* to have a stronger or weaker meaning than the speaker intended, they'll probably never notice. Quite useful. The bad news is: people might be misunderstanding you. Quite frustrating.

They have a word for it

Lisa: Dad, do you know what Schadenfreude is?

Homer: No, I do not know what Schadenfreude is. Please tell me, because I'm dying to know!

Lisa: It's a German term for 'shameful joy,' taking pleasure in the suffering of others.

Homer: Oh, come on Lisa. I'm just glad to see him fall flat on his butt!

"When Flanders Failed,"
The Simpsons (1991)

English speakers have been discovering and rediscovering the apt utility of the German word *Schadenfreude* since the mid-1800s. After Lisa Simpson pointed it out again in the 1990s, English speakers got a bit obsessed with the idea that other languages have words for things we haven't managed to label. A fad for books and websites about "untranslatable" words followed, and English got a new idiom related to complex emotions:[54]

- "Ricky Gervais returns to host the Golden Globes. We're **a weird combination of excited and scared for it**. We're not sure what that is, but **the Germans probably have a word for it**." (*Conan* talk show schedule, 2016)
- "I love the look on Jasper's face when Brownie scampers up his neck and into his hair. It's **a wonderful mix of joy, tenderness,**

218

and disgust. The Germans probably have a word for it."
(A. J. Jacobs, *Drop Dead Healthy,* 2012)

- "I feel **a special sort of weariness** looking at his site; one so heavy and distinct that **the Germans probably have a word for it.**" (Hugo Rifkind in *The Spectator,* 2011)

Linguists usually have little patience with the fascination with "untranslatable" words. If the words were really untranslatable, you'd have to know the language before you could understand the word—and yet every article about "untranslatables" explains the meaning of the foreign words in a language its readers understand. But while I have to professionally frown (in one sense or the other) at "untranslatable" claims, I completely understand the fascination with them because I seem to have wound up with a vocabulary that can hit the mark in one country while being very difficult to explain in the other. I marvel at the British expressions that I somehow lived decades without but now find indispensable, like *naff*. It takes the *Oxford English Dictionary* six adjectives to describe *naff* ("unfashionable, vulgar; lacking in style, inept; worthless, faulty"), but it can't quite communicate the unattractive uncoolness of *naff*ness. I love saying *plonk* for 'cheap but serviceable wine' and *bumf* for 'a quantity of unneeded papers,' as in *my recycling bin is full of election bumf.* I also mourn the American expressions that take too much explanation to use in Britain. Being *nickel-and-dimed* ('strained by many small expenses'), being in a *snit* ('small fit of temper'), or going to the house *kitty-corner* ('at a diagonal') to ours (*catercorner* or *catty-corner* in other regions of the US).

Wanting to celebrate these words that don't work in half my conversations, I declared October 2011 "Untranslatable October." Each day I tweeted one American or British expression that has no equivalent in the other nationlect. By the end of the month, I was relieved to be relieved of the duty to come up with more untranslatables. But by the following October, I had collected enough for another month. "Just one more Untranslatable October, then," I thought. By the third year, I thought I was really pushing it. Would I get through another month? I did. And the next October and the next and the next. As I write this, I'm gearing up for the seventh Untranslatable October. There are just *that many* meanings that one country or another has not bothered to put into a word.

British *moreish* is an adjective that communicates 'you can't help having more of it': *These truffles are really moreish*. American *to make nice with (someone)* means 'to be friendly or cooperative just because you've been told to do so': *I have to make nice with Jones while the boss is on-site*. American doesn't have a word for *moreish*. British doesn't have an expression for *make nice with*. It's cheating to call them *untranslatable*, since I have translated them. Yet they are special, and it's that specialness that "untranslatable" lists try to capture. *Untranslatable* serves as a snappier way to say 'one language or dialect has a word or idiom for something, and some other language or dialect doesn't have a ready-made way of expressing the same idea.' With my linguist hat on, I call that ready-madeness **lexicalization** (putting a word or idiom to a concept). What's thrilling about lexicalization is that every language does it differently. Our world is complex. Our experience of it is multifaceted. That's a big old mess that needs some organization, and we get it by picking out parts of our experience and naming them. Take an emotion, a relationship, an object, anything, and give it a name, and you make it more available for talking about, more available for thinking about.

Of course, American and British English share most of that lexicalization (except when we don't, as we've discovered for *frowns* and *twangs* and *sandwiches*). The things that one English has a word for and the other doesn't are generally not everyday concepts. Sometimes, you learn these words and think: "Well, yes, I can see why that culture needed that word." British *jobsworth* for 'a person who takes satisfaction from sticking to their job description to an unhelpful and nonsensical degree' seems fitting for a country where customer service often has a tinge of resentment about it. American English has many specific terms related to eating in restaurants, such as *to bus* for clearing and cleaning tables between seatings, *family style* for serving food in dishes from which everyone takes their own portion, and a whole range of terms for telling a waiter whether and for how long you want your fried egg flipped over in the pan: *sunny-side up, over easy, over medium, over hard.* (Flipping is not an issue in the traditional English breakfast; cooking fat is spooned over the egg to cook the top—or not.) The specificity of the egg vocabulary conjures up the stereotype of the American customer who follows each restaurant order with a long list of particulars: "Could I have the fish broiled, not fried? And could I substitute broccoli for the potatoes? And the salad dressing on the side?"

Sometimes the untranslatables don't translate because they rely on things or institutions in one country but not the other. (Recall the sports metaphors in chapter 2.) British has *marmite*, meaning 'something that people have firmly positive or negative opinions about': *Big Brother is television marmite.* It doesn't work in the US because the pungent yeast spread *marmite* is not something everyone knows about, and thus not something that everyone can be expected to have an opinion on. The American *101* means 'the basics of a subject': *It's journalism 101 to look at a candidate's voting record.* This comes from how US college courses are numbered. In Britain the number is more associated with *Room 101*, where prisoners are tortured with their greatest fears in George Orwell's *1984* (and which is kept in the popular imagination by a BBC television program in which celebrities describe their personal Room 101– the things that get them into a tizz).

Some of the "untranslatables" almost have translations, but they still *feel* a bit different. Maybe British *dodgy* is a lot like a particular use of *sketchy* in American, but for me they just miss each other.

Is it the woody sound of the British word versus the reediness of the American one? Or could it be the connotations contributed by their related nouns: *a dodge* being a cheat, *a sketch* being quick and incomplete? Whatever it is, for me *a dodgy neighborhood* has a slightly different shade of unsafety than *a sketchy neighborhood*.

If Americans wanted a word for *jobsworth*, they could make one up. But why bother? English has a good track record of stealing the words it needs—we might as well pilfer each other's words. We already do, of course. One of the pleasures of writing the *Separated by a Common Language* blog has been to declare transatlantic Words of the Year. I ask: Which American word has particularly made its way in Britain, and which British word has been important to America in the past year? More often than not, the words that make the trip into another nationlect are not replacing existing words, but are filling semantic spaces that haven't yet been filled.

In the past decade, UK-to-US Words of the Year have included **gutted** ('emotionally devastated'), **to vet** (a candidate, etc.; originally horse-racing jargon), and **gap year** ('a year off between school and university'). For those who have these words, it's hard to imagine how we lived without them. US-to-UK examples include **staycation** ('holidaying at or close to home'), **(policy) wonk** ('someone who's passionate about the detail of political process and policy'), and **bake-off**. *Bake-off* almost seems like a native British word now, thanks to the hugely successful *Great British Bake Off* on television. In the US it's been renamed *The Great British Baking Show*—not because *bake-off* is too British, but because the Pillsbury Company, which invented the term for its promotions, has a trademark on it in the US.

I'd like to nominate a few more for Anglo-American sharing. My husband was suffering from muscle spasms in his calves on a visit to the US. Americans offered immediate sympathy: "Oh a **charley horse**—those are the worst!" British people: You really need a word for that pain, so you'll get that kind of sympathy.

And lazy Americans, you need a noun for not getting out of bed in the morning (but not necessarily sleeping in): the very British *lie-in*. If only I'd had that expression when I was missing so many physics lectures in college. I'd still have missed the 9:15 lectures. But I would have had a noun for it, and that's the important thing.

Doomed to difference

The English never say entirely what they mean. Do I mean that? Not entirely.

Alan Bennett, *The Old Country* (1977)

People who are worried about the homogenization of English often point to the spread of American words as evidence. But when words are borrowed, they come into ready-made linguistic and cultural systems that have to make room for the new words and ideas. In the process, the new words can get squeezed into a new shape in their new locale. We saw this for *burger* and *hot dog*. British English imported the words and then did British things with them. They are not isolated examples.

Borrowed words undergo meaning change for two reasons. The first is that they just haven't been fully understood. I loved this commenter on the UK *Telegraph* newspaper website who tried to school his compatriots on the correct use of the Americanism *rain check*:

Take a rain check—which is used now by Brits to mean check on something, instead of the true meaning of obtaining a refund (cheque) for bad weather.[55]

It's true that some British people erroneously used *rain check* to mean 'check for rain.' It is also true that quite a few used it to mean 'a refund for bad weather.' But they were wrong too. In the US *rain check* means: 'a ticket given to those attending a rained-out event, allowing them entrance to the rescheduled event'. You can see how British folk, when faced with a new-to-them expression, tried to reconstruct its meaning by looking at the parts of the expression, *rain* and *check*. But in doing so, they changed the meaning of the word.

Americans, of course, do the same things with British expressions. The British phrase *chat up* has been on the rise in the US since the 1990s, and it has been used in all sorts of ways:

> Tyra Banks proves she's mastered the "smize" [smiling with the eyes] (and her balancing skills) after **chatting up** her roundtable show FABLife. (*People*, August 24, 2015)

> I had always wanted children. [...] I frequently passed the time in airports by **chatting up** frazzled mothers and babbling toddlers (Jean Twenge in *The Atlantic*, July/August 2013)

> [Journalist Ted] Koppel has **chatted up**—often grilled—a who's who of U.S. policymakers, presidents and world leaders over the years (*USA Today*, November 14, 2005)

People magazine seems to use *chat up* as a synonym of *talk up* or *promote*, while in the other cases it means 'talk to' or possibly 'interview'. None of these have much to do with the British meaning 'hit on; flirt with'. To British ears, these American uses sound a bit racy—or just plain wrong.

Borrowed words also have to compete with existing words in the language. As linguist Alan Cruse once wrote, "languages abhor absolute synonyms just as nature abhors a vacuum."[56] So when a language ends up with exact synonyms, either one of the synonyms dies out or they move apart in meaning or usage. And so it is for the British adoption of *cookie*. Many sources will tell you that the British word for American *cookie* is **biscuit**. Do not trust these sources, as they demonstrate an impoverished knowledge of the words.

American *cookie* comes to us from Dutch, and it can indeed refer to what British people would call *biscuits*. But key to the British *biscuit* is that it is hard (after all, it comes to English from the French for 'twice-baked'). This fact was underscored by a court case to decide whether there should be a tax on **Jaffa cakes** (a small sponge cake disc topped with orange jelly and dark chocolate). Cakes, being a necessity of life, are not taxed in Britain, while chocolate-covered biscuits, being a luxury, are. (I can't explain it, but I won't complain about tax-free cake.) Despite their name, Jaffa cakes are the size of a traditional British biscuit, they're eaten with the hands in biscuit-eating situations, and they're usually found among the biscuits in shops. That was enough for the authorities to deem them taxable. The manufacturer argued they were cakes, on the basis that biscuits start out hard and soften when they get stale, whereas cakes start out soft and harden as they get old. Jaffa cakes are soft; therefore they can't be biscuits. The court agreed. (Pringles, the extruded potato snack, were briefly untaxed for the same reason. The manufacturer argued that since they're made from a dough that is only 42% potato, they're more of a cake than a taxable potato crisp. That was a cakewalk too far for the Court of Appeal.)

The British have imported the word *cookie*, but they've not imported the American meaning of the word (just as happened for *burger* and *hot dog*). When I bring **snickerdoodles** (a soft, raised cookie rolled in cinnamon and sugar) to British gatherings, I am invariably complimented on my "cakes." Though they are American *cookies*, they are not British *cookies*. A **hobnob** (a crunchy, sweet oat-based disc) is not a *cookie* in Britain, though it would be in America, if such things could be found in America. The British meaning of *cookie* is restricted by the existence of the word *biscuit*.

Newfangled things from America are called *cookies* (but only if they are uncakey enough).

And so it goes. Some British folk will insist that a **bathrobe** must be terrycloth because otherwise it conflicts with the British term **dressing gown**. Some Americans (I've been one of them) differentiate a *vase* in the American pronunciation (rhymes with *case*) from a *vase* with the British pronunciation (rhymes with *bras*)—the first is for putting flowers in; the second, perhaps a Ming vase, belongs in a museum. Where we have words, we have meaning. And we're never short of new meanings when new words or pronunciations come our way.

8

THE STANDARD BEARERS

To let thee at once into a secret, unknown to these [American] people themselves, their government is a pure unadulterated LOGOCRACY or government of words.

Washington Irving,
Salmagundi (1807)[1]

It's not just that English words mean different things in Britain and America. English itself means different things *to* Britain and America. We have different "cultures of language"—the assumptions and values we hold about which aspects of language are important, who the linguistic authorities are, what's "normal" English. You could call these our *everyday language ideologies*: the assumptions about language that are so deep-seated we don't even know that we assume them.

For instance, in England I teach "English Language." In other countries, that would mean that I teach people to speak English. But in England,[2] English Language is a school subject taught to mostly native English speakers. At school level, it involves text analysis, creative writing, and some practical linguistics. Carried on to university level, it can become an in-depth course in English linguistics. So, I teach English Language. But I don't teach English, because at our university *English* means 'English literature' and just English literature. The *English* students take none of the English Language classes. American degrees in English also concentrate on literature, but not so exclusively. They require courses in argumentative writing and may require students to take courses on the history of the language or English linguistics. Journalism is an option in the English degree of some American universities, while in the UK it's relegated to Media Studies. The academic idea of *English* is, to use an Anglican expression, a broader church in American universities than in English ones. Though the differences in British and American language cultures are subtle, the ENGLISH = LITERATURE equation is a thread running through the ideology of English in England.

I felt this particularly when I first moved to England in 2000. It struck me that when the BBC needed commentary on some aspect of language change, they tended to turn to poets and other creative writers rather than linguists or lexicographers. At that time, the teacher qualification courses for those who wanted to be secondary school English teachers only accepted graduates of literature programs, not those with English Language degrees. Those literature-adept teachers would be expected to teach their charges about adverbs and relative clauses, but it was assumed they had learned about those things by osmosis—from reading and talking about literature. While linguists and English Language graduates have improved their profiles in the media and in schools since then, there are plenty of other places to see *literature* eclipsing *language* in Britain. In America *language* is associated with more practical communication.

How we talk about English, who does the talking about English, our worries about the language and how we cope with those worries—all, like the language itself, overlap and differ in the UK and US. The ownership of English is divvied up in different ways in the two countries, which may reflect deeper cultural beliefs about the individual's place in the world and the potential for education to shape it.

Whose standard?

> When I read some of the rules for speaking and writing the English language correctly ... I think—any fool can make a rule and every fool will mind it.
>
> Henry David Thoreau (1860)[3]

The notion that we're all "created equal" is one of the most frequent tropes of American political speech. America imprints its children with the message that if you're good and you try hard, you can do anything. Anyone can grow up to be president. ("And anyone who doesn't grow up," quipped Johnny Carson, "can be vice president.") Underlying the "anyone can succeed" belief are British values that came over with the early settlers: the value of hard work, the importance of fairness, and the primacy of the individual. Yet the British in general are less sold on the optimistic message of possibility—and understandably so. Living in a monarchy makes it quite obvious that anyone cannot grow up to be anything. Unless a zombie infestation wipes out at least 98% of the UK population (not to mention all the distant royal relations from other European dynasties), my British child has no chance of being the British head of state. In Britain, "anyone can grow up to be ..." is *only* found as a setup to jokes: "It's said that in Britain anyone can grow up to be Prime Minister and, looking at Tony Blair, you can't argue," went one newspaper opinion piece.[4]

Britain has more a sense, as we saw in chapter 7, that social class is almost genetic—that if your parents were working class, then you are (and ever will be) working class too. That's a fairly realistic estimation. Among twelve industrialized countries, Britain comes last in one of the best measures of social mobility: whether your economic status is better than your parents'.[5] The US doesn't fare much better—it's two notches above the UK, with Italy between them. But the *stories* we tell ourselves about social class and opportunity differ, and that comes through in how we talk about the English language and whose English is "good." In Britain, the notion of "good English" is inextricably linked to social class. In the US, less so.

For England, "correct" English is **the Queen's English** (or **the King's**, depending on who's on the throne). You can't get any higher up the social ladder than that. "Proper" English is also called **Received English**, in the sense that it's accepted by some sector of society, and **public-school English**, after the most exclusive and expensive schools in the country. The word *grammar* itself can signal exclusivity. Recent, impassioned debates in the UK have given rise to headlines like these—which can be quite alarming to a news-reading, grammar-loving linguist like me:

Leave grammars in the past (*Guardian*)
Give poor white children their own grammars (*Times*)
Grammars 'out of bounds for too many families' (*Daily Mail*)

My first reaction to these headlines was "Grammar is wonderful! What have you got against it? Why control access to it?" I got my breath back when I realized that *grammar* here is short for **grammar school** (a type of free, state secondary school that has admissions by exam) and that these headlines were about controversial government proposals to open more grammar schools. British grammar schools are so-called because they traditionally taught Latin and Greek. (The very small number of similar schools in the US are called **Latin schools** or **classical schools**.) The subject matter and the entrance exam make grammar schools exclusive (though not as exclusive as the **independent** or **public** schools, which cost money). In the US, **grammar school** is anything but exclusive: it's a synonym for **elementary school** or **primary school**. Today much less grammar is taught in either of those kinds of grammar school—or indeed any school. But it is nevertheless symbolic that in Britain, *grammar (school)* is only for some, but in America *grammar (school)* is for everybody.

The US doesn't have *Presidential English* or *Prep School English*. It's just *Standard*. **Standard American English** meets a standard of acceptability, but not a "royal standard." It sounds educated, but not necessarily elite. It's "normal" English, cookie-cutter English. It's the English that teachers and journalists and politicians are meant to write or speak, conforming to certain grammatical, spelling, and vocabulary norms.

In Britain *standard English* is a less neutral term. It's often used in a way that ignores the possibility of standards outside England, as in the BBC's advice against Americanisms: "In the UK, people throw *stones* not *rocks*, because in **standard English** [that is, unlike American English] a *rock* is too large to pick up."[6] Beyond the "standard is our English, not their English" criterion, talk of *standard English* in Britain creates "considerable confusion between an élite accent and a standard language."[7] A UK educational report in 1925 unironically defined *standard English* as "the kind of English spoken by a simple, unaffected young Englishman like the Prince of Wales."[8] This British association of *standard* with the socioeconomic heights remains. My middle-class, southern English colleagues protest when I refer to their language as *standard English*, though it is an English no one would consider nonstandard. Somehow calling how they talk *standard* feels uncomfortable to them. Yet it's not uncommon for English people to say, "I speak RP," as if Received Pronunciation is the name of a language, rather than a way of pronouncing English. The difference between having a standard language and having a certain accent is more important to mark in Scotland, where Scottish Standard English refers to the kind of English one would use in school or professional situations—but with a Scottish accent.

Americans don't talk about accents being "received," but instead have *Network English* or *Broadcast English*: the range of accents used on the national television news. It's not the accent of a New England yacht club or a southern debutante ball; Network English is somewhere in the middle. Middle class, Midwest, middle America. The reference to broadcast networks in talking about accent is telling: it was only in the age of radio and television that a distinctly American standard accent arose. Watch early Hollywood movies, and you'll hear accents that aspire to the Old World. (*Aspire* is the key word here. One dialectologist noted in 1931 that, despite their zeal, American actors and radio presenters "seldom succeed in imitating British pronunciation, beyond two or three vowel sounds."[9]) After World War II, Americans preferred the accents that had developed through westward dialect leveling, in the middle of the country rather than at the edges. As the US became a world power, its citizens no longer needed to look to England for linguistic approval. While RP still holds a certain cachet in America, it sounds like morning coats and top hats. Network English sounds like a mid-price business suit. Above all, Network English is perceived as neutral.

Accents were never so neutral in British broadcasting. Sir John Reith, the first director-general of the BBC, thought it the broad-caster's responsibility to improve listeners' English:

> Even the commonest and simplest words are subjected to horrible and grotesque abuse. One hears the most appalling travesties of vowel pronunciation. This is a matter in which broadcasting may be of immense assistance.[10]

To aid with this public service, Reith set up the Advisory Committee on Spoken English in 1926. Committee members had different opinions about what good English might be, and some were keen to rein in the excesses of RP. (One member, George Bernard Shaw, proposed that the committee should have "an age limit of 30 and a few taxi drivers on it."[11]) But Reith's goal

232

was to disseminate a standard of pronunciation for the nation. The result is **BBC English**, which is often treated as a synonym of **Received Pronunciation**. RP is generally thought to be an accent that all English speakers can understand, so to some extent BBC English might be thought of as meeting in the middle. But it is not the geographic middle or the socioeconomic middle. The signals BBC English sent were southern and upper class—going down a notch or two after the Second World War, to what we might think of as upper middle class. Social change in the 1960s brought more regional voices to the airwaves, but fifty years later the BBC is still called upon to address the London bias in broadcast voices. Correcting that bias seems to create as much unease as it alleviates. Not too long ago, BBC journalist Steph McGovern received this note in the post:

> Dear Ms McGovern, I watched you on BBC Breakfast. I'm sorry about your terrible affliction. Here's £20 towards correction therapy.[12]

The "affliction" was McGovern's northern accent: Middlesbrough, precisely. She cites this letter as one of the more polite expressions of opinion about her presence on television.[13] Other non-RP speakers in the British public eye tell similar stories.

As the linguistic model in Britain shifted toward the (southern) middle class, some started to see speaking RP or "talking posh" as a liability. The actor Benedict Cumberbatch and *Downton Abbey* creator Julian Fellowes, for instance, have complained in the press about the discrimination they suffer due to their accents (while hardly seeming to suffer; Fellowes was made a lord in the very year when he complained about "poshism"). For many, the RP accent carries with it the worst stereotypes of the British upper classes: that they are snobbish, overprivileged, out of touch. Who would want to aspire to that? So, in its place came a more classless (but still not universally admired) range of London-centric accents, now commonly called Estuary English, after the estuary of the River Thames.[14] English teacher David Rosewarne coined the term in 1984:

> It is a mixture of non-regional and local south-eastern English pronunciation and intonation. If one imagines a continuum with RP and [more working-class] London speech at either end, "Estuary English" speakers are to be found grouped in the middle ground.[15]

The term has never been popular with linguists. It conflates many accents under one name, and it provides a focal point for what phonetician John Maidment calls Disgusted-of-Tunbridge-Wells Syndrome:

> Disgusted of Tunbridge Wells is a mythical figure, very probably ex-military or married to such, retired, living in Tunbridge Wells in Kent, a town, so I'm told, amply supplied with inhabitants of this sort. DTW's main hobby in retirement is writing outraged letters to the local and national newspapers [...] The furore in the press and on the radio about [Estuary English] has really given DTW something to rage about.[16]

Estuary speakers are sometimes derided as "Mockneys" (fake Cockneys), since some of their pronunciations are reminiscent of East London. Traditionalists are up in arms about Estuary's glottalized *t*'s and vowel-like *l*'s (which you can listen for when Adele sings *Skyfall*). What's interesting is *who* gets grief for these pronunciations. The critic Malcolm Bradbury, writing in 1994, supposed that Estuary English was "learnt in the backs of taxis or from alternative comedians."[17] It's not the poor who are riding in the backs of taxis. Bradbury seems to neither wonder nor care how working-class Londoners pronounce their *t*'s, but the well-to-do are expected to distinguish themselves from their drivers, and so Bradbury urges his readers to "eschew the Estuary."

In both countries, prejudice against "nonstandard" speakers is one of the last acceptable forms of discrimination. Speak a non-standard English and you may not be "well spoken" enough to get that job as a sales rep or a teacher. In the UK, language standards and social class are so tied up that some people have argued that a person with a decidedly northern accent cannot be considered "middle class." By that view, the accent is more important than education level, wealth, or social status in determining which class a person belongs to. Lancashire native Rebecca Hardy contrasted her very Britishly middle-class belongings with her decidedly northern accent:

> There must be millions of us—the strangely classless—all walking around with our daft dialects and John Lewis bags, our National Trust cards and gardening clogs, wondering where exactly our place is in British society now that our voices have been deemed not middle-class enough. Which, really, of course, means: not standardised south-east.[18]

It's not just that southerners don't consider northerners "classy" enough to be middle class. Many northerners—including a few faculty members I know—have a very hard time thinking of themselves as middle class. Being northern working class is a badge of pride—or *covert prestige*, as sociolinguists call it.

In the US, region and class often take a backseat to race. Standard American English isn't necessarily "upper class," but it sure sounds "white" to many people. Thus, in the US, the term *Standard English* is often contrasted with *Black English* or *African-American English*. Keith Powell, who played "Toofer" on the sitcom *30 Rock* (so called because "with him you get a two-for-one; he's a black guy and a Harvard guy"), has written about the whiteness of speaking "standard" in America:

> All of my black friends have been told at some point or another during their lifetime that they "talk white." I've been told it so many times, I've lost count. In some perverse way, though, I believe it's said as a way to come to an understanding: the person who says it doesn't know many different types of black people. Black people are generally seen as uneducated thugs. I do not appear to be an uneducated thug. Therefore, I must talk white.[19]

The racial nature of Standard American English can be heard in the favored pronunciations of America. Many linguists think that both the vowel changes of the northern cities and the spread of rhotic (/r/-ful) pronunciations in New York and the South over the 20th century were triggered by white Americans' increased perception of some sounds as "more black" and therefore to be avoided.[20]

All of this is to say that the notion of "standard" English is complicated—and it is complicated in different ways in the UK and the US. What we can say for sure is that neither country has an "official" English. There is no governmental linguistic oversight. We don't manage our language by committee. Even committees with more modest aims, like the Advisory Committee on Spoken English and the Simplified Spelling Board, have lasted two or three decades at most.

Our allergy to academy-style language regulation doesn't mean English speakers want linguistic anarchy—far from it. Instead, the individual is expected to regulate their own language. Perfect it, even. There is no shortage of role models and teachers and books to help us along the way. Both countries' publishers churn out dictionaries and grammars and style guides. If you look at enough of these (as I have), you'll start to notice the different tones taken by many such language resources, and how these align along national lines.

In the beginning was the word (and the dictionary)

It is hazardous to embark on topics as enmeshed in folklore as the influence of the dictionary or Anglo-American differences; to embark on both simultaneously is little short of foolhardy.

Randolph Quirk (1973)[21]

A week into my first expatriation from the US, I was invited to dinner at a colleague's home, where I met his wife, Jill, and their twentysomething son. Upon meeting me, the son excitedly asked: "You're from the US? Are there any serial killers from your town?" Unfortunately, my answer had to satisfy his stereotype. But it was Jill's stereotype of Americans that really threw me: "I'm always impressed by how articulate Americans are." In her experience, if you asked an American a question on any subject, they could come up with an answer on the spot and argue their point effectively. With hindsight, I have to wonder if she had been moved to say this because I'd spent the evening talking out of my hat. But at the time, I took it as a compliment—and, through the filter of my youthful American verbal insecurity, a strange thing to say.

It's not uncommon to hear Americans being stereotyped as inarticulate—what with the *likes* and the *y'know*s and the *and stuff*s peppering some American speech. And many Americans believe that the English will always trump them linguistically. But those who listen carefully often praise American orality. "I'm always amazed at how erudite the vox pop interviews on [US] TV news are," wrote the critic A. A. Gill. "When Americans talk, they talk with ease and confidence. They seem more comfortable in their own mouths than the English do."[22] That American lack of self-consciousness is helped by the American acceptance of a variety of speech types as reasonable and persuasive: the down-home expression can be as valuable as the grand oratory. The two types seem to take turns getting elected president.

The American ease of speech is seated in the democratic urge—
the freedom of speech that is also seen as a responsibility to speak.
It's supported by the low-church experience of congregants tes-
tifying, where anyone and everyone is expected to bear witness
for all to hear. Freedom of speech doesn't feel quite the same in
the UK, where everyone from Middlesbrough-born journalists to
Benedict Cumberbatch is ridiculed for their accents. When those
who dare to speak are mocked for their audacity, it's no wonder
that few are comfortable doing it. In Gill's view, Britain ends up
with a "mumbled reticence."

Gill supposed that American comfort in speech is the product
of a culture that doesn't read much, that instead tells its stories
aloud. He sees that orality as dividing British and American
literature.

The great distinguishing feature of American writing is that it
almost always sounds like a voice in your ear. Words on the
page are spoken. Most European writing—all English English
writing—is about writing. It's silent, cerebral. It has never been
said out loud. It's never meant to be heard. But read Twain or
Steinbeck, Mailer, Hemingway, Updike or Wolfe, and you can
hear it. It's constantly repeated that we are countries separated by
a common language, but that doesn't sound right. What is more
likely is that the Old World's English is a written language, and
the New World's a spoken one.[23]

By doing that British thing of conflating *literacy* and *literature*, Gill
misses the New World's deep and deeply *practical* relationship with
the written word. By romanticizing an oral tradition, Gill misses
America's informed replacement of the English *literary* tradition
with the American *literate* tradition. Benjamin Rush, founding
father and a leading intellectual figure in the revolution, noted this
in his 1788 proposal for a federal university:

The present is the age of simplicity in writing in America. The turgid style of Johnson, the purple glare of Gibbon, and even the studied and thick set metaphors of Junius, are all equally unnatural, and should not be admitted into our country.[24]

The United States was founded on the written word. The first shot in the American Revolution was fired in 1775 and the last in 1783, but neither bullet marks the anniversary of the country's independence. The withdrawal of British troops didn't make the US independent. Independence was to be found in the thirty-two paragraphs and fifty-six signatures of the Declaration of Independence, ratified on the Fourth of July 1776. A document gave the country its birthday.

The United States was born literate, while Britain is old enough to have had literacy thrust upon it. The nonconformist denominations that settled and thrived in the US—Congregationalists, Quakers, Methodists, and Presbyterians—aimed for a direct relationship with God, not mediated by priests and ritual, but through prayer and scripture. In order to be saved, you had to take literacy seriously. A 1642 Massachusetts law saw illiteracy as child abuse. Parents could lose custody of their children if they were not taught to read.[25] By the end of that century, most of the northern colonies had similar laws. By 1800 the United States had the highest literacy rate in the world.[26] "Nearly every child, even those of beggars and blacks in considerable numbers, can read, write, and keep accounts," reported the president of Yale College in 1823.[27] This was less true in the South, where several colonies, starting in the mid-1700s, had made it a crime to teach slaves to write.[28] But until the decades just before the Civil War, it was no crime to teach enslaved people to *read*. Writing could be a tool for rebellion, but reading was a spiritual necessity.

For as long as there has been a United States, Britain has lagged just a bit behind it on many measures of literacy. Throughout its history, the US comes ahead in mass literacy, in the introduction and uptake of free and compulsory childhood education, and in the extension of higher education beyond the elite. American reverence for the written word comes in many forms—for instance, the US has almost twice as many public librarians per capita as the UK.[29] The US may be the country responsible for monster-truck rallies and fast-food hamburgers, but it also invented Scrabble and the spelling bee. America's First Lexicographer, Noah Webster, is considered a founding father.[30] His "Blue-Back Speller" and his *American Dictionary* have been described as a "secular catechism to the nation-state."[31] For a nation whose literacy was motivated by personal relationships with the Bible, the written word is sacred, but accessible. Revered, but approached practically. Literacy ensures salvation, communication, and regulation.

This practical reverence for the written word is not copied from Britain—as our legal systems reveal. The US Constitution, the highest law of the land, was set out in 4,543 words in 1787. Amendments over the years have brought the word count up to 7,591. That's shorter than this chapter and shorter than any other nation's written constitution, yet it defines government and human rights and responsibilities in the American context. The wording of the Constitution is sacrosanct—the amendments are tacked onto the end of the document rather than edited into the existing text. And changing the Constitution is not easy: the most recent amendment (restricting Congress's ability to give themselves pay raises) took 202 years to ratify. Americans of my generation grew up able to sing a slightly edited version of the Constitution's preamble (*We the people . . . in order to form a more perfect union . . .*), and we cite the amendments by number in arguments. We know our rights because they're written down for all to see. That's what democracy's about, right? Who wouldn't want that?

Well, the British, for the most part. The United Kingdom is a constitutional monarchy, but you can't point to anything and call it "the British constitution." Instead an aggregation of statutes, treaties, and unwritten tradition is treated as an "uncodified" constitution. The effect is that "no Act of Parliament can be unconstitutional, for the law of the land knows not the word or the idea."[32] A UK parliamentary committee recently considered whether modern times demanded a written constitution. Their report sums up the case against in three adjectives: "unnecessary, undesirable, and un-British."[33] The intangible patchwork of Britain's uncodified constitution testifies to a long history, dating back to the Magna Carta in 1215. The resulting legal flexibility means that Britain need not be stuck with the poor wording or peculiar ideas of hundreds of years ago. When I express my deep, American discomfort with the changeability of the British constitution, my English friends cite American gun deaths as a cautionary tale against making laws as incontrovertible as the US "right to bear arms." They make an excellent point, but I still find some comfort in the fact that my rights as an American are eminently knowable and unlikely to change (unlike my rights as a British citizen, which, as I write this, are changing rather radically due to the 2016 referendum to leave the European Union).

As our laws go, so goes our language. The American relationship to the written word of dictionaries is more literal, more biblical than the British. You can see this in the intersection of dictionaries and the law. In the first ten years of this century, the US Supreme Court cited 295 dictionary definitions in 225 of its opinions.[34] The UK Supreme Court is fairly new. In seven years of its decisions, I could find only seventeen that mentioned specific dictionary definitions—though the UK and US Supreme Courts hear similar numbers of cases per year.[35] Before 2009, the House of Lords served as the court of final appeal, with much the same attitude toward dictionaries. A 1998 House of Lords' decision warned that the meaning of a text "is not the same thing as the meaning of its words. The meaning of words is a matter of dictionaries and grammars."[36] That is to say, a UK court's responsibility is to interpret documents contextually, rather than literally. Legal scholars and lexicographers are concerned about American courts' willingness to employ dictionary definitions in interpreting laws, patents, and contracts. Dictionaries differ. Justices might cherry-pick definitions, using a dictionary that suits their biases, then present it as "objective" evidence. But in spite of those repeated objections, the US Supreme Court's use of dictionaries has increased about tenfold since the 1960s.

I don't want to overstate the differences between the dictionary cultures of Britain and the United States. There's plenty of back-and-forth in their lexicographical traditions, and dictionaries are dictionaries. They've got common structures with common goals and they're recording our common language, so we mostly use them similarly. But then again, cheese is cheese and although both countries make cheese and eat cheese, I could easily list half a dozen differences in how we *relate* to cheese. (To give just one example, a cheese course at the end of a meal is a much more British institution than an American one.) Similarly, our relations to dictionaries have different tinges: the American more legalistic and literal, the British more leisurely and literary. British lexicographer Jonathon Green stereotypes British dictionary users as wanting "the story of words," "whereas Americans like to know their status—can I use it thus, is it right or wrong?"[37] This comes out in Green's area of expertise: slang. The well-known dictionaries of English slang—first Eric Partridge's, later Green's—are British. They're objects that can be read for their great word stories. The most comparable American dictionary only got to the letter O before its publisher killed it. It wasn't the type of practical dictionary that American publishers are willing to get behind.

Green's stereotype is also reflected in general dictionary usage. In surveys of university students in the 1970s and '80s, more Americans than Britons were found to own dictionaries. (I imagine that, like me, many of the American students received a dictionary as a high school graduation gift.) The American students were twice as likely as British students to consult a dictionary at least once a week, and they used them mostly to look up spelling, pronunciation, meaning, or usage advice.[38] The British students didn't look up those things as much as the Americans did, but used their dictionaries to look up more word histories.

Dictionary publishers market to these contrasting behaviors. American dictionary covers advertise:

- *the words you need today*
- *expert guidance on correct usage*
- *The Clearest Advice on Avoiding Offensive Language*
- *The Best Guidance on Grammar and Usage*
- *The Official Dictionary of the ASSOCIATED PRESS*[39]

In contrast, the cover of the British *Chambers Dictionary* offers a quotation by the author Melvyn Bragg, claiming that Chambers "stands out like a baroque mansion against a city of faceless concrete." Their website proclaims, "Chambers—For Word Lovers." *Collins English Dictionary* similarly touts itself as "the language lover's dictionary." Oxford's tagline, "the world's most trusted dictionary," comes closest to the American claims of correctness and certainty, but not very close. It tells us how people see Oxford dictionaries, but not what those dictionaries can do for us. American dictionary advertisements tell you which newspapers and government organizations use their dictionary. They tell you the places you should have a dictionary: home, school, and office. British dictionary marketing name-checks famous novelists and poets, and while they may mention study, they hardly ever refer to mundane work. American publishers pitch their dictionaries to the aspirational, the linguistically insecure who want reassurance when they write term papers or business letters. British dictionaries, on the other hand, are marketed to the arrived, offering them words to love, rather than words they need.

The LITERACY = LITERATURE equation can be seen in British dictionaries more than American ones. Johnson supported the definitions in his *Dictionary of the English Language* (1755) with literary quotations by the likes of Milton, Dryden, and Shakespeare. His definitions sometimes provided more entertainment than practical language help, making the book a piece of literature itself:

Lexicographer
A writer of dictionaries; a harmless drudge, that busies himself in tracing the original, and detailing the signification of words.

Monsieur
A term of reproach for a Frenchman.

Oats
A grain, which in England is generally given to horses, but in Scotland supports the people.

After a very quiet century, the next big thing in British lexicography expanded upon Johnson's approach. The "dictionary on historical principles," proposed at the Philological Society of London in 1857, took seventy-one years to complete and was published in 125 installments between 1884 and 1928, by which time it was known as the *Oxford English Dictionary*. The OED followed Johnson in including quotations to illustrate words' usage, but arranged them to show the development of a word's meanings over time. In a state of constant revision and updating, it is one of the great works in the humanities of any time or place: "a scholarly Everest," according to *Time* magazine; "one of the wonders of the world," according to the *Guardian*. But it was never intended for everyday use by the general public. At twenty volumes, it would challenge the bookcase, the pocketbook, and the patience of most dictionary users. The Oxford University Press used its OED materials to start producing dictionaries for the general user in 1911. Competitors for these dictionaries have come and gone, but they bear the hallmarks of a literary view of English. The publishers of *Chambers Dictionary*, for instance, bragged of its inclusion of "obsolete and rare words in the works of our greatest writers" and so they give space to words like *forswatt* ('sweaty') and *forswonck* ('overworked'). You will only ever find yourself needing those definitions if you're reading Edmund Spenser's *Shepheard's Calendar*, published in 1579.

American dictionary culture does not prioritize the literary. Rather than following Johnson in quoting literary authors and philosophers, Noah Webster's 1828 *American Dictionary of the English Language* illustrated definitions wherever possible with quotations from the Bible or American statesmen, instilling a sense of the dictionary as a moral and patriotic document—a bible to go alongside the Bible. This is still literally true, as the Foundation for American Christian Education has revived Webster's 1828 dictionary for their "Noah plan" home-schooling curriculum.[40]

The 19th-century Dictionary Wars between Webster's and Worcester's dictionaries set the commercial tone for dictionary culture in America. Worcester's *A Comprehensive Pronouncing and Explanatory English Dictionary* (1830) focused on the "best usage" of words, which for Worcester meant "as close as possible to educated London usage." Dictionaries were in high demand: the US population was growing rapidly and the spread of public education, and the future of American English, needed to be decided: Should it stay loyal to the crown like Worcester or declare its independence with Webster?

After the Dictionary Wars ended with Worcester's death in 1865, Merriam-Webster prevailed, though the victory was tempered by the fact that, without a trademark on *Webster*, other publishers could come along and trade on the hard-won fame of the name. But the "war" propaganda established the role of the dictionary in the United States. The campaigns pushed the idea of the dictionary's relevance to everyday life. They taught Americans that every home, every schoolroom, and every place of business should have a dictionary sitting alongside the Bible, ready to educate and to authorize.

The grammar infrastructure

You can write charmlessly without insulting the reader. But to write ungrammatically, and not realise it, is to insult the English language. [. . .] And in this respect the British are a long way ahead of the Americans: a long way ahead, that is, on the road to perdition.

Clive James (2006)[41]

The American "can-do" spirit applies to language. In the States, it's taken as a given that writing and speaking are improvable skills that can be boiled down to some simple advice and self-discipline. We have some good role models on this account—like Abraham Lincoln. Though he's remembered for his moving rhetoric, Lincoln's humble beginnings on the frontier meant that he got little formal education beyond the barest basics. Instead, his learning was mostly self-driven. Lincoln read whatever spellers, grammars, and readers he could find and committed long passages to memory. Rosemary Ostler, in her book *Founding Grammars*, observes: "None of the formal grammar rules that Lincoln applies in his speeches would have been acquired naturally while growing up on the Indiana frontier."[42] It's hard to imagine a character like Lincoln making it to the highest office of the United Kingdom. But I find it even harder to imagine a British Rosemary Ostler writing a well-received book about the grammar books that shaped the nation's highest political office.[43]

The belief that anyone, like Lincoln, can school themselves into articulacy is fundamental to American education. Communication skills are explicitly taught. This can be clearly seen in higher education, where nearly every degree requires courses dedicated to the teaching and practice of written composition. This makes Rhetoric and Composition, as it is called, one of the more lucrative areas of humanities research and textbook publishing in the US. In the UK, there is no such discipline.

I hadn't realized this when I started teaching in England, so I innocently asked an English colleague at what point in our curriculum the essay writing was taught. (I'd been there long enough to ascertain that my students hadn't come to that point.) My colleague seemed puzzled by my question, then replied that the able students would pick up a good writing style from reading. And the less able students? They'd be the ones getting the poorer marks. I had to remind myself that this was a colleague who would wish no student ill. He and I had just been indoctrinated by different educational systems. To me, his response seemed to reflect the "knowing your place" aspects of British society (writing well isn't for everybody), whereas mine reflected an American optimistic gumption (anyone can write well; they just have to keep at it).

The point of Rhetoric and Composition teaching is to develop skills in research, critical thinking, and writing clear, factual argumentative prose in standard American English. The students who pay attention leave the course with a common vocabulary for discussing essay structure. Sitting as it does in the first term of higher education, Freshman Composition is seen as the chassis on which the American liberal-arts education is carried forward. Although there are plenty of academics arguing about whether it is effective and complaining about teaching it (grading that many essays is no picnic), Freshman Composition is so institutionalized now that it hardly budges.

Explicit first-year writing courses were first taught in the late 1800s, starting at Harvard. American organizations dedicated to the teaching of college writing were in place by the 1950s. But many count 1963 as the year in which American rhetoric and composition studies became a proper academic discipline.[44] Part of the engine for making it a discipline in its own right was divorcing it from the teaching of grammar—to make it clear that composition courses were teaching big thinking and communication skills rather than just telling people where to put commas.[45] That year saw the publication of *Research in Written Composition*, commonly known as "The Braddock Report." This report sounded the death knell for formal grammar teaching. Braddock and colleagues argued that:

> The teaching of grammar has a negligible or, because it usually displaces some instruction and practice in actual composition, even a harmful effect on the improvement of writing.[46]

With the simultaneous rise of child-centered educational styles and descriptive linguistics as an academic discipline, teaching young people about semicolons and dangling participles seemed less pressing and more oppressive. Yet in writing courses teachers and students still sometimes needed to have conversations about semicolons and dangling participles. The teaching of grammar became much less organized at this point, but the emphasis on explicit teaching of writing meant that it could never go away completely. The textbooks for Freshman Composition have chapters on grammar. The teachers rarely cover them in class, but they refer the students to them as needed. Freshman Composition thus contributes to what I think of as the grammar infrastructure of the United States, part of the reason that when grammar teaching started to drop in the 1960s, it fell more quickly and more resolutely in the UK than in the US. With less historical interest in the English language and little specialized teaching on written communication, England had less of an infrastructure for approaching English as a linguistic and communicative system, separate from literary study.

Education in England had always been slow to take an interest in English grammar, preferring instead Latin and Greek as serious subjects of study. A British government report in 1921 concluded that it is "impossible at the present juncture to teach English grammar in the schools for the simple reason that no one knows exactly what it is."[47] Grammarians from other European countries took on the mantle of writing English grammar books. As one Dutch grammarian noted, "we can hardly look to our *English* colleagues for much guidance" since in Britain "the study of English, apart perhaps from that of English phonetics, may be said to be non-existent."[48] English literature and English composition were also neglected in England until the 19th century. The English educated classes felt free to assume that English language, literature, and culture would be acquired naturally at home, and so attention focused on less domestic subjects.[49]

Scotland, on the other hand, introduced English language, literature, and composition as school subjects in the 1700s. The Scots could not assume that knowledge of English language and culture would seep into children at home, but could see that knowledge of these things would help them get ahead in the newly united kingdom. American education followed the Scottish model, taking English very seriously. Noah Webster urged Americans not to emulate England's emphasis on Greek and Latin in education. Thomas Jefferson made sure that the University of Virginia taught Anglo-Saxon, so that its students would better understand their own language.[50] Benjamin Rush saw Philology as central to the American curriculum, emphasizing the "cultivation and perfection of our language," since English "will probably be spoken by more people in the course of two or three centuries, than ever spoke any one language at one time since the creation of the world."[51]

And Americans continued to take explicit study of English seriously. In the 1870s Alonzo Reed and Brainerd Kellogg of the Brooklyn Polytechnic Institute developed their method for sentence diagramming.[52] One hundred years later, after the supposed death of grammar teaching, my sixth-grade self was at the blackboard showing off work like this:[53]

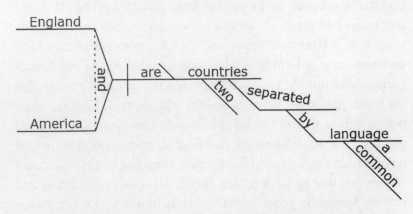

Another twenty years later in Texas, I was teaching that system to another generation of students who were required to pass an English grammar course as part of their Education degrees. Today, another twenty years later, that course, Modern English Grammar, is still required and still teaches sentence diagrams. News of the death of grammar teaching in America has been somewhat exaggerated.

While it served fewer and fewer people as the 21st century approached, the grammar infrastructure was still there to a great extent, and still influencing the culture. At least one court case has been decided on the basis of Reed-Kellogg diagrams.[54] Characters argue about sentence diagrams in Anne Tyler's fiction. You can go on Etsy and buy a poster with the first lines of twenty-five novels diagrammed, or a pendant with "Diagrams sentences for fun" diagrammed onto it. Americans are often surprised to discover that Reed-Kellogg-style diagrams are unknown outside the US and that no equivalent system takes their place in the UK.

American grammar study was never much removed from the goal of educating the citizenry. For instance, Charles Fries'

American English Grammar (1940), the first corpus-based English grammar, was financed by the National Council of Teachers of English with support from the Linguistic Society of America and the Modern Language Association. The project bridged practical educational goals with the burgeoning academic field of linguistics—a link that came decades later in the UK. The continued publication of grammar and writing textbooks for native speakers (the equivalents of which are barely found in the UK), the training of teachers, and the opportunity to talk about grammar in writing classes all contribute to the grammar infrastructure. This gives the US a slight advantage when educators or governments try to revive grammar teaching.

In England, attempts to revive grammar teaching have been sudden, under-resourced, and controversial: sudden due to the institution of a National Curriculum starting in the late 1980s, under-resourced because the generation of teachers responsible for instituting the curriculum had been taught no grammar, and controversial because grammar teaching is often seen as a left–right political issue in England. The Conservative party has been the main mover in promoting formal grammar teaching—with a clear ideological bent in which *grammar* is

> the metaphorical correlate for a cluster of related political and moral terms: *order, tradition, authority, hierarchy* and *rules*. In the ideological world that conservatives inhabit, these terms are not only positive, they define the conditions for any civil society, while their opposites—*disorder, change, fragmentation, anarchy* and *lawlessness*—signify the breakdown of social relations.[55]

More liberal politicians and educationists either opposed grammar teaching altogether or favored a more descriptive approach that values nonstandard varieties of English. Disagreements about values and methods meant that the first national curriculum for

English took eight years to finalize—longer, I understand, than for any other subject. When the Conservatives regained power in 2010, they immediately went about adding far more specific grammar demands to the curriculum. By 2014, mentions of grammar in the national curriculum had multiplied sixfold. Seven-year-olds were to be examined on the difference between subordinate and coordinate clauses. By age eleven, children are tested on whether the *after* in *You can stop after running a mile* is a subordinating conjunction or a preposition (answer: preposition) and on the meanings of Latinate roots, like the *struct* in *construction* (answer: 'pile up, build').[56] Given the emphasis on learning testable terminology, parents and teachers soon came to associate grammar with unnecessary standardized testing.[57] In the first year of the new grammar tests, parent groups organized a children's strike on exam day, holding placards on which "grammar" was presented as the opposite of "fun" and "learning."

While the government gave some lip service to the notion that labeling parts of sentences would better students' practical communication, neither their actions nor their rhetoric indicated a strong link between actual literacy and the grammar teaching proposed.[58] The Conservative rhetoric on grammar is about civilization, not communication—about order, high culture, and a "best" English at the top of society. Norman Tebbit, a member of Margaret Thatcher's cabinet, went so far as to see linguistic prescriptivism as crime prevention: "If you allow standards to slip to the stage where good English is no better than bad English, [it] tends to cause people to have no standards at all, and once you lose standards there's no imperative to stay out of crime." Prince Charles, speaking to a business consortium in 1989, suggested that grammar teaching was necessary for the supply of "people who write good English and write plays for the future." He'd started talking about business writing, but couldn't help but make the British association of "good English" with "great literature." The most recent curricular reforms were accompanied by promotion of Latin and classical Greek as subjects and the removal of American and digital texts from the English curriculum. Guidance on exam marking includes specific instructions to teachers to not accept American spellings or the word *gotten*. In this context, English grammar study looks less like a way to make a Lincoln of yourself and more like a Tardis aimed at the late days of empire.

You can find the permissive and the pedant in both countries, but the differing infrastructures and the tones of the debates divulge underlying ideas about how and why we should learn about language. Literary Britain versus literate America. Culture versus communication.

By the rules

If you go to an American bookshop by far the biggest section is "Self Help and Improvement." [...] There's an unbelievable sense that life is improvable, that you can be lectured at or indeed given a sermon at. It's the Protestant base of America that things are done by text and by works, as opposed to by submission and by doctrine in the way [of] the High Church European rump that we still believe.

Stephen Fry (2009)[59]

Britain and America both love instructional nonfiction. But while similar numbers of how-to books populate the national bestseller lists, their titles tell different cultural stories. Faced with the insecurities of modern life, the US book-buying public asks, "How can I change *myself* in order to change this situation?" Americans want to know how to reduce stress, how to organize their lives, how to win friends and influence people. The British book-buying public, on the other hand, takes comfort in food. Cookbooks overwhelm the British bestseller lists, with a few dieting books providing a corrective measure. Instructions on living, thinking, or doing business and instructions on cooking or eating sell in inverse proportions in the two countries:

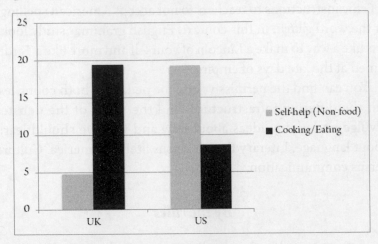

Average number of instructional books in
Amazon's top 100, 2011–2016

The self-help industry is founded on values inherited from Britain, but taken to new extremes in America:

Optimism: Things can always get better.
Responsibility: It's up to me to make things better.
Order: The path to success can be mapped.
Egalitarianism: Everyone has a right to that map.

In America, the secret to success is no secret. The path to the good life can usually be boiled down to fewer than twelve steps.

This is no less true in the area of language. Americans want help. And the best help is the help that is clear and simple. Recall the differing solutions to collective noun agreement (*the government is/ are*, chapter 6). The British style guides ask the writer to consider the context and decide whether the singular or plural verb sounds best. Americans are given a one-size-fits-all rule: use a singular verb. Easy to teach. Easy to follow. A bit authoritarian, but at least we get to choose our authorities. No quasi-governmental language academy for us, just an array of advice books. In the land of Lincoln, dictionaries and usage guides are seen as self-help books that can give anyone the means to use standard English. This point of view helps explain the second Dictionary War.

In 1961, Merriam-Webster published *Webster's Third International Dictionary*, the biggest revision of their unabridged dictionary since the 1800s. Its editor, Philip Gove, was determined that the dictionary would describe the language as it is, rather than telling readers which words are good and which bad. *Webster's Third* defined words like *ain't* and *irregardless* without explicitly saying they were mistakes to be avoided. The advertising promised "the living language: vivid, exciting, and warm."[60] This was a little too intimate for many, who preferred their words sober and still. The headlines of American newspaper reviews sum up the general feeling about *Webster's Third*:

Sabotage in Springfield
A Non-Word Deluge
Anarchy in Language
The Death of Meaning[61]

And then it got nasty.[62] The publisher of the *American Heritage* history magazine, James Parton, was so incensed by the new dictionary that his company attempted a hostile takeover of Merriam-Webster, with the aim of restoring to print the 1934 *Webster's Second International Dictionary*.[63] The takeover failed, so Parton founded a competitor dictionary that would take the judgmental role that *Webster's Third* had abdicated—relying not just on the authority of the editor, but on a consultant Usage Panel of 105 learned writers, professors, and editors. For controversial words, *The American Heritage Dictionary* published paragraphs on usage. In these, readers could learn, for example, that just 67% of the Usage Panel were happy for you to use the verb **to shake down**.[64] Today the panel is chaired by linguist and style-guide author Steven Pinker; its nearly 180 members include 73 professors, three former US poet laureates, the *New York Times* crossword-puzzle editor, and leading lights of American journalism and literature, united in an effort to help Americans help themselves in deciding whether they should risk using **hopefully** to mean 'I hope.' (In the 1999 edition, 34% of the panel said it was acceptable. In 2012, that proportion was up to 63%.)

Americans didn't invent English dictionaries or grammars or usage books or style guides. The British got there first, and there are still excellent British style guides as well as not-so-excellent grumpy books justifying silly rules with silly reasons (as exemplified throughout the earlier chapters of this book). But it's a measure of the strength of American usage guides that they seem to have actually changed the language on that side of the Atlantic.

A case in hand is the decline of the passive voice in American writing. Passive voice changes the focus of a sentence by putting the object of the verb in the subject position. With the subject position now occupied by the object, the former subject—usually the *agent* of an action—can go unmentioned:

Active: We made mistakes.
Passive, with agent: Mistakes were made by us.
Passive (agentless): Mistakes were made.

Between 1960 and 1990, use of the passive decreased by 28.2% in American writing, while in British writing the decline was a gentler 14%.[65] If you've ever used a word processor's grammar checker, you've probably received the wrist-slapping message: "Passive

Voice (consider revising)." But how did we get to the point where software chides us for our passives? The blame rests particularly on one book: William Strunk's *The Elements of Style* (1918).

Strunk, like many a professor I know (like many a professor I *am*), seems to have been easily annoyed by his students' essays. As a prophylactic against further insult to his writerly sensibilities, he wrote and self-published a booklet of dos and don'ts for his students at Cornell University. That would have been the end of it, except that one of those students was E. B. White, later a staff member of *The New Yorker* magazine and the author of *Charlotte's Web* and *Stuart Little*. After an old friend nostalgically sent White a copy of Strunk's "little book," White wrote a fond recollection of it for *The New Yorker* in the summer of 1957. Jack Case, an editor at Macmillan, immediately saw the potential for the little book and wrote to White to propose that he edit a new edition of his beloved teacher's book. Case saw Freshman Composition courses as a key market for the book; the popularity of White's novels would make it an easy sell to teachers. After eighteen months of revisions, the book was published in April 1959. Before the year was over, it had been a Book of the Month Club selection and number 3 on the *New York Times* bestseller list. The reviewers gushed. *The Elements* was "a public service of the greatest magnitude," according to the *Boston Daily Globe*. It has been in print (with some updating) ever since, selling over ten million copies to generations of college students, journalists, and wannabe novelists who've read Stephen King singing its praises in his autobiography. *The Elements of Style* is probably the only writing manual to have inspired an operatic song cycle and a ballet. Such is its cultural importance in the US.[66]

Following his own advice to "put statements in positive form," Strunk couldn't say, "Don't use the passive voice." Instead he advised readers to "use the active voice," because it is, among other things, "vigorous and direct," "concise," "lively," and "emphatic." Like many teachers (mea culpa, mea culpa), Strunk expected his students to do as he said and not as he did. The very first sentence of his *Elements* has two passive verbs: "This book **is intended** for use in English courses in which the practice of composition **is combined** with the study of literature."

Strunk and White were not alone in discriminating against the passive. George Orwell, for one, preached, "never use the passive where you can use the active," in his 1946 essay "Politics and the English Language." But Strunk and White tend to get the blame for the downfall of the passive in America due to their book's perpetual ubiquity in classrooms and editorial offices.[67] The swifter decline of the passive in the US seems to be symptomatic of both a greater hunger for language advice and a greater opportunity for particular advice to be spread through the formal teaching of writing—that American grammar infrastructure.

The passive is hardly the only example of American language changing due to an enthusiasm for following usage advice—let me tell you about *that* and *which*. Essentially: *that* introduces a clause that tells you *which* thing the noun refers to (a restrictive relative clause), and *which* can introduce clauses that sneak a bit of extra information into the sentence (a nonrestrictive relative clause):

Restrictive:
The law that forbids jaywalking is fifty years old today. (tells you which law)
Nonrestrictive:
That law, which passed by only five votes, is controversial. (gives an extra fact about the law)

You'll have a natural intuition for the two types of relative clauses, even if the terminology (or my explanation of it) sounds like gibberish to you. The intuition is revealed by the facts that (a) we use different intonations and punctuation for the two types (whether or not we've been taught to) and (b) we never put a *that* before a nonrestrictive clause. English can use *which* for both types, though. Since there are two words (*that*, *which*) and two jobs for those words to do (restrictive/nonrestrictive clauses), usage mavens and grammar pedants love to try to make a one-word/one-job rule. *That* can't go with nonrestrictive relative clauses, so, they reason, *which* shouldn't go with restrictive ones.

This "phony but ubiquitous rule," says Steven Pinker, "sprang from a daydream by Henry Fowler."[68] Fowler's *Dictionary of Modern English Usage*, published in Britain in 1926, has five dense pages on restricting *which* to nonrestrictive clauses, which Fowler saw as a "line of improvement" for the language. But despite Fowler's fine reputation in the UK, his rule has had little effect there: in the 1990s still more than half of written restrictive relative clauses had *which*. On the other hand, the US (which was already using more *that*s than Britain) took the distinction seriously. By the 1960s, slightly more than half of American restrictive relative clauses used *that*. By the 1990s, more than 85% followed the rule.[69] The American usage guides had taken over from Fowler. Linguist Deborah Cameron attributes the British–American *that*–*which* gap to the "absolute dominance" of the *Chicago Manual of Style* in US publishing and "the zeal with which copy editors enforce its prescriptions."[70] I wouldn't put all the blame on *Chicago*, since *Garner's Modern American Usage* and the style manuals for the *New York Times* and the Associated Press all have the same rule. British usage guides are much less bossy about *which* since Fowler left the scene, but no one seems to be paying much attention to them anyway.

A final case for your consideration is ***try and*** rather than ***try to***. The BBC News style guide, for instance, is pretty clear on this: "Correct usage is **try to** do something, and **not** 'try and' do something." But the style guide is swimming against the BBC tide. Their television listings include things like "Francis goes undercover to **try and** solve a mysterious outbreak of vandalism," their view-on-demand platform says "**try and** get a password," and occasionally even the news division forgets its own style guide: "proposals to **try and** increase house-building."

One study found that Brits used *try and* (where they could have said *try to*) over 71% of the time in speech and 24% of the time in writing. The American figures were 24% for speech and 5% in writing.[71] Older, educated Brits prefer *try to* a bit more, but those under forty-five say *try and* 85% of the time, regardless of their level of education.[72] The usage guides are having little effect in Britain—and many have reasonably given up on the matter. Oliver Kamm's 2015 *Accidence Will Happen* goes so far as to call *try and* "standard English," while only 55% of the *American Heritage* Usage Panel see it as acceptable.[73]

Perhaps because of their Verbal Inferiority Complex, Americans often follow the rules in British style guides better than their British readers do. You can see the rule-following as sheepish American conformity, or you can see it as a way of democratizing the language. If everyone has access to the rules, then everyone can use them. If everyone uses them, then we are linguistically equal. There's no need to be blessed with the "good ear" that comes with breeding or education. The rules do the language no great service, but they help people feel like they have the key to speaking and writing well.

9

THE PROGNOSIS

England will never have any more honor, excepting now and then that of imitating the Americans.

John Adams (1780)[1]

The previous chapters have challenged a number of myths about American and British English, but we're still left with the assumption that our transatlantic linguistic relationship is lopsided. I won't argue that it's not—relationships are rarely symmetrical, and they wouldn't be very interesting if they were. But relationships evolve, and perhaps this one needs a little counseling. The two parties have got stuck in a groove, telling themselves the same stories about each other while not noticing that they and their partners have changed. Here are a couple of stories that seem to be particularly steadfast in our conceptions of American and British English.

- British English is the highest-status English, so Americans inevitably hold it in high esteem.
- Britain suffers a severe trade deficit in the transatlantic language exchange, importing from but almost never exporting to America.

These stories are less defensible than they were a few decades ago. Both countries have undergone great social changes in the past fifty years, and how we interact with each other has changed too.

The 20th century brought America to Britain in a way that had not happened before: American troops stationed in Europe, American voices recorded in the latest media technologies, and American consumer products flowing out of a dynamic economy that had hardly suffered the privations of war. The postwar Marshall Plan ensured that American loans for European recovery were repaid in part through import of American goods. It was a soft invasion of British culture, and a shock to the system of a nation that over the previous centuries had become accustomed to being the cultural imposer, rather than the imposed-upon.

The US has certainly built up some momentum in cultural exports. But the 21st century is looking rather different. The rise of the internet means it's much easier for people to have all kinds of relationships across borders. And the thing about internet communication is that it's almost entirely in words. Americans are able to consume more British media now than they ever could in the 20th century, when newspapers were on paper, books came from bookshops, and British television had just a few slots a week on the "educational" television station. Now short-run British dramas and comedies have a second life on Netflix, and British chat shows, adventures, and reality television are broadcast on BBC America. On American television, Brits including John Oliver, Piers Morgan, Craig Ferguson, and James Corden have stepped into high-profile host positions previously held by Americans. The online versions of newspapers like the gossipy *Daily Mail* and the serious *Guardian* have millions of American readers. And British editors have been in charge of the *Wall Street Journal*, American *Vogue*, *Cosmopolitan*, the *New York Daily News*, *Gawker*, and the *Daily Beast* in the past decade. Americans have more immediate access to more British English than they have ever had. So what does this mean for our relationship? Does exposure give rise to intimacy? Or does familiarity breed contempt? Are we talking more similarly? Or will we always be different?

AVIC: Cured in our lifetime?

Before I came to America from England three months ago, I asked an American journalist in London what kind of reactions to expect. "Well, when they hear an English accent Americans usually add about 20 points to your IQ. But when they see a black face they usually don't," he said. "You'll be an anomaly."

Recalling that the authors of the book *The Bell Curve* had claimed that black people have an IQ 15 points lower than whites, I was heartened to think that even in the eyes of the most hardened racist I would still come out at least five points ahead.

Gary Younge (1996)[2]

No one has ever measured the number of extra IQ points that Americans accord the owner of an English accent. I doubt that anyone could measure it. The sense that such things are quantifiable might have started with a 1985 study in which Americans were asked to rate personality traits of four men reading the same passage, two with standard American and two with Received Pronunciation accents.[3] Americans rated the British voices as higher in personal status than the American accents—with ratings for intelligence, confidence, success, and ambition contributing to the overall status score. In the thirty years since that study, it's been easy to find claims of ten, fifteen, or even twenty extra IQ points. But while we see IQ-point inflation in the retelling of the tale, the British advantage might not be what it used to be. While expat advice resources assure Brits abroad that "the merest murmur of a British accent turns the average American into a heap of delighted, obliging mush,"[4] there is some evidence that this is less true with each decade.

In a 2001 study, American subjects rated American voices as at least as intelligent as the English accents, with the female American voice rated as both more intelligent and better educated than both English accents in the study.[5] While the male English accent sounded no more intelligent than the American accents, it was rated higher than both American accents for education, social class, and income. In other words, the American subjects thought the English accent sounded more well-to-do than the American accents, but not any smarter.[6] A 2005 study explored the same issue by asking English speakers from several countries to give their impressions of national accents. Americans tended to describe British accents as "cultured." That was as good as it got, though. The Americans commented little on the interpersonal and emotional connotations of British accents, but when they did, they made three times as many negative comments as positive ones, with descriptions like "stuffy," "they feel they are better than we are," "conceited," and "full-of-yourself attitude."[7] In other words, sounding "cultured" is not necessarily an advantage in the US, with its social imperative to sound friendly and egalitarian in all interactions. As we've seen in chapter 4, the value Americans put on being *smart* is rather distinct from the value of formal education. Informal education—street smarts, self-help, the school of hard knocks—requires more gumption, and the self-schooled are often seen as more trustworthy than those in the ivory tower.

This was a theme of all the accent-attitude studies. While Americans associated English accents with high social status, they scored the same accents low on friendliness, sincerity, and trustworthiness. Sure, Americans may admire British accents and they may be friendly to British tourists (but then Americans act friendly by default). They might not, however, be able to imagine folks with British accents as real friends. They might not be all that comfortable hanging out with them.

These stereotypes are used for effect in American television and film. Hollywood evil geniuses often sound like they have had an Oxford education (even if they're supposed to be Nazis or ancient Romans). On television, English accents often signal a disruptive interloper—like the English Emily in *Friends*, whose engagement to Ross threatened the reconciliation with Rachel that fans hoped for.[8] Let's not exaggerate the effect, though. Patrick Stewart has used his actorly RP accent to heroic effect in both *Star Trek* and *X-Men*. *Star Wars'* good guys Obi-Wan Kenobi and C-3PO sound English. American filmmaking often employs British accents as a shortcut to signalling a distant place or distant time—whether that be the revolutionary France of *Les Misérables* or the fantasy worlds of *Game of Thrones* and *Lord of the Rings*.

If they're disappointed with their declining intelligence ratings, British readers may now be reassuring themselves with the belief that their accents are still undeniably sexy in America. I'm afraid I have more bad news. Only 35% of Americans in a 2014 poll claimed to find British accents attractive. Many more (49%) were simply indifferent to the UK sound. (This didn't stop the British pollsters from trying to reinvigorate the myth with their headline "It's true! Americans love British accents.")[9] Irish and Australian seem to impress Americans more these days, perhaps because they are exotic (like the British), but without the perceived stuffiness and condescension.

A 2007 accent-attitude study may hold a clue as to why Americans are falling out of love with British accents.[10] Investigators at Brigham Young University asked American participants to listen to a passage read in accents that the study called *Standard American*, *Middle Eastern*, *Latin American*, and *British*. One group of subjects rated a "British"-accented recording as the most intelligent of the four accents. The second group rated it the *least* intelligent. The key difference between the groups was experience. Group one had not spent much time outside the US, while group two consisted of Americans who had lived abroad for at least three months. In other words, the Americans who had the most opportunity to speak with people from other countries were less positively impressed by a British accent, while their estimation of other accents (including their own accent) went up. The RP accent suffered particularly because it had a very high pedestal to fall from. Now, this was a small study that has to be taken with several grains of salt, but I can't help but wonder if these Americans who went abroad had heard ridiculous claims like "*mathematics* is plural" or "Americans say *conTROVersy*" uttered in RP accents. Such experiences were certainly enough to make me question the intelligence behind the accents after I moved to England.

American Verbal Insecurity Complex was rooted in the feeling that the US had yet to fully develop its own culture separate from the former colonial power. Americans felt theirs was a substandard version of the language, rather than just a different version. But now the US has enough history and enough cultural products (including entire genres of literature, music, film, and theater) that we can associate "American" with all sorts of interesting things, including a standard language that doesn't have to look to England for direction. The United States' "superpower" status in the 20th century had a lot to do with American feelings of legitimacy in the world. In the 21st century, many Americans find that life has become more international, with the internet, media, and travel bringing more British people and their language into our circles. That allows us to hear more accents associated with more kinds of individuals, reducing the need to stereotype. At the same time, there are plenty of Americans who don't have much interest in Britain or anywhere else in the world, really. They don't care what the British think of their language, so they have no reason to fret that American English is not as "good" as British. Much as this might offend some British egos, it's a healthy state of linguistic affairs for Americans to not be measuring their English against that of another country.

Amerilexicophobia on the wane?

The one thing we seem to think we have left is the ability to sneer at Americans.

Stephen Fry (2009)[11]

The prognosis for Amerilexicophobia is less clear, but I'm optimistic. British attitudes toward American English are often negative—there's no escaping that. In the 2001 study mentioned earlier in this chapter, 15% of American comments about British accents mentioned negative interpersonal characteristics. The equivalent figure for negative British-on-American comments in that study was 45%: that's three times more bad-mouthing from Britain than from America.[12] But when the comparison is a bit broader, Brits seem more tolerant of American accents. In 2004, the BBC Voices project asked over five thousand Britons to score each of thirty-four British and "foreign" accents. On the "pleasantness" scale, "Standard English," "accent identical to my own," and "Southern Irish" fared best. In terms of social prestige, "the Queen's English," "Standard English," and "accent identical to my own" were the top three. But the "North American" accent[13] didn't fare badly at all: 8th in prestige (behind Edinburgh, Scottish, and London, but just ahead of "French accent") and 15th in pleasantness, tied with Lancashire and well ahead of German, the Black Country (in the Midlands, west of Birmingham), and Birmingham.[14] Among the English nationlects, New Zealand fared better in both categories, South African much worse, and Australian slightly more pleasant, but not as prestigious.

What's clear from these studies is that accent attitudes are not really about language. Only about 10% of the negative comments about US accents in the first study were really about the sound of the accent ("ugly," "harsh," or "not very nice to listen to"). The rest had little to do with American pronunciation and more to do with stereotyped American personalities, with comments like "over the top," "phoney," and "imperialistic." Given the current political climate, I can't imagine that such stereotypes of Americans will dissipate any time soon. But I still have hope about the language.

Certainly, the moral panic about American English is still played out regularly in Britain. As I finish writing this book, another book is being promoted as "a call to arms against the linguistic impoverishment that happens when one language [American English] dominates another [British English]."[15] (I'm sure the Scots, Welsh, and Irish will find this ironic, given that the English have historically done their best to dominate and wipe out their languages.) Nevertheless, while this crusade has been fought in Britain for decades, the calls to arms are increasingly met with calls for tolerance and even appreciation of American English.

"That the US speaks the same language has helped many Britons thrive during America's ascendancy," notes Michael Skapinker in the *Financial Times*. The spread of English, largely due to the economic and cultural power of the United States in the 20th century, has allowed British actors to gain lucrative Hollywood careers, British newspapers to gain worldwide readership, and British authors, like J. K. Rowling, to be among the world's bestsellers. Skapinker therefore urges the British to "thank America for saving our language."[16] Similar opinions can be heard from a broad range of language commentators in Britain. Those who aren't afraid of American words often express admiration of the perceived dynamism of American English, which they fear British English lacks. (I'll come back to this point.)

This willingness to tolerate and give credit to American English is probably less to do with appreciation of the United States and more to do with changing attitudes about social class, language change, and linguistic prescriptivism. Western societies have become more open, with the result that more voices are heard in public forums. Meanwhile, the academic field of linguistics has been increasingly effective in getting its messages out beyond university walls. The more people have access to information about English's constantly changing past, the more they might be willing to accept linguistic change as part of life. The more they hear about the futility of previous efforts to stop linguistic change, the less willing they might be to invest much rhetorical effort in trying to keep English still. The more we talk about the fact that no form of English has a greater claim to logic or beauty than other forms, the more we might tolerate variation in language. These days, there may be as many journalist-cum-usage-experts who cite linguistic evidence and preach against "zombie rules" (such as "don't split an infinitive") as those who get grumpy about the language going to hell, with Americans leading the way. Sure, journalists, broadcasters, and Prince Charles are still hating on Americanisms (including *to hate on* meaning 'to disparage'). But others, including Skapinker at the *Financial Times* and Oliver Kamm at *The Times*, are working as linguistic peacemakers. Skapinker and Kamm are not alone, but they are worth particular mention because they write for fairly staid, traditional British publications. Those aren't the first places one might think to look for tolerance of Americanisms. But there it blossoms.

Will we all write the same English soon?

There is no such thing as the Queen's English. The property has gone into the hands of a joint stock company and we own the bulk of the shares!

Mark Twain (1897)[17]

In his book *Twentieth-Century English*, Christian Mair, chair of English linguistics at Freiburg University, concludes:

a dispassionate look at contemporary linguistic developments shows that popular discussions hopelessly overemphasize the influence of American English on the development of the language as a whole.[18]

It's not just the popular discussions that overemphasize American influence. Mair gives several examples of serious academics jumping to conclusions about the Americanization of British English. Sidney Greenbaum, when he was director of the Survey of English Usage, "tended to exaggerate the speed" of American-influenced changes, "probably because of preconceived ideas he [held] about the globally dominant role of American English."[19] Mair concluded that these linguists often cherry-pick instances of language change that support their preconceptions and overlook other possible explanations for language change, while often displaying a dogged ignorance of American English.

I mention Mair's conclusion because I know what's coming when I say that British English is at no risk of becoming indistinguishable from American. I'm used to the eye rolls. I'm used to the trotting out of well-worn examples. I'm used to being ignored. But look! A dispassionate observer in Germany has done systematic research and come to the same conclusion that this passionate American in Britain has: that the fear of Americanization has led British folk to misjudge their own language. Amerilexicosis is real.

Mair was looking at grammar, in which American and British English are clearly more similar than they are different—even where they differ. Take, for example, prepositions after *different*. American English often uses **different than**. If Britain were on a clear road to Americanization, you might expect to hear and read more *different than*s in the UK nowadays. Instead, it's **different to** that is on the increase in British speech and informal writing.[20] Usage guides and English teachers in both countries will tell you to prefer **different from**, and for the most part we all do—though some British linguists seem to think that Americans have given up on *from*.[21] *Different* mostly has the same preposition in the two countries. Where it's changing, it's not getting more similar.

We've seen other examples of drifting apart in this book. Collective noun agreement was one, with the British increasingly saying **the team are** where Americans would say **the team is**. We've also seen examples of coming together, such as the British perhaps following Americans in asking *Do you have . . .?* rather than *Have you got . . .?* Surveying linguistic changes in 2003, dialectologist Peter Trudgill came to the conclusion that the grammatical scene was very mixed, with British English seeming to affect American English as much as American was affecting British.

After a book's worth of analysis of many grammatical trends, Christian Mair concluded that any American effect on British grammar is modest. We tend to come together in formal writing but continue to diverge in speech. His *different* example is a case in point: we tend to see *different from* in formal writing, but in speech, we're free, and more apt, to let our local linguistic flags fly with *different than* or *different to*.

Mair's finding makes sense. Writing tends toward the standard form, so that the greatest number of people may be able to understand it without the distraction of unfamiliar phrasings. The written form lasts. Whether it's an information pamphlet, a newspaper article, a book, or a law, its author will have little control over who gets to read it. And so they put on the English that they think will travel furthest and that will age the best. The written form also allows us more opportunity to "correct" our natural language in the direction of the standard form. If I write *different than*, I can backspace over it and write *from*. Or an editor might do it for me when I'm writing for publication. The spoken form isn't afforded the luxury of editing, and needs to be understood where we are. When we speak, we adjust the language to suit our audience, to assume a particular social position, to express solidarity, or to distance ourselves. We don't have to be as careful, because we're getting feedback from our audience and can see whether they understand us. We can gauge how well we're being understood and rephrase if necessary.

But even in writing, we can still see divergence. The decisive shift from *-ize* to *-ise* seems to be a technology-enhanced Britishization. British spell-checkers increasingly reject *-ize*, not because it's wrong, but because allowing both -*ize* and -*ise* would introduce the possibility of inconsistency in your document. For consistency's sake, they had to choose one spelling, and for not-getting-angry-letters-from-Brits' sake, they chose the spelling that looked least American. The shift toward plural collective noun agreement (*the team are*) is visible in British newspapers as well as in speech—though it's probably relevant that that tendency is particularly strong in the sports pages, a part of the newspaper that is more directed at the local audience and perhaps more apt to want to signal local allegiance (go team!) than other news, much of which may come from international wire services.

Newswires gave newspapers across the world the opportunity to have the same content, though their articles were usually (or ideally, at this point) put through the linguistic sieve of a local editor. But these days, even the most local content may become international because publication is increasingly on the worldwide web (emphasis on the *worldwide*). This has made news organizations more conscious of communicating in a general, standard English, while at the same time making them more sensitive to the linguistic traditions of other places. In 2009, the *New York Times* finally abandoned the American **labor** spelling for the British **Labour** Party, citing its increasingly international audience.[22] The British *Guardian* newspaper followed in 2014 with the decision to spell American proper names in American spelling, as in the **Centers** (not **Centres**) *for Disease Control* and the US *Department of* **Defense** (not **Defence**). Their production editor, David Marsh, defended the change:

> the old argument that "the *Guardian* is a British newspaper so we use British spellings" has served us well but no longer holds; we remain a British newspaper but one with many more readers outside the UK, especially in the United States. "Translating" World Trade Centre, as we used to do, is simply inaccurate: that's

not what it's called. Readers who can cope with, say, *Académie française* should be able to manage the occasional "center."[23]

These newspapers still expect their international readers to tolerate their national spellings. But they've compromised on the spelling of proper names because spelling names correctly is accurate and respectful. (Or they just got tired of the transatlantic letters-to-the-editor complaining about the issue.) These newspapers are neither Americanizing nor Britishizing; they are modernizing for their global audiences.

Are American words taking over Britain?

In England, save for the impetus given by the war, the word-coining power has lapsed [...]. It is significant that when we want to freshen our speech we borrow from America—poppycock, rambunctious, flipflop, booster, good mixer—all the expressive ugly vigorous slang which creeps into use among us first in talk, later in writing, comes from across the Atlantic. Nor does it need much foresight to predict that when words are being made, a literature will be made out of them.

Virginia Woolf (1925)[24]

Vocabulary is the easiest and the most noticeable way for one English to affect another. Words change all the time and they migrate easily—in part because we can never get enough. No one ever says, "I really need to go on a verbal diet; I've taken on too much extra vocabulary." Having more words increases the number of things we can talk about, the level of nuance in our descriptions, and the poetry of our expression. Nevertheless, some people worry that some words are "bad," and in particular some Brits worry that bad American words are taking over their language. Certainly, British English does get a lot of new vocabulary from America, but there's still plenty of variance between the two countries. In fact, if we want to look at vocabulary loss, the more immediate risk comes from within our own countries, rather than across the pond. While some worry that they hear *fall* more often in Britain these days, *fall* hasn't done the damage that *autumn* has done to British vocabulary. *Autumn*—being the dominant word in the powerful south—has completely replaced *backend* (as in the "back end" of the calendar), which as recently as the 1950s was the preferred term for the season in much of the north of England.[25] The same is happening across the US, as regional words are replaced by the "standard" words of the more populous or more powerful parts of the country.

At the international level, an awful lot of American vocabulary hasn't migrated. *Diaper* has not replaced *nappy*. *Emcee* has not displaced *compere*. The American term *sheetrock* has not touched the British *plasterboard*, nor has *baseboard* supplanted *skirting board*. American expressions that have taken up permanent residence in the UK are but a selection of American words and phrases. They're the words that we're likely to come across in the news, in a corporate boardroom, or with the import of things. For instance, influx of American food words in the past decade has been rapid, because baking and barbecue have surged in popularity as cooking shows and dining out have become more widespread. But words to do with more private domestic activities or national institutions are far more likely to stay put. I know this from my own experience. If Britain were really all that Americanized, I wouldn't have to learn new vocabulary every time I go to the **hardware store** (an errand for which I had to learn the old-fashioned British word *ironmonger*). I'd get what I craved when I ordered a bacon sandwich, and I wouldn't have to explain myself when I gossiped about **earthy-crunchies** (people with hippy tendencies) and **wet noodles** (wimpy naysayers). We're still different enough that we miscommunicate. Having a baby in England required me to get a whole new vocabulary of **muslins** (all-purpose soft cloths, like American **burp cloths**), **babygros** (onesies), **pushchairs** (strollers), and **health visitors** (community nurses who look after newborns and their mothers). Buying a house in England meant I needed to learn what **gazumping, gazundering**, and **snagging** are.* Traveling in England meant a new vocabulary of **return** (not *round-trip*) **tickets**, **platform** numbers (unlike the American *track 29*), **coaches** (long-distance buses), and **lay-bys** (for which the US has many regional terms, including *rest area*, *pullout*, and *turnout*). These words haven't crossed the Atlantic because we mostly use them with people near us. Most of the Americanisms that Brits worried about fifty years ago have not yet displaced British words. For instance, a 1964 book cited *meet up with, movie, canned*, and *elevator* as Americanisms that British speakers worried about.[26] Fifty years later, though Britons are very aware of those Americanisms and sometimes use them, they still mostly say *meet, film* and *cinema, tinned*, and *lift*.

Where words do move, it's often because there's a gap in the local word ecology. These words enrich the language with new concepts to discuss. *Monobrow, mileage, chunky, tween*, to *out* someone—none of these had direct British equivalents, and so they threatened no British vocabulary when they crossed the Atlantic. Sometimes efficiencies are introduced, much to some people's distaste. But adding words like *hospitalize* and *alphabetize* to the British vocabulary has not erased the option of saying *admit to hospital* or *put in alphabetical order*. The verbose are free to use them.

And despite the cries of "Americanization!" the British have their own way with these words, making them un-American. *Cookie* and *hot dog* may be American words, but the way British

---

* To **gazump** is to 'steal' a house from an agreed buyer by offering a higher price to the seller. To **gazunder** is to offer a lower price just before the contract exchange. **Snagging** is identifying the little fixes (from a **snag list**) that need to be finished before a building contract or house sale is complete.

people use them, as we've seen, is not American. The same goes for *fries*, which in British has come to refer to thin-cut fried potatoes. *Chips* remains the word for the more traditionally British type (closer to the size of American *steak fries*). And British English has taken over some American words. Anyone today who says *the dog's breakfast* (a mess) or *mobile phone* sounds more British than American, despite the fact that those expressions started out in the U S of A. The fact that most people don't know they're Americanisms shows how little the provenance of an expression matters once people start using it.

Finally, contrary to Virginia Woolf's fear, British English still makes its own words for itself. The *Oxford English Dictionary* records hundreds of British words that are less than fifty years old, and the lexicographers hold hundreds more in the wings, waiting to see if they stand the test of time. British English is making new words by blending old words, as in *alcopop, chugger* (from *charity + mugger*), *trustafarian* (rich kid with bohemian lifestyle), and *moobs* (man boobs). It clips the ends off words to make *pap* (paparazzo), *boyf* (boyfriend), and *bruv* (rather than adopting the American *bro*). It adds prefixes, as in *mis-selling* (selling on the basis of bad advice) and *mini-break*, and suffixes, as in *(metal) detectorist, bestie* (best friend), and *ladette*. There are new acronyms, like *BOGOF* (Buy One, Get One Free) and *quango* (QUasi-Autonomous Non-Governmental Organization). There are plenty of compounded nouns, like *house-share* and *awayday* (US *work retreat*), and verbs like *to longlist, to hot-desk*, and *to gobsmack* (to surprise; metaphorically smacking in the gob, or mouth). There's even new onomatopoeia, like *fnarr fnarr* (a stifled laugh) and *phwoar* (an expression of sexual appreciation). As well as verbing some nouns, the British are nouning verbs: *an overspend, a stitch-up*.

These new British words (and the many more I don't have space for) don't always get the love and appreciation they deserve. Some would complain that many are "just slang"—but that's not a fair complaint. Slang is English's laboratory, where many new words are tried out before some rise to the top. Like *to burgle* and *to vet* before them, some will transcend their humble, humorous, or jargon origins to be plain old English. Others will remain on the edges of "proper" English. A striking number of new British words refer to unethical or criminal activities: *dead-leg*, 'to strike someone hard in an attempt to cripple them'; *dogging*, 'public sex'; *happy-slap*, 'to strike a stranger and post a video of the assault online.' A good number are ways of insulting people: *minger*, 'ugly person'; *chav*, 'loutish person of lower social class'; *slap-head*, 'bald man'; *wazzock*, 'idiot.' A few are for more respectable British inventions: *banoffee pie*, *gastropub*, *E-fit* (computerized composite drawings, for police work). Some have been exported to the US; some remain UK-only. The chief thing to remember about them is that they exist. Every young British person's day is full of Britishisms—don't let the American *awesomes* and the *you guys* distract you. The children practice *joined-up writing* (not *cursive*) and *maths*. They look forward to *breaking up* (stopping school) for *half-term* (midterm break). Those who are a little older seek out *banging* club nights, where they'll do *crep checks* (judge people by their footwear), hoping to *pull* (go home with) someone *fit* (attractive). All very British things to say and do.

Yes, Americans invent words that come to be used in other English-speaking countries. Using a sample of fifty words first recorded in 1913 and 1933 in the *Oxford English Dictionary*, lexicographer Jeremy Butterfield found that 66% were first cited in use by Americans (the rest but one were first used in Britain).[27] Replicating Butterfield's methodology, I looked at randomly selected words from 1953 and 1973.[28] What you can see there is the waxing and waning of our fortunes. In 1953, when Britain was still in recovery from the war, twenty-five of the thirty words were American in origin, one Australian, four British. In 1973, the US contributed only half the new words. Except for two Australian words, the rest were British. (It's worth keeping in mind at this point that the OED has a New York office and an American reading program. They know about American words.) The 1953 number feels high, but if we consider the relative populations of the US and the UK, it's the only year in which the two countries contributed to the dictionary in proportion to their populations. As far as the OED is concerned, the UK may be punching above its weight vocabulary-wise.

How American words travel the globe, on the wings of capitalism and militarism, has been at the root of the discomfort about them. But the increased traffic of British people and communications to the US means that there is more opportunity for British words to show up in American contexts. Some, like *gobsmacked* and *bloody brilliant*, are the calling card of the *Anglocreep*—a disparaging term coined by *The Atlantic* magazine for the type of American anglophile who revels in dropping obviously British words into conversation.

But many more Britishisms come in under the radar without showing their passport. American news contains more and more Britishisms like *knock-on effect* (consequence), *the run-up* to an event, and *short-listing* for awards. Informal expressions like *kerfuffle*, *peckish*, *get no joy* (have no luck), and *to flummox* (confound) seem to be coming in through the media or military. American business-speak is using more Britishisms like *one-off*, *year-on-year*, *to liaise*, and *to second* (temporarily reassign to a different position or department; accent on the second syllable). The celebrity magazines are full of *baby bumps*, *dodgy* performances, *cheeky* poses, and actors being *sacked*. The fashion magazines say we're *spoiled for choice* (adjusting the British *spoilt*) in our search for a good *trouser*, stylish *trainers*, or a *bespoke* skin treatment, which you can buy from particular *stockists*. British sports clichés have been transplanted, including: *the long game*, *on the back foot* (from cricket), *to punch above one's weight*, and *credit to* ... (frequently heard in postgame interviews).[29] *New York Times* sports editor Jack Bell complains that as soccer has become more popular in the US:

> every chip is *cheeky*, every player on the wing is *nippy*, every field is a *pitch*, every pair of cleats are *boots*, every uniform a *kit* and every big play is *massive, just massive*. [...] some pooh-bahs somewhere (ESPN, Major League Soccer, Fox Soccer to name three) have come to the conclusion that to sound authentic the game in the United States has to [...] adopt the Britlingo of the game.[30]

Other English inventions have made their way to America with their names intact: ***pantos***, ***Boxing Day sales***, and ***scones***. While some people equate globalization with Americanization, there's a clue in the name: it's ***global***. It's not just that people around the world are eating American hamburgers and watching American films. We're eating Thai food and reading Scandinavian murder mysteries, collecting Japanese Pokémon, and drinking Italian coffees. People, things, and ideas are moving all over the world, not just to and from the US. And words are going in all directions. Some are more likely to spread out; some are more likely to stay at home. It's an exciting time to be a word lover.

Will we have the same accent?

> It is one thing to pronounce *can't* so that it rhymes with *ant* instead of *aunt*, but a whole other order to do that without feeling like a fraud.
>
> Rebecca Tan (2016)[31]

National linguistic divergence is clearest, of course, when it comes to pronunciation. Fears about accents fading away often make the news—especially in Britain, where accents have particular social meaning.

Television often gets the blame for the loss of local accent features. It's a convenient scapegoat, but there's very little evidence that it's much of a culprit. I know of just one study that has raised the possibility that television has some effect on English accents. The researchers found that Glaswegian working-class teenage fans of the London-based soap opera *Eastenders* had taken on some London working-class dialect pronunciations, like "fink" for *think*.[32] Since the pronunciation of working-class teens in Glasgow is unlikely to take over the Scottish establishment anytime soon, this seems less like television making us all sound alike and more like television giving people the option to be "different" in less local ways.

In general, accents are becoming less local and more regional. People from the villages sound more like the people from the towns, and people from the towns sound more like people from the nearest city. This isn't because they all watch the same TV shows, but because they talk with one another. Many of the people in the village go to work in the town. People from the town move to the city, or vice versa. And people from the city marry people from the villages, and vice versa. The media may bring more voices into our lives, but it's the roads and rails that bring people into our lives—people we talk with and people we grow to talk like.

Nevertheless, American television and voice technologies are still treated as prime suspects in discussions of accent change in Britain—even by linguists who should know better. When HSBC bank launched their "voice biometrics" security system, they commissioned two linguists to forecast what British English would sound like in 2066—a nice little publicity stunt that got them into every UK newspaper. The report covered the likely direction of sound change in six British cities, and it had a section about the causes of sound change, with the heading "Talking to machines and listening to Americans."[33] In spite of that title, not a single one of their predictions had British English sounds becoming more American. And yet someone stuck in a section heading that insinuated American culpability. Never mind whether there's any evidence of Americanization in the accents—it's a post-truth approach to language headlines. Another symptom of Amerilexicosis.

"Siri might be killing your accent!" headlines are popular in any news market where a non-American or regional English is spoken.[34] They just go to show how little people have learned from decades of experience with language technology. Ten years ago, the pundits predicted that students would soon be submitting essays with *are* spelled *R* and *great* as *GR8*. That hasn't happened. Young people now use smartphones that auto-complete the correct spelling. They would only type *C U L8R* with irony. People worried that word processors would Americanize all spelling, but today's computers are much better at using the location (or the preferences the user has set) to predict which spelling of *colo(u)r* is needed. Language change is gradual, but technological adaptations have been springing up quickly. So rather than the language changing to suit the technology, the technology changes to suit the language. The entrepreneurs in Silicon Valley don't want to change your English. They want to sell you—and all the people with all the Englishes around the world—products you'll find useful.

But the proof of our accent independence is in the pronouncing, not the predicting. In 1930 the *Manchester Guardian* ran a competition for four-line poems about a child going to the "talkies" and coming back with an American accent. Publishing a selection of the submissions, they noted the "real feeling" the topic inspired. My favorite entry managed to mock American and working-class English accents at the same time:

> Don't speak to me o' "talkies!"
> Them nasty low-class shows!
> Wot made my little 'Enery
> Start talking through 'is nose!

The winner ingeniously found an American city to rhyme with *talkie*:

"Peggy, my little one, where did you go?"
"I parked at the 'movies'—I'll say it's some show!"
"But child, you're in London, you're not in Milwaukee!"
"Aw, gee! All the stars speak like that in a 'talkie.'"[35]

The filmgoers of London have had ninety years to acquire a good Milwaukee accent. And yet they haven't. Since the advent of the talkies, even more American voices have been heard round the world from television, pop music, and talking computers. And yet American and British accents continue to diverge, not converge.

Think of the /r/ in *car*—or the lack of it. Over the course of the 20th century, the *r*-ful pronunciation has become the prestigious pronunciation in the US. Fewer and fewer New Yorkers, Southerners, and New Englanders leave off the /r/. But while /r/ made its comeback in the US, the *r*-less pronunciation spread further west and north in England. If American English were influencing British English, we should hear more /r/s in England. But there is no indication here that the UK is looking to the US for its accent trends.

The /t/ "tap" that Americans use in words like *butter* is another pronunciation that Brits hear often in American media. To the relatively small extent that the tap is heard in UK speakers, there's no particular evidence that it's due to "Americanization." Americans use the tap as part of standard pronunciation. It's not lazy; it's just how the words are pronounced there. But it can turn up outside the US because making a consonant voiced (in this case *d*-like) in between vowels is the kind of thing that happens naturally in informal speech. It takes effort to turn your vocal cords on for a vowel and off for a consonant and on again for the next vowel, and so those between-vowel consonants can get a "reduced" tap pronunciation in any dialect. A 2006 study of British television presenters showed they used taps in faster, less formal speech but not when reading the news.[36] That's not the American use-it-always tap, but a side effect of more casual speech contexts. A 2015 study found twice as many taps in older RP speakers than in teenage RP users, and again mostly in fast speech.[37] Taps have been around for decades in such British contexts.[38] If they were on the rise, we'd expect to hear lots from teens.

We don't hear taps as much from British teens because British /t/s are increasingly replaced by glottal stops, including in the between-vowel contexts where American use taps. That is to say, rather than closing the breath stream with the tongue for the /t/ sound, the closure happens in the throat. The result is a little hiccup of a non-sound in the same position where Americans would tap. *Getting* becomes "ge'ing"; *British* is "Bri'ish." Glottal *t*'s are common to many areas of Britain, from Scotland to East London, and have been increasing since the 19th century. So, rather than imitating the American tapped *t*, many British speakers are taking their *t*'s to the other end of the vocal tract.[39] There is some evidence that there is increased tapping in upper-class British English as a reaction to glottal stops. Not wanting to sound as stuffy with crisp *t*'s, but also not wanting to sound "street" with glottal *t*'s, male teenagers at exclusive boarding schools seem to use more taps than other British teens.[40] But that doesn't necessarily mean they're Americanizing: *t*'s have been tapped in East London for a long time—and East London is the source of many current changes to southern British English.

Another British pronunciation trend is "*th*-fronting," in which the *th* sounds becomes /f/ or /v/. Where I live in Sussex, it's sometimes hard to tell whether a speaker is saying *three* or *free*. British folk didn't get this idea from America, where *th*-fronting is only found in some forms of African-American English. And before you say, "Aha! Rap music did it!" consider a musical comedy about Cockney life, staged in London in 1960. It was called *Fings Ain't Wot They Used to Be*. Neither Cockneys nor African-Americans needed to learn *th*-fronting from another country. The *th* sound is probably the hardest sound to pronounce in English (which is why it's one of the last sounds for children to get right). So it's not uncommon for English speakers to do something or other to *th* to make it easier to pronounce. Only so many solutions are available for this problem. The sound can go forward to the *f/v* position in the mouth, backward to the *s/z* position, or it can "harden" into *t* or *d*. These are common phonological processes, and they can turn up anywhere. But while *th*-fronting is spreading in the UK, it doesn't seem to be spreading in the US.

American and British vowels are moving apart too, though they are difficult to discuss briefly, since changes are ongoing in many regions of both countries. But if we take Received Pronunciation as one case study and compare it to the inland north of the US (which includes Chicago and my own Rochester, New York, accent), the vowels are going in different directions.[41] While the vowel in *bit* has been moving higher in the mouth in RP, it's been going lower in northern-cities American, getting closer to *bet*. For the Queen, the *u* in *but* seems to be heading lower in the mouth, towards the vowel in *bat*, but for my American family it's headed backwards in the mouth, toward the sound in *bought*. Our sounds seem to repel each other.

Exposure to American English makes some southeastern Englanders jump to conclusions about unfamiliar regional forms. For instance, I saw a local advertisement in Birmingham suggesting that you *treat your mom* to some pampering. Someone had defaced it with a "correction" to *mum*, presumably because *mom* was seen as an American incursion. But *mom* is the traditional form in parts of the West Midlands, where Birmingham is. *Mom* and other British regionalisms are nowadays more willing to make themselves known because speakers of regional Englishes are "less ready to defer to the upper-class and country-wide norm."[42] *Yod*-dropping, a name for not saying a *y* sound before *u* in words like *suit* or *news* ("nooz" instead of "nyooz"), is another American-like pronunciation that didn't have to come from America. It's found in several dialects of England. In some of them, yod-dropping goes even further than in America: saying *few* as "foo" and *beautiful* as "bootiful," as in a traditional Norfolk dialect.

Pop-music accents are often raised as evidence of successful American accent imperialism. Again, the truth is not so straight-forward. Sometimes British singers sound American not because they want to, but because the melody neutralizes some of their accent features.[43] For instance, some complex London vowels are difficult to sustain in long notes, so they get simplified to more American-like sounds. "You can't sing something like 'Tracks of My Tears' in a London accent," says Billy Bragg (who should know). "The cadences are all wrong."[44] Some British singers, in some songs, do "put on" an American accent, often to match a particularly American genre of music. But if we're going to get het up about that, then we should also take the time to notice that Americans do the same in the reverse. Brandon Flowers' imitation of his musical heroes' accents meant that many British listeners thought the Killers were an English band, rather than a Las Vegas one. The American pop-punk sound has a definite London lilt. "I'm an American guy faking an English accent faking an American accent," says Billie Joe Armstrong of Green Day.[45]

Today in the UK, authenticity is the key, and so the trend is toward more local UK accents. Alex Turner of the Arctic Monkeys sounds like someone from Sheffield (and when he doesn't, he's given hell for it).[46] Lily Allen sounds like a Londoner. A range of particularly British musical styles, most recently grime music, have emerged with particularly British-sounding voices, whether they be from London, Birmingham, Manchester, or Cardiff.[47] British hip-hop artist Sway reports that American audiences thinks he raps "like Harry Potter," but he'll keep at it because "I feel so British, and it's a great selling point."[48]

If our accents aren't coming together, what about individual word pronunciations? This is something that Jonnie Robinson, the British Library's curator of spoken English, paid attention to when collecting over ten thousand recordings of Britons speaking in 2010–11. He concluded that for pronunciations "British English, for whatever reason, is innovating and changing, while American English remains very conservative and traditional," as we've seen for *controversy* and *garage*.[49] Two words whose British pronunciations do seem to be converging with the American are *schedule* and *privacy*. In both cases, American English can't take all the blame. British kids don't hear *schedule* much—certainly not as much as American children do—because British English uses the words *timetable* and *programme* more.[50] If you don't hear *schedule* but come across it in writing, it would be natural to interpret the *sch* as in *scheme* or *school*. Rather than chiding young people for talking "like Americans," perhaps "shedule"-loving Brits should stop saying *timetable*, so that youngsters will hear the *sh* pronunciation more often.

While it's easy to perceive "*pry*-vacy" as American in contrast to "privvacy," that pronunciation has long existed in the UK and was even the preferred pronunciation in the *Oxford English Dictionary* during the 20th century. But as use of the word has rocketed in the internet age, people tend to come across it in writing. Those who learn the word from print might reasonably assume that *privacy* sounds like *private*.

More than any other part of language, pronunciations reveal our identities. We find comfort in hearing ones like our own. We feel we're being "fake" if we try on another. Accents are changing, but they're still with us because we still need them—not just to show who we are, but to show who we aren't. For that reason, we can expect that Americans and Brits (and northerners and southerners, and English and Scots . . .) will sound different for as long as we see ourselves as distinct from the others.

Same difference

Above all, remember that many Americans read *The Economist* because they like to read good English. They do not want to read prose loaded with Americanisms.

The Economist Pocket Style Book (1986)[51]

The physical distance between North America and Britain was a key factor in our Englishes drifting apart. Communication and travel technologies seem to reduce that distance because we can see and hear each other more often. But their effect on language is still limited because we acquire language from the people we interact with, and most Americans and Britons still interact mostly within their own countries. Our children don't learn English from the television or the internet—they learn it from their families. As they get older, they may be more influenced by the music or the video games of another country, but the people they're really trying to sound like are more local—the cool kids in the next school year up. You might impress them with your ability to throw a few cool transatlantic words around, but you can't impress them by mimicking people from another country, because to do so would make you seem phony. Even if you wanted to, you couldn't, since your exposure to the other nationlect is not immersive enough to allow all the words, meanings, structures, and connotations to transfer unscathed from one country to another.

Besides distance, strong national identities were a key factor in getting our Englishes as different as they have been. As Americans became more secure in their identity as American English speakers, standards of spelling, pronunciation, and grammar were allowed to shift from the British-English model. Standard British English hadn't felt the pressure of an external English until recently. And now that that there is pressure from the American side, we sometimes see British English recoiling from it.

I am not the kind of person who likes to predict the future. I can't tell you what anyone is going to sound like in a hundred years, which words will fall out of fashion, or which punctuation mark will suddenly become popular. But I am willing to assert that as long as national identity is important to us, our languages will differ. As long as people want to feel American or British, they're going to want to sound American or British. And since we generally establish our own identity by contrasting ourselves with those who are like us but not us, sounding American is going to involve not sounding British, and sounding British is going to involve not sounding American. Accent is the most obvious place for this to happen, as differences in accent allow us to communicate with each other while still strutting our local stuff. But I wouldn't put it past us to maintain many other differences—our slangs, our preferences for particular phrasings, our minor yet emblematic spelling variations.

It's not a given that national identities will remain as important to our personal identities as they are now. If geography and national borders become less a factor in individual identity, other identities—political, cultural, sexual—might take a heightened role in determining how we want to talk and be heard. But in the short-to-medium term, nationalism does not seem to be going anywhere, and so we shouldn't expect nationlects to go away either.

10

BEYOND BRITAIN AND AMERICA

I have undertaken the prophesy that English will be the most respectable language in the world, and the most universally read and spoken, in the next century, if not before the close of this.

John Adams (1780)[1]

In his book *Globish*, the British journalist Robert McCrum describes a 21st century in which English no longer belongs to the native speaker from the UK or the US. It is a *lingua franca*, a language used throughout the world to bring people together in business, in education, in entertainment, in diplomacy.

The American century is the essential precursor to the Globish millennium. It was a two-stage process. First, there was the worldwide development of a common print culture, in which American language and cultural values became widely available. Secondly, the IT revolution and its infinity of data globalized these resources while at the same time splicing them with a multiplicity of competing traditions.[2]

But the essential precursor to that essential precursor is the British Empire. There would be no American English without it—and yet it is often erased from discussions of the spread of English in the 20th century. English would not have become a global success if the British hadn't planted its seeds far and wide. Today over sixty countries, most with British colonial pasts, have English as an official language.[3] No continent is English-free, even Antarctica. And on every continent, it was the British who first deposited English, not Americans. British spelling has a far greater geographical claim than American, and it's sometimes claimed that people in former British colonies "speak British English." Really, they speak their own English. But it's fair to say that Commonwealth Englishes are closely related to British English.

English's spread around the world is rooted in British imperialism, but postwar English learning in Europe and East Asia has more to do with the size and influence of the US than with Britain. The English that's being spread is not necessarily American English, however. While American economic power, media, and consumer goods were raising the profile of the English language in the 20th century, the UK was making the language an export product. The British Council, for instance, was founded by the British Foreign Office in the 1930s to promote British culture (and thereby fight fascism). This has increasingly meant, as Prince Charles has described it, ensuring "that English (and that, to my way of thinking, means *English English*) maintains its position as the world language."[4]

While Americans are good at exporting, they haven't cared as much about exporting their language, content to piggyback on British linguistic expansionism. For instance, British dictionary publishers put a large proportion of their resources into making dictionaries for learners of English as a foreign language (in fact, that's the only kind of dictionary that some UK publishers now produce). American dictionary makers have come very late to that party, if they've bothered to show up at all. When the Iron Curtain opened and China liberalized, the British dictionaries were there, ready to sell to new, large markets of English learners.

English testing is another linguistic export. The tests are required for entry to many English-speaking schools, universities, and workplaces, as well as for immigration to some countries. The British Council–founded International English Language Testing System (IELTS) was taken by 2.9 million people in 2016.[5] The American equivalent, the Test of English as a Foreign Language (TOEFL), probably does at least as much business (they choose to remain mysterious about this), but IELTS scores are accepted as evidence of English ability by more organizations.[6] Other British organizations, including Pearson educational publishers and Cambridge English, contribute to and compete in the testing and test-preparation market. The US has five times as many English speakers as Britain and an economy six times the size of the UK's. Considering these measures, the UK seems to have a disproportionate share of the language-export market.[7]

The vocabulary of English teaching (and teacher training) in the two countries reveals their historical situations and differing current attitudes. In the UK, people talk mostly about EFL: English as a Foreign Language. In the US, it's ESL: English as a Second Language.[8] Many "British teachers use EFL as a blanket term whereas many US teachers use ESL" for both domestic and foreign language learners.[9] The UK terminology gives a clearer sense of English as an export product—the English learner is framed as foreign, not British. In the US, with its history of immigration and linguistic integration, the terminology does not place learners of English abroad. Despite its reputation for cultural imperialism, the US just doesn't have much interest in proselytizing English. Pew Research described this mind-set:

> Americans are accused of believing "Aren't we great? Do as we do!" In reality, they are far more likely to say, "We think the American way is great; we assume you want to be like us, but, if you don't, that's really not our concern."[10]

In contrast, it's the British discourse of global English that regularly describes the language in terms a missionary might use to describe the word of God. English is "the UK's greatest gift to the world," according to the British Council's director of English and exams,[11] and "the greatest legacy the English have bequeathed the rest of humanity," according to broadcaster Jeremy Paxman.[12]

British institutions that export English have a clear awareness of the differing importance of English nationlects in other parts of the world. At the same time, by referring to these nationlects, they feed the presumption that "real English" is native-speaker English. Part of IELTS's marketing strategy is to make clear that they accept "all standard varieties of native-speaker English, including North American, British, Australian and New Zealand English." The British learner dictionaries are fairly good at presenting and marking American usages. The American institutions seem less concerned about pointing out national differences. While TOEFL accepts British spellings and presents a few non-American accents in its listening tasks, its marketing does little to inform test takers about this. One way to see this is that the English-promoters from Britain are more worldly, more generous in their definition of "English," while the Americans are more parochial, with only one English (theirs) coming to mind when they talk about English testing. But another way to see it is that TOEFL is mostly a test for people in or coming to North America to study or work. America is a big enough pull for its test; it doesn't need to push its influence beyond that in an attempt to stake a claim on English as a whole.

Which is to say, if there is an international English arms race (do I mean a *tongues race*?), it's not terribly clear that American English is putting up a fight. But is it winning anyway?

Which English rules the waves?

America won the world by winning it over.
Peter Conrad, *How the World Was Won* (2014)[13]

Globally more people now speak English as a second (or third or fourth or seventh) language than speak it as their first. This should make talking about "British" and "American" English less relevant—it's a global language that works beyond borders. Nevertheless, the nationlect terms remain important to many. At the very least, a spelling system needs to be chosen—and whether or not *favo(u)rite* has a *u* is most often described as "British" versus "American" spelling. Students and teachers around the world debate which English is better to learn, speak, or write, inspired in no small part by the "native is best" discourse of English teaching and English testing. The testing organizations tell students that they can take the tests in whichever "native" English they like, but test coaches emphasize the firmness of the nationlect categories: "You should not change between American and British English," says one. "If you try to switch, your language will just be confusing to the listener or reader. Use one or the other; don't mix."[14]

This means that learners of English are meant to be conscious about which English they're aiming for and which one they're getting. I look back at my school experience of learning Latin American Spanish with a Puerto Rican twist and my teacher's Brooklyn accent, and I wonder at that expectation. Still, learners often express strong preferences about British versus American English. In a 2014 market research survey by Pearson English, American English came out ahead in student preferences. Seeing as their poll was conducted in only twelve countries, including just one Commonwealth member (India) and the US itself (but not the UK), this is not a particularly surprising result. But though American English came out ahead in East Asian and Latin American countries, British English did better in Turkey, India, and Poland. (Germany and Russia were too close to call.) British English was most popular among those under twenty-five years old—indicating that American popular culture is not enough to win the hearts and minds of young language learners.[15]

Learners often express strong feelings about British and American accents, and even talk up one by disparaging the other, much like British and American folk do. The stereotypes are familiar: British (RP) as "high class" or "snobbish," American as "cool" or "show-off."[16] But despite the willingness to stereotype, it's all just English when you're learning it. In one rather typical study, less than a third of students learning English in Oregon could identify a recorded local accent as American.[17] The easiest English for most learners to understand is the English of people who talk like them—with the same kind of non-native accent. Anyone who's ever aced a French class with an Anglophone teacher, then struggled to understand even six-year-olds in Paris, knows what I'm talking about.

In countries where English has a long history as a language of education, media, or government, people are increasingly willing to acknowledge a local standard English. For instance, in a 2002 study, about two-thirds of English-language students in India, Pakistan, and South Africa wanted to sound like they were from their own country, rather than aiming to sound British or American.[18] Other studies, from Nigeria and Singapore, reveal similar feelings (among students at least; English teachers, as you probably know, often have very conservative ideas about language).[19] Immigrants to the UK or US may want their accents to blend in (particularly if their ethnic group is discriminated against), but where English has made a home abroad, there's every reason for the people to want to speak their own English—just as happened over the generations in the United States. Even where English does not have a long history, people are making it their own. In Norway, for example, sociolinguists Ulrikke Rindal and Caroline Piercy interviewed English-learning adolescents about their language-learning aims. A "large minority" said they would rather have a "neutral" accent—to "be thought of as someone who knows the language," rather than trying to pass for British or American. (The others were split between 34% who aimed for British and 41% who preferred American.)[20]

This gives us even more Englishes to enjoy, but at the same time internationalization creates pressures for English to homogenize. It's fine if you're speaking Nigerian English to other Nigerians, but if you have to converse with people from China and France—who learned and speak English with a different accent—using Nigerian English is not going to be terribly efficient. When we want to communicate, we try to adjust our language to make ourselves understood. And so people in the English education and language planning fields talk more and more about "Global English," "English as an International Language," or "English as a Lingua Franca," a form (or, more reasonably, a range of forms) of English used for intercultural communication. Lingua-franca English might use a smaller range of vocabulary. It might tend toward more literal language. It might be slightly slower and more enunciated. Talk of such things makes some worry that we'll all be speaking the same way someday, that English will be reduced to its lowest common denominator.

But the existence of English as an international lingua franca does not entail that national or local Englishes are going to go away. Arabic might provide a reasonable comparison. Modern Standard Arabic is the language of Al-Jazeera television, newspapers, and books. It's a pan-regional version of Arabic, but it's not everyday Arabic. The colloquial Arabics differ to the extent that "a rural Moroccan and a rural Iraqi cannot have a conversation and reliably understand each other. An urban Algerian and an urban Jordanian would struggle to speak to each other."[21] Arabic is in this position because it has different roles to play in different contexts. So has English. And among the speakers of English around the world, new ways of Englishing emerge.

Brits and Americans aren't very good at taking part in International English. The monolingualism of the typical native English speaker is a factor. Not having much experience at communicating in a second language, Brits and Americans tend to speak to English learners just the same as they would to native speakers, or to exaggerate their speech in some unhelpful, unnatural way. International English is happy to go on without us. In fact, International English might be better off without us. As one intercultural communication trainer told the BBC:

> often you have a boardroom full of people from different countries communicating in English and all understanding each other and then suddenly the American or Brit walks into the room and nobody can understand them.[22]

The more that people from Africa, Asia, Europe, and Latin America can talk with each other in English, the less they need Britain and America as any kind of go-between. Korean Airlines "reportedly chose a French supplier for its flight simulators because its 'offshore' international English was more comprehensible and clearer than that of the UK competitor."[23]

Native speakers in Britain and the US make the mistake of thinking they have no language learning to do: everyone speaks English, so we've got it made. This monolingual monomania stands to leave our countries sidelined from the very benefits our language has brought us in the postwar era. International students studying English in the UK and US now will go back to their countries and train the next generation of English teachers there. The UK language export market will shrink while English grows.[24] If the 19th century was the British century and the 20th the American century, perhaps the 21st is the English language's century.

At the moment, English looks too big to fail. Even Britain's exit from the European Union is not enough to shift the linguistic balance toward the former language of diplomacy, French. The world has invested heavily in English education, and it wants return on that investment. That's not to say that English will always be in that position. But for the moment, there are no clear up-and-comers waiting in the wings to replace it. While that may feel good for us English-native speakers, like our language is "winning," we've got to let go of that. The Englishes of the European Union, the Chinese boardroom, the Korean flight school—they're not ours to claim. But that shouldn't stop us from admiring those Englishes and learning to communicate with their speakers.

English doesn't need saving

English? Who needs that? I'm never going to England!

Homer Simpson[25]

My daughter was born in 2007. Shortly into my maternity leave, I had to cancel my subscription to *New Scientist*. Reading about climate change, the precariousness of the world economy, and horrific viral epidemics left me with too many mental images of my child fighting for survival in an apocalyptic world. With that kind of context, I do not care whether her generation or the next use the subjunctive, how they spell *colo(u)r*, or whether they pronounce the *r* at the end of it. Instead I worry very much about those people who fill the radio airwaves and the newspaper columns with their worries about the future of the English language. If they have time for that worry, then they're not worrying properly about the things that need worrying about. Great thinkers don't worry about which vowels or which words the next generation will use—busybodies do.

The English of the future isn't our English; it's our children's and our grandchildren's. What's British to them might be American to us, and vice versa. There's an expiration date on the annoyance of a pension-aged Englishman who complains that British children say *poop* rather than *poo*[26] or of an American fulminating against the use of *nil* in sports scores.[27] Those new incursions are only new incursions for as long as people perceive them as new; for people who've grown up with them, they're just English. Few Brits today would take linguistic offense if someone's heart *raced* (mid-1800s US), and Americans wouldn't think it unduly British to *brunch* (late-1800s UK). The two countries have enriched the language we share, while keeping distinct identities.

Our Englishes will continue to grow and change in ways that bring us together. But for as long as our sense of identity derives in part from our nationality, we can also expect corrective measures that push our Englishes apart. As long as an English accent helps road trippers get out of US speeding tickets, there will be British tourists in America "going the full Hugh Grant," as an Englishman I know claims to do. (I am hoping he just means the speech style, and not the other activity that Grant was once arrested for in America.) For as long as there are Brits who don't want to be mistaken for Americans or Americans who don't want to be mistaken for Brits, our vowels and our colloquialisms will serve as our identity badges.

But our Englishes being different doesn't mean we have to be chauvinistic about them. We don't have to devalue one to value the other. We shouldn't guard them jealously from contamination. English deserves our love. But it doesn't deserve our worry. We should let it go and see where it takes us. It may be a small world, but English is a big language.

NOTES

1. The Queen's English, Corrupted

1 The English language deterioration in usage. 1979 (Nov 21). House of Lords debate. *Hansard* vol. 403, cc156–96. http://hansard.millbanksystems .com/lords/1979/nov/21/the-english-language-deterioration-in -1#S5LV0403P0_19791121_HOL_162 [April 8, 2017].

2 Engel 2010.

3 Engel 2011.

4 Stevens 2012.

5 Singh Kohli, Hardeep. 2008 (Nov 7). The influx of Americanisms in British English. *The Times.* http://www.thetimes.co.uk/tto/arts/books /article2453530.ece [April 1, 2017].

6 HRH Charles, Prince of Wales, speaking at the British Council, reported in the *Chicago Tribune*, April 7, 1995.

7 Humphrys, John. 2007 (Sept 24). I h8 txt msgs: How texting is wrecking our language. *Daily Mail.*

8 Watson 2004, cover.

9 Visser, Wessel. 2009. The credit crisis has its roots in Main Street, not Wall Street. *Clarity* 62. http://clarity-international.net/journals/62.pdf [April 1, 2017].

10 Call for debate on children's TV. 2007 (Oct 3). *BBC News.* http://news .bbc.co.uk/1/hi/uk/7025301.stm [April 1, 2017].

11 Wilde 1894.

12 @Queen_UK on Twitter. 2014 (June 11). https://twitter.com/queen_uk /status/476630784108134400?lang=en [Aug 11, 2017].

13 Trevelyan 1912, p. 5.

14 Obama, Barack and David Cameron. 2012 (March 12). The U.S. and Britain still enjoy special relationship. *The Washington Post.*

15 Conversation reported by Dr. T. Campbell in 1781, in Boswell 1791, vol. 2, fn. 923.

16 Schulte Nordholt 1986, p. 9.

17 In an 1842 letter to John Forster, quoted in Forster 1872, p. 357.

18 Mencken 1922, p. 22.

19 Chancellor 1999, p. 4

20 Cited in Mencken 1921, p. 48.

21 Jefferson 1787, p. 70.

22 Bryson 2004.

23 Pew Research Center. 2014. *Global attitudes and trends*. http://www .pewglobal.org/database/indicator/1/ [April 8, 2017].

24 Letter from Pat Bynam, published in *Waitrose Food Illustrated*, July 2006.

25 Frankel, Eddy. 2015 (Aug 16). Top five worst sounds in London. *Time Out*. http://www.timeout.com/london/blog/top-five-worst-sounds-in -london-081615 [April 1, 2017].

26 Blinder, Scott. 2014. *UK public opinion toward immigration: Overall attitudes and level of concern*. (Briefing paper.) The Migration Observatory, University of Oxford.

27 Stevens 2012.

28 Booth, George. 2015 (Oct 28). For a country bereft of butchers . . . they've certainly butchered our language. *Press and Journal* (Aberdeen). https:// www.pressandjournal.co.uk/fp/lifestyle/lifestyle-columnists/735373 /george-booth-country-bereft-butchers-theyve-certainly-butchered -language/ [April 1, 2017].

29 British children "turn to American English." 2012 (May 29). *BBC News*. http://www.bbc.co.uk/news/entertainment-arts-18247748 [April 8, 2017].

30 Cheerio pussy cat, hi there awesome English. 2014 (Aug 26). *The Telegraph*. http://www.telegraph.co.uk/news/newstopics/howaboutthat/11055412 /Cheerio-pussy-cat-hi-there-awesome-English.html [April 1, 2017].

31 Wherever dates for words or other expressions are given, the source is the online *Oxford English Dictionary* (as it appeared at the time of writing).

32 Everything is awesome: It's cheerio to some old faves as Britain bows to the rise of American English. *Cambridge News*, Aug 28, 2014.

33 British spelling sometimes suffers because of the loss of the /r/ after vowels, a pronunciation change that has slowly spread through England over more than 500 years. Since people no longer hear the *r*, they sometimes leave it out of the written form, as in *draw(er)s*. It then reappears in places where it shouldn't, such as in a discussion on the Mumsnet site about where to find a "green Parker with an oversized hood"—that is to say, a *parka*.

34 Peanut butter sales up as marmalade falls from favour. 2013 (March 27). *BBC News*. http://www.bbc.co.uk/news/uk-21953090 [April 1, 2017].

35 Khan, Urmee. 2010 (April 4). BBC criticised for creeping "Americanisms." *The Sunday Telegraph*. http://www.telegraph.co.uk/culture/tvandradio /bbc/7553057/BBC-criticised-for-creeping-Americanisms.html [April 23, 2017].

36 BBC News 2011.

37 The number is approximate because some of the "Americanisms" are not words but changes to word meaning, and meanings are difficult to separate and count.

NOTES

38 Miller et al. 2015.

39 Witherspoon 1803, p. 181, cited in Longmore 2005, p. 281.

40 *Monthly Anthology, and Boston Review* 1809, pp. 263–4; quoted in Burkett 1979, pp. 130–31.

41 Orac. 2007 (Sept 3). Signs, signs, everywhere a sign... *Science Blogs*. http://scienceblogs.com/insolence/2007/09/03/signs-signs-everywhere-a-sign/ [April 1, 2017].

42 Jones 2001, p. 86.

43 Yagoda, Ben. 2011 (Jan 2). The elements of clunk. *The Chronicle of Higher Education*. http://chronicle.com/article/The-Elements-of-Clunk/125757/ [April 1, 2017].

44 English expatriates do this too. See Jones 2001.

45 Aristides 1997.

46 Reported in Jones's sociological study of English expatriates in the US: Jones 2001, p. 121.

47 Spotted in London, Feb 2016.

48 Wattenberg, Laura. 2015 (May 12). Survey reveals smartest baby names. *Baby Name Wizard* blog. http://www.babynamewizard.com/archives/2015/3/survey-reveals-smartest-baby-names [April 1, 2017].
      Wattenberg, Laura. 2015 (Feb 12). Survey reveals the most sophisticated names. *Baby Name Wizard* blog. http://www.babynamewizard.com/archives/2015/2/survey-reveals-the-most-sophisticated-baby-names [April 1, 2017].

49 Truss, Lynne. 2006. Books. *LynneTruss.com*. http://www.lynnetruss.com/pages/content/index.asp?PageID=76 [April 1, 2017].

50 Menand, Louis. 2004 (June 28). Bad comma. *The New Yorker*. http://www.newyorker.com/magazine/2004/06/28/bad-comma [April 1, 2017].

51 Harvey, Giles. 2011 (Aug 2). Original English. *The New Yorker*. http://www.newyorker.com/books/page-turner/original-english [April 1, 2017].

52 Lerner, Alan Jay. 1964. Why can't the English? [song lyric]. *My Fair Lady*. Columbia Pictures.

53 Sarah Palin tells immigrants to the US to 'speak American' [video]. 2015 (Sept 7). *The Guardian*. http://www.theguardian.com/us-news/video/2015/sep/07/sarah-palin-tells-immigrants-to-the-us-to-speak-american-video [April 8, 2017].

54 How many continents there are is a fraught question, dependent on historical, political, and geological factors. Anglophone countries generally use a seven-continent system: there is no continent called *America*, but two called *North America* and *South America*. (If we need to refer to both, they're *the Americas*.) France, Spain, and Portugal use a six-continent model, with one continent in the western hemisphere, *America*. *American* can seem more ambiguous and problematic for those who use that model.

NOTES

55 Some people use the term *RP* as if it refers to any relatively standard southeastern accent, but it can more specifically refer to a set of vowels and consonants that is associated with public (US = private) school education. Trudgill and Hannah (2013) estimate that only 3–5% of the UK population speak with true RP accents.

2. The Wrong End of the Bumbershoot: Stereotypes and Getting Things Wrong

1 Jaspistos. 1987 (Oct 2). Competition 1491. *The Spectator*. The winning contribution can be found at: http://archive.spectator.co.uk/article/3rd-october-1987/44/competition [April 3, 2017].

2 Horwill 1939, Moss 1991, Moore 1997.

3 Moore 1997.

4 Quoted in: Pullum, Geoffrey. 2013 (Nov 5). Was it really, Oscar? *Lingua Franca* (blog). *The Chronicle of Higher Education*. http://www.chronicle.com/blogs/linguafranca/2013/11/05/was-it-really-oscar/ [Aug 2, 2017]

5 Gonçalves et al. 2017.

6 The content of the law goes way back, but the name **Murphy's Law** is an American military-ism from the 1940s. The British equivalent, *Sod's Law*, has only been dated to 1970. Since I'm a Murphy and not a Sod (which comes from the word *Sodomite*), I'm sticking with the American version.

7 Bloomingdale, Hayley. 2016 (Feb 17). Britishisms 101: An American's guide to decoding British English. *Vogue*. http://www.vogue.com/13401276/britishism-dictionary-translating-american-british-english/ [April 3, 2017].

8 BBC News 2011.

9 Sidebar: You say lootenant, we say leftenant . . . two nations divided by a common language. 2011 (March 13). *Daily Mail*. http://www.dailymail.co.uk/news/article-1365751/How-British-English-Americanisms-ARENT-taking-language-research-shows.html [April 17, 2017].

10 Zatat, Narjas. 2016 (April). 41 things Americans say wrong. The Indy 100. *The Independent*. http://indy100.independent.co.uk/article/41-things-americans-say-wrong--WJC98FgggW [April 3, 2017].

11 Shaw, George Bernard. 1912. Preface to *Pygmalion*. Project Gutenberg edition. https://archive.org/stream/pygmalion03825gut/pygml10.txt [April 3, 2017].

12 Travis, Alan. 2016 (Jan 21). Homicides in England and Wales up 14%. *The Guardian* https://www.theguardian.com/uk-news/2016/jan/21/england-wales-homicides-rise-knife-gun-crime [Aug 5, 2017].

13 The claim is found in Heffer 2011 and 2014. In the *Corpus of Contemporary American English*, the ratio is 1899 *repetitive* to 214 *repetitious*; in *TIME*

302

magazine (since 2000) it's 19:2; in the *Corpus of American Soap Operas* it's 17:6 (Davies 2008–, 2007–, and 2011–, respectively).

14 Jones et al. 1981.

15 Mitchell 2010; Cleese, John. 2007 (Nov 29). A careless rant. *John Cleese's podcast* 18. https://www.youtube.com/watch?v=FpVpIaC6QrM [Oct 16, 2017].

16 *My* (then more often spelled *mi*) was pronounced like *me* before the Great English Vowel Shift, a seismic change in English long vowels that marks the boundary between Middle English and Modern English. Since the change only happened to long vowels, it's thought that in some dialect areas of England the vowel in *my* had shortened before the vowel shift got to those areas, and therefore their *me* [mi] pronunciation of *my* escaped unchanged.

17 Haigh, Chris. n.d. 30 awesome British slang terms you should start using immediately. http://www.lifehack.org/articles/communication/30-awesome-british-slang-terms-you-should-start-using-immediately.html [Aug 11, 2017].

18 Lottie Mullan sings "Would you be so kind." 2011 (Oct 20). *The Delete Bin.* https://thedeletebin.com/2011/05/12/lotte-mullan-sings-would-you-be-so-kind/ [April 3, 2017].

19 @minifiliawarde on Twitter. 2017 (July 10). https://twitter.com/minfiliawarde/status/884523970481008640 [Aug 8, 2017].

20 Yagoda, Ben. 2011. *Not One-Off Britishisms.* https://britishisms.wordpress.com/ [April 8, 2017].

21 Yagoda, Ben. 2011 (Sept 20). The Britishism Invasion. *Slate.* http://www.slate.com/articles/life/the_good_word/2011/09/the_britishism_invasion.single.html [April 8, 2017].

22 Sherman, Robert B. and Richard M. Sherman. 1968. Me Ol' Bamboo [song]. In *Chitty Chitty Bang Bang,* United Artists.

23 Angell, David and Peter Casey. 1994. My coffee with Niles. *Frasier,* season 1, episode 24. National Broadcasting Company.

24 Yagoda, Ben. 2011 (Nov 4). Cheerio *Bumbershoot! Slate.* http://www.slate.com/articles/life/the_good_word/2011/11/bumbershoot_it_means_umbrella_but_it_s_not_british_for_umbrella.html [April 30, 2017].

25 Lavine, Harold and James Wechsler, *War propaganda and the United States* (1940), cited in the OED entry for *bumbershoot.*

26 Barry, Dave. 1990 (Dec 16). On the loose in London. *The Baltimore Sun.* http://articles.baltimoresun.com/1990-12-16/features/1990350149_1_london-underground-week-in-london-british-person [April 18, 2017].

27 Inman, Matthew. ©2016. Minor differences, part four. *The Oatmeal.* http://theoatmeal.com/comics/minor_differences4 [Aug 2, 2017].

28 The film provides subtitles: "Is this true? If you were aroused, why didn't you pleasure yourself?" *Austin Powers in Goldmember.* 2002. USA: New Line Cinema.

29 Webb 2011, p. 135.

30 Fry, D. B. 1947. The frequency of occurrence of speech sounds in Southern English. *Archives Néerlandaises de Phonétique Experimentales*, 20. Cited in Crystal 1995.

31 Winter-Hébert, Lana. n.d. 75 simple British slang phrases you should probably start using. *Lifehack*. http://www.lifehack.org/articles/lifestyle/simple-british-slangs-you-probably-should-start-using.html [March 30, 2017].

32 Ilson 1990, p. 37.

33 Boyle, Darren. 2015 (March 23). It's Late Late Showtime for James Corden. 2015. *MailOnline*. http://www.dailymail.co.uk/news/article-3007460/The-stars-don-t-want-sit-couch-producers-nervous-viewers-won-t-eyes-James-Corden-makes-debut-host-Late-Late-Show.html [April 8, 2017].

Goldhill, Olivia. 2015 (March 23). A blagger's guide to British slang: Charming or bonkers? *The Telegraph*. http://www.telegraph.co.uk/news/celebritynews/11490076/A-blaggers-guide-to-British-slang-charming-or-bonkers.html [April 3, 2017].

Harlow, John. 2015 (March 22). One man, two guv'nors, no slang, please. *The Sunday Times* (London), p. 3.

34 Advertisements for Cottonelle, Newcastle Brown Ale, and Budweiser, respectively.

35 Radford, Ceri (writing as Constance Harding). 2012 (March 29). A guide to help Americans speak the Queen's English. *The Telegraph*. http://www.telegraph.co.uk/culture/books/9174003/A-guide-to-help-Americans-speak-the-Queens-English.html [April 8, 2017].

36 Jonnie Robinson, quoted in: Copping, Jasper. 2011 (Feb 5). The "conTROversy" over changing pronunciations. *The Telegraph*. http://www.telegraph.co.uk/news/newstopics/howaboutthat/8305645/The-conTROversy-over-changing-pronunciations.html [April 8, 2017].

37 It's rare to see arguments in favour of "garridge" but the BBC tried—for a while. The 1931 edition of the BBC *Pronunciation Guide* says:

> *Garage* has been granted unconditional British nationality, and may now be rhymed with *marriage* and *carriage*. There are people who maintain that this is an uneducated pronunciation; but if the word is ever to become an English word—and it is difficult nowadays to do without it—then it must shed its foreign "zh" ending.

By the 1935 edition, the more French(ish) pronunciation had reasserted itself (Pointon 1988).

38 Denison 2007, p. 122.

39 In the *Corpus of Global Web-Based English* (Davies 2013a), the UK/US numbers are, respectively: *might* of 672/392; *would* of 1634/926; *could* of 821/458; *should* of 683/442. I discuss this at more length at: http://

separatedbyacommonlanguage.blogspot.co.uk/2016/02/might-of-would
-of-could-of-should-of.html [April 8, 2017].

40 As of August 2017, Twitter still divides English into "English" and "English
UK (British English)." When I drafted this chapter in spring 2016, "whom
to follow" was visible on the profile page when preferences were set
to English UK. (I learned of the difference from editor Tom Freeman,
aka @snoozeinbrief.) The screenshot I took of "whom to follow" was,
unfortunately, not of sufficient quality to be reprinted here.

41 *Train_drops* blog. https://www.facebook.com/train_drops-4001637
90096768 [April 8, 2017].

42 The correction read:

> Last Saturday's profile contained this: 'Gawker published a post
> about a married media executive from a rival firm, whom it alleged
> had solicited a gay porn star for sex.' Whom had solicited a gay porn
> star? No, of course not.

Keleney, Guy. 2016 (March 26). Errors & Omissions: Mistakes—we've made
a few, but not too few to mention. *The Independent.* http://www.independent
.co.uk/voices/comment/errors-omissions-mistakes-we-ve-made-a-few
-but-not-too-few-to-mention-a6952516.html [April 3, 2017].

43 Hutchinson, John. 2015 (June 18). Why THIS PICTURE upsets
Brits. *MailOnline.* http://www.dailymail.co.uk/travel/travel_news
/article-3128430/Why-picture-upset-Brits-Survey-reveals-UK-tourists
-prudes-beach-won-t-entertain-going-commando-highly-likely-offended
-partners-went-topless.html [April 3, 2017].

44 Pinker, Steven. 1994 (April 5). The game of the name. *The New York Times.*

45 54% of American versus 64% of British lavatorial leave-takings involve
formulae like "I'm going to go to the ___," according to Levin 2014.

46 Davies, Caroline. 2010 (Aug 31). I want to spend a penny, not go to the shop:
Nurses to be taught euphemisms. *The Guardian.* http://www.theguardian
.com/society/2010/aug/31/foreign-nurses-taught-english-euphemisms
[April 8, 2017].

47 Fairman 1994.

48 I counted words starting with *cock* in the vicinity of the word *hen(s)* in the
GloWBE corpus (Davies 2013a). Once I took out ones that didn't refer to
chickens (e.g. the *hen parties* with their *cocktails*), there were 21 *cocks*, 10
cockerels and 1 *cock-bird*, which seems another way to avoid referring to a
male organ. That is to say, British folk seem to be avoiding *cock* at least half
the time.

49 Mitchell 2010.

50 Though such numbers are often bandied about in discussions of Shakespeare's
greatness, about 60% of those "Shakespearean coinings" have been found in

earlier documents (Shea 2014). Even if Shakespeare was the first to *write down* some of those words, he may well have learned them by listening to other people speak.

51 Massie, Allan. 2012 (May 29). There's nothing wrong with Americanisms: It's management-speak that is the enemy of English. *Telegraph Blogs*. [last viewed Sept 15, 2015; no longer on *Telegraph* site]

52 Ivory, Chris, Peter Miskell, Helen Shipton, Andrew White, Kathrin Moeslein, and Andy Neely. 2006. *UK business schools: Historical contexts and future scenarios*. Summary report from an EBK/AIM Management Research Forum. Advanced Institute of Management Research.

53 Allport 1979.

54 See Kövecses 2000, chapter 17.

55 The published list had 20 most despised businessisms, but number 4, "all of it," does not seem to be a businessism. I would guess that when asked what business jargon they hate, some respondents replied, "All of it," i.e. 'All business jargon.'

   Simpson, Aislinn. 2008 (Nov 28). "Thinking outside the box" is most despised business jargon. *The Telegraph*. http://www.telegraph.co.uk/news/newstopics/howaboutthat/3532338/Thinking-outside-the-box-is-most-despised-business-jargon.html [April 18, 2017].

56 According to a search of the *Corpus of Global Web-based English* (Davies 2013a). Included in my counting are hyphenated and hyphen-less spellings.

57 Don't brainstorm, take a "thought shower." 2008 (June 20). *Metro*. http://metro.co.uk/2008/06/20/dont-brainstorm-take-a-thought-shower-204354/ [April 8, 2017].

58 Quoted in Webb 2008, p. 14.

59 Hargis, Toni. 2015 (Aug 19). In quotes: What do Brits think about Americans? *Anglophenia*. BBC America. http://www.bbcamerica.com/anglophenia/2015/08/19/in-quotes-what-do-brits-think-about-americans/ [April 8, 2017].

60 @GlennyRodge on Twitter. 2016 (Sept 28). https://twitter.com/glennyrodge/status/781028828839833601 [April 8, 2017].

61 Based on a search of *The Times* newspaper archive.

62 Table of American and British English words. n.d. *Textfiles.com*. http://www.textfiles.com/fun/brittish.txt [April 8, 2017].

   Lieberman, Becca. 2015 (Aug 14). Just British things: An American's perspective. *Verge*. http://vergemagazine.co.uk/just-british-things-an-americans-perspective/ [April 8, 2017].

   Brown, Laurence. 2015 (Jan 9). 12 American words and phrases beginning with "H" not widely used in the UK. *Lost in the Pond*. http://www.lostinthepond.com/2015/01/12-american-words-and-phrases-beginning.html#.VsZeSBhi9b0 [April 8, 2017].

UK Terminology Supplementum. n.d. *Harry Potter Places.*
harrypotterplaces.com/tips/UKterminology.pdf [April 8, 2017].
British Terms: Miscellaneous. n.d. *Dumka.us.* http://www.dumka.us
/BritEng.html [April 8, 2017].
English language varieties. n.d. *wiki voyage.* https://en.wikivoyage.org
/wiki/English_language_varieties [April 3, 2017].
63 Rubenstein 2006.

3. Separated by a Common Language?

1 Culpeper 2005, p. 84.
2 Taps also replace the /r/ sound between vowels in some British Englishes. You sometimes see *dd* as an attempt to represent (and mock) it, as in *veddy teddible* for 'very terrible.' This tap has mostly died out in Received Pronunciation, but lives on in some parts of Scotland and the north of England (and in Ireland as well).
3 This pronunciation difference is restricted to a set of adjectives from French whose vowels changed in British. For nouns like *reptile* or *textile*, *-ile* is pronounced the same in the US and UK. Even among the adjectives it's an irregular difference. For instance, both countries prefer the "aisle" pronunciation for *infantile* and "ill" for the last syllable of *imbecile* (though a more French-like "eel" pronunciation is also possible in British).
4 Berg 1999, p. 126.
5 Algeo 2006, p. 2.
6 Bolinger 1998, p. 54.
7 Banana bread. *Betty Crocker.* http://www.bettycrocker.com/recipes/banana-bread/51427396-6764-4b0a-a73a-78c683c703d2 [April 18, 2017].
8 Banana bread. *BBC Food.* http://www.bbc.co.uk/food/recipes/bananabread_85720 [April 18, 2017].
9 From the *Corpus of Contemporary American English* (Davies 2008–).
10 @paulmcmc on Twitter. 2016 (May 17). https://twitter.com/paul_mcmc/status/732472428031442949 [Aug 2, 2017].
11 Lane Greene, language columnist at *The Economist* and fellow American in Britain, once pointed out to me that in two randomly chosen *Economist* articles (about 1,400 words), he could find only one Britishism (*make a fist of*). So British and American English can't be *that* different, right? I responded by picking the first article off the *Brighton and Hove News* website, which happened to be about a *doctor's surgery* (US *doctor's office*) moving. The article was 635 words long and had, by my count, 17 Britishisms (not counting repetitions). These had to do with property (US *real estate*), local government structures, building work (US *construction work*), and simple things like the surgery being *in* a street rather than *on* it.

NOTES

12 Ruette, Ehret, and Szmrecsanyi 2016.

13 Martin, Katherine. 2017. A multidialect model for monolingual dictionary data. Paper presented at the 21st Conference of the Dictionary Society of North America, Barbados, June 9–11.

14 Both Landau's and Ilson's figures are cited in Ilson 1990.

15 *Light verb* is a grammatical term for verbs that are fairly empty of meaning, but which support the use of an action noun in a sentence. So, for example, **to take a look** and **to have a look** mean much the same thing as *to look*. Nothing is really 'taken' or 'had.'

16 See Johnson 2006 for insightful and entertaining discussion of obituary language.

17 Pareles, Jon. 2016 (April 21). Prince, an artist who defied genre, is dead at 57. *The New York Times*. http://www.nytimes.com/2016/04/22/arts/music/prince-dead.html [April 18, 2017].

18 Italie, Hillel, Nekesa Mumbi Moody, and Jeff Baenen (Associated Press). 2016 (April 22). Pop superstar Prince, 57, visionary who transcended genres. *The Boston Globe*. https://www.bostonglobe.com/metro/obituaries/2016/04/21/pop-superstar-prince-dies-his-minnesota-home-age/8btYydwVriZVwp2gTCHaYK/story.html [April 18, 2017].

19 Khatchatourian, Maane and Andrew Barker. 2016 (April 21). Prince found dead at 57. *Variety*. http://variety.com/2016/music/news/prince-dead-dies-1201758325/ [April 18, 2017].

20 Prince—obituary. 2016 (April 21). *The Telegraph*. http://www.telegraph.co.uk/obituaries/2016/04/21/prince--obituary/ [April 18, 2017].

21 Sweeting, Adam. 2016 (April 21). Prince obituary. *The Guardian*. http://www.theguardian.com/music/2016/apr/22/prince-obituary [April 18, 2017].

22 Obituary: Prince. 2016 (April 21). *BBC News*. http://www.bbc.co.uk/news/entertainment-arts-36107155 [April 18, 2017].

23 Anonymous. 1815. Essay on American language and literature. *North American Review and Miscellaneous Journal* 1, 307–14, p. 309.

24 Letter to John Waldo Monticello, Aug 16, 1813. *The letters of Thomas Jefferson*. http://www.let.rug.nl/usa/presidents/thomas-jefferson/letters-of-thomas-jefferson/jefl221.php [April 18, 2017].

25 **Deputize** did occur in the 2nd edition of Nathan Bailey's *Dictionarium Britannicum* in 1736, but there is not much evidence of it being used in Britain. John Pickering's *Vocabulary* of Americanisms (1816) claims that it was sometimes heard in England, but not written. There **depute** was preferred.

26 Görlach 1991 provides a statistical analysis of vocabulary growth in Early Modern English.

27 U.S. Bureau of the Census. 1975. *Historical statistics of the United States, colonial times to 1970*, Bicentennial edn. Washington, DC.

28 **Devil**: *deule, de'ule, diuell.* **Dew**: *daew, deaw, dew, dewe* (Queiroz de Barros 2007).

29 Historian C. P. Stacey described the War of 1812 as "an episode in history that makes everybody happy." Canada thinks of it as a nation-defining moment. In the US, it is glorified as the "second war of independence." But "the English are happiest of all, because they don't even know it happened" (Stacey 1964, p. 331).

30 Webster 1789, p. 20.

31 Ibid.

32 Ibid., p. 397.

33 Sweetland, James H. 2001. *Fundamental reference sources*, 3rd ed. Chicago: American Library Association, p. 264.

34 Letter to Edmund Jennings, Sept 23, 1780. In Adams 1852, vol. 9, p. 509.

35 See Metcalf 2004.

36 Review of *A philosophical and practical grammar of the English language* by Noah Webster. In *Monthly Anthology and Boston Review*, May 1, 1808, p. 277.

37 Letter to W. Strahan, Nov 29, 1769, in William Temple Franklin (ed.) 1819, *The posthumous and other writings of Benjamin Franklin*. London: Harry Colburn, p. 401.

38 British Airways. 2017. Spanish: https://www.britishairways.com/es-es/information/atom/food-and-drink/special-meals. Portuguese: https://www.britishairways.com/pt-pt/information/atom/food-and-drink/special-meals. US English: https://www.britishairways.com/en-us/information/food-and-drink/special-meals. UK English: https://www.britishairways.com/en-gb/information/food-and-drink/special-meals [Aug 22, 2017].

39 Pickering 1816, p. 10.

40 Webster 1789, pp. 22–3.

41 Gooskens 2007.

42 Laird 1970, p. 195.

43 The origins of African-American Vernacular English continue to be debated. Is it a creole, with features of West African language? Or are its particular grammatical properties reflective of British northern dialects brought to the American South? As evidence is gathered, increasingly it points toward England.

44 "C." 1800. On the scheme of an American language. *Monthly Magazine and American Review*, III (July), 1–4.

45 de Tocqueville 1840, p. 68.

46 Particularly George P. Knapp's *The pronunciation of Standard English in America* (1919).

47 Webster 1790, p. xi.

48 Given the uninspired updates of Johnson's dictionary available at the time, American dictionaries indeed sold well in Britain. But when the Merriams advertised to Americans that *The Times* of London called Webster's the "best and most useful Dictionary of the English language ever published,"

they declined to mention that the praise was in a paid advertisement for the dictionary itself.

49 Roane, A. 1860. Worcester's and Webster's Dictionaries. *Debow's Review* 28(5), 566–73.

50 Channing 1856.

4. America: Saving the English Language Since 1607

1 Mencken 1921, p. 608.

2 Crashaw in Whitaker 1613, p. A2.

3 Marckwardt 1958, p. 80.

4 Beck 1830, p. 26.

5 Ibid., p. 29.

6 Fowler and Fowler 1908, p. 24.

7 Study catches two bird populations as they split into separate species. *Science Daily*, July 30, 2009. https://www.sciencedaily.com/releases/2009/07/090714104000.htm [April 20, 2017].

8 The Obama and Thiessen examples are quoted in: Green, Jeff. 2014 (June 4). "Period. Full stop" is the new "at the end of the day." *Bloomberg News*. http://www.bloomberg.com/news/articles/2014-06-04/-period-full-stop-is-the-new-at-the-end-of-the-day- [April 18, 2017].

9 *Huffington Post*, May 24, 2011. Cited on Ben Yagoda's *Not One-Off Britishisms* blog: https://britishisms.wordpress.com/2011/06/08/full-stop/ [April 18, 2017].

10 McCutcheon, Chuck and David Mark. 2015 (July 22). How "full stop" got to be the new "period" in Washington. *Christian Science Monitor.* http://www.csmonitor.com/USA/Politics/Politics-Voices/2015/0722/How-full-stop-got-to-be-the-new-period-in-Washington [April 18, 2017].

11 Norris 2015, p. 95.

12 183 *autumn leaves* versus 53 *fall leaves* in COCA (Davies 2008). In the *TIME* magazine corpus (Davies 2007–), *autumn leaves* occurs 45 times and *fall leaves* only once.

13 In Pownall's *Topographical account of the middle British colonies in North America*, London 1776, p. 44; cited in Beck 1830, p. 29.

14 Letter in *The Mirror* (Edinburgh) by Mary Muslin No. 96, April 8, 1780, p. 383. Quoted in Read 1980, p. 16.

15 Fall foliage is worth billions to New England's economy. 2014 (Oct 20). *Mashable* (Associated Press). http://mashable.com/2014/10/20/fall-foliage-tourism/#GLeFVb6vDqq7 [April 18, 2017].

16 Spring forward, fall back. *The Phrase Finder*. http://www.phrases.org.uk/meanings/spring-forward-fall-back.html [April 18, 2017].

17 *The Druid* 1781, reprinted in Witherspoon 1802, p. 463.

NOTES

18 In Freeman 2009, p. 121.

19 Sante, Luc. 1995 (Jan 30). Smart city. *New York Magazine*, 34–7, p. 34.

20 *The Economist* 2010, p. 130.

21 In Kemble 1890.

22 It's possible that the 'heed' sense of *mind* survives in the US because waves of Irish immigration brought people who still used it. But if that were the case, we'd expect it to be much more prevalent in the areas of the US with heavy Irish immigration, such as the Northeast. That doesn't seem to be the case.

23 Wells 1996.

24 Lord Adam Gordon, traveling through the colonies 1764–65, on Philadelphia. Cited in Read 1980.

25 Cresswell 1924, p. 271.

26 Read 1938, pp. 73–6.

27 Brockett 1829.

28 1994 (July 5). House of Commons debate. *Hansard* vol. 246, cc150–5.

29 Rosengarten, Theodore. 1974. *All God's dangers: The life of Nate Shaw*. New York: Knopf.

30 Mitchell 2010.

31 Smith 1866.

32 Quoted in Pickering 1816, p. 156.

33 In the *News on the Web* corpus (July 25, 2016; Davies 2013b) the American past participle form is *proven* by a 2:1 margin, and the British is *proved* by nearly a 3:1 margin. In the passive, *proven* is much stronger in both countries, preferred in the US by nearly 5:1, and roughly equal with *proved* in the UK. The adjective has gone more decisively in the direction of *proven*—it would be rare to hear a noun phrase like *a proved remedy* in either country now.

34 Pickering 1816, p. 156.

35 Hundt 2009, pp. 22–4.

36 Engel 2010.

37 Whibley 1908, p. 119.

38 Hundt 2009, p. 21.

39 In Freeman 2009, p. 86.

40 American English still has *have got* as well as *have gotten*. This allows for a distinction that British English has lost. If an American says *I've got a cake*, it means she has a cake. If she says *I've gotten a cake* it means she's acquired a cake. Both these interpretations are folded into *got* in British.

41 F. Th. Visser's *An historical syntax of the English language* (4 vols., 1963–73), as cited in Burchfield 2004, p. 746.

42 Fowler and Fowler 1908, p. 154.

43 In the *Frown* corpus, according to Serpollet 2001, p. 541.

44 For more on these hypotheses, see Kjellmer 2009. The final suggestion, that subjunctive was a case of "colonial lag" in some regional dialects, is the least

likely of the bunch. If that were the case, we'd expect to see the subjunctive in informal writing, e.g. personal letters, but there's little evidence of that.

45 Blount 2008, p. 8.

46 Corbett, Philip B. 2008 (Oct 13). Subjunctivitis. *After Deadline.* http:// afterdeadline.blogs.nytimes.com/2008/10/13/subjunctivitis/ [April 18, 2017].

    Corbett, Philip B. 2009 (Sept 29). Save the subjunctive! *After Deadline.* http://afterdeadline.blogs.nytimes.com/2009/09/29/save-the -subjunctive/ [April 18, 2017].

47 Williams, Patricia J. 1998 (June 15/22). Invictus. *The Nation,* p. 10.

48 Amis 1997, p. 260.

49 Westbrook, Caroline. 2016 (March 9). This schoolboy's letter to Justin Bieber correcting his grammar in hit song Boyfriend has gone viral. *Metro.* http://metro.co.uk/2016/03/09/this-schoolboys-letter-to-justin -bieber-correcting-his-grammar-in-hit-song-boyfriend-has-gone-viral -5743173/#ixzz4ekEsZyNg [April 18, 2017].

    Giordano, Chiara. 2016 (March 9). Justin Bieber told off by British schoolboy for his poor grammar and letter goes viral. *Mirror.* http:// www.mirror.co.uk/3am/celebrity-news/justin-bieber-told-british -schoolboy-7526102 [April 18, 2017].

50 Williams, Zoe. 2015 (Sept 11). Brewsters are women; brewers are men: Inside the micropub world. *The Guardian.* https://www.theguardian .com/lifeandstyle/2015/sep/11/brewsters-women-brewers-men-inside -micropub-world-dancing-man [April 18, 2017].

51 Stockwell, Tom. 2015 (Sept 7). How to piss off a Brit. http://matadornetwork .com/abroad/how-to-piss-off-a-brit/3/ [April 18, 2017].

52 Hundt 2009, but I'm afraid I must take responsibility for the twerking and the lambada.

5. More American, More Ænglisc?

1 In the First Hundred Years' War (1337–1453), the House of Plantagenet in England sought to expand their territories in France, with varied success and ultimate failure. The Second Hundred Years' War (1689–1815) was a series of loosely connected conflicts that concerned, variously: religion, power and trade in the New World, French republicanism, and, finally, Napoleon's invasive empire.

2 Tombs and Tombs 2006.

3 Wilson 1533.

4 Meritt 1940. Since *cross* was borrowed from French way back in the 1300s, it probably didn't strike Cheke as a borrowing.

5 Dickens 1858, p. 1.

6   Anderson, Poul. 1989. Uncleftish beholding. *Analog Science Fiction/Science Fact* 109(13), 132–5.

7   Orwell 1946.

8   Coulmas 1994.

9   Scholfield 1994.

10 I've seen British copy editors lop all the *-ue*'s off *-ogue* words in the belief that they were Americanizing the text. But only one *-og(ue)* word is found more often in its shorter form in American English: *catalog*. *Dialog* is common in the computing term *dialog box*. Ignoring that usage, Americans prefer the *dialogue* spelling by a margin of 38 to 1 (in Davies 2008–). *Prologue, epilogue,* and *pedagogue* are similarly more often found in their longer forms in America.

11 Cited in Horobin 2013, p. 203.

12 Izzard, Eddie. 1999. *Dress to Kill* (stand-up performance). Vision Video.
    Some Brits seem to think that **thru** is standard US spelling. It is not, despite attempts to make it so. *Thru* is used where space is at a premium—on signage or road markings or in tweets—but not in spelling tests or newspaper articles. The fast-food term of art *drive-thru*, however, has the abbreviated spelling as standard.

13 Comprehensive list of American and British spelling differences. http:// www.tysto.com/uk-us-spelling-list.html [April 15, 2017].

14 Ball, Nick. n.d. How Collins differs. *North American SCRABBLE® Players Association.* http://www.scrabbleplayers.org/w/How_Collins_differs [April 15, 2017].

15 The æ in "encyclopædia" might look like the respectably Old English letter ash (æ), but ash had been removed from English spelling long before Modern English speakers started importing such words from classical languages.

16 The British *oe* seems like it's doing something at the beginnings of words, since there the British and American versions are pronounced differently in their respective countries: British **oestrogen**, for example, has the *even* vowel ("eestrogen"), while American **estrogen** has the *etch* vowel. But British English doesn't actually need the *oe* spelling to signal the "ee" pronunciation, since other Latin-derived words that start with just *e* get the "ee" pronunciation for many British speakers, including *evolution* and *ecological* ("eevolution" and "eecological").

17 Napier, L. Everard. 1952. The correct spelling of medical terms (Letter to the Editor). *The Lancet* vol. 260, pp. 885–6.

18 See my blog: http://separatedbyacommonlanguage.blogspot.co.uk /2015/05/foetus-and-foetal-and-bit-on.html.

19 Bolton, Barry. 2008, 2013. *NHS Choices Editorial Style Guide.* http://www .nhs.uk/aboutNHSChoices/aboutnhschoices/Aboutus/Documents/NHS -Choices-Editorial-Style-Guide-V3.pdf [April 15, 2017].

NOTES

Bolton, Barry. 2014. *Foetal/Foetus vs Fetal/Fetus*. Internal document, NHS Choices. (Received with thanks from the author.)

20 Farley, Christopher John. 1997 (June 9). Not Nirvana: Foo Fighters offers up an uneven second album. *Time*, vol. 149.

21 In the interest of having just three groups, I've included some arguable cases. *Enamo(u)r* is a borrowing from French that did not exist in Latin, but it is derived from Latin *amor*, so I have put it with the "Latin" cases. The French *saveur* derived from the Latin *sapor*, showing the same relation between Modern French *-eur*, Old French (and British English) *–our*, and Latin (and American English) *-or*. *Parlo(u)r* and *savio(u)r* have equivalents only in postclassical Latin. There they have an *-or* but also more syllables than the borrowed French word: *parlatorium* and *salvator*.

22 Eden, Terence. 2014. *Shakespeare's Honor. Terence Eden's Blog.* https://shkspr.mobi/blog/2014/12/shakespeares-honor/ [April 15, 2017].

23 Wesley 1826, p. 225.

24 English didn't take *arbor* from Latin, though John Ash believed it had and therefore spelled it *u*-lessly. English had borrowed the French word *herbier*, referring to a lawn, and its form was anglicized into *herbor, herber*, or *herbour*. The *h* was never pronounced, and its meaning extended over time to include gardens and orchards. At that point, scribes probably started confusing it with the Latin word and "borrowed" its spelling.

25 About his more radical spelling reform agenda, Webster (1789, p. 397) wrote: "Such a reform would diminish the number of letters about one sixteenth or eighteenth. This would save a page in eighteen; and a saving of an eighteenth in the expense of the books, is an advantage that should not be overlooked."

26 @enanram on Twitter. 2013 (Jan 7). https://twitter.com/enanram/status/288094104536096768 [April 15, 2017].

27 Humphrys 2004, p. 135.

28 This number is surely inflated by the fact that the earlier OED editors were happier to include neologisms than later ones were. Still, I mention the large number because many people seem to think of *-ize* suffixation as a 20th-century thing.

29 That hasn't stopped words with *-ize* being singled out as horrible Americanisms—from **jeopardize** in the early 1800s to **alphabetize** as one of the BBC's "noted" Americanisms in 2011. Both are first found in 17th-century Britain.

30 In spelling, Americans distinguish **vise**, 'a tool for gripping,' from **vice**, 'sin, crime,' though they are pronounced the same. British uses *vice* for both. Unusually in this case, the American spelling is more French than the British. The name of the tool comes from the French word *vis*, while *vice* comes from the French *vice*.

31 Ishikawa 2011, using data from the *Collins Bank of English*.

32 This study is based on the *Collins Bank of English* corpus, on which Collins dictionaries are based. Studies of other data sets don't show as steep a decline, but they do show a reversal in preference and end up at about the same place in the mid-1990s. For instance, examining the spelling of ten words in the British National corpus, Mäki (2015, p. 41) found 71% -*ize* in the period 1960–74. By 1985–93, it was down to 31%.

33 Hepworth, David. 2012 (March 8). Why do Americans pronounce non-English words in such a pretentious way? *David Hepworth's Blog*. http://whatsheonaboutnow.blogspot.co.uk/2012/03/why-do-americans-pronounce-non-english.html [April 15, 2017].

34 "BwanaBob." 2003 (Aug 29). British pronunciation of "foreign" words. *Straight Dope Message Board*. http://boards.straightdope.com/sdmb/archive/index.php/t-207928.html [April 15, 2017].

35 In Spanish, the pronunciation of *ll* varies a lot, both across dialects and across words. It can range from a bit like the English "y" sound to something more like "sh." American pronunciations of it, unsurprisingly, are closer to Latin American than European.

36 Orwell 1941.

37 "A Gentleman." 1836. *The laws of etiquette; or, short rules and reflections on conduct in society*. Philadelphia: Carey, Lea, and Blanchard. http://www.gutenberg.org/ebooks/5681?msg=welcome_stranger [April 15, 2017].

38 Pronunciation. n.d. *Debretts*. http://www.debretts.com/debretts-a-to-z/p/pronunciation/ [April 15, 2017].

39 Hall-Lew, Coppock, and Starr 2010.

40 Matevi. 2009 (May 27). PSA: The entree comes before the main course (a small rant about language). *Ars Technica Openforum*. http://arstechnica.com/civis/viewtopic.php?f=23&t=60130 [April 15, 2017].

41 Reed, Jessica. 2015 (March 13). The battle to keep French pure is doomed. *The Guardian*. https://www.theguardian.com/commentisfree/2015/mar/13/the-battle-to-keep-french-pure-is-doomed [April 20, 2017].

42 (My translation.) Statuts et reglements. n.d. Académie Française. http://www.academie-francaise.fr/linstitution/statuts-et-reglements [April 20, 2017].

43 Les missions. n.d. Académie Française. http://www.academie-francaise.fr/linstitution/les-missions [April 15, 2017].

44 This is not to say that the Académie has forgotten about repressing local languages. They vehemently opposed constitutional protection for regional languages (including Alsatian, Breton, Corse, and Basque) in 2008, on the grounds that supporting regional languages is damaging to the unity of the nation.

45 Carrère d'Encausse, Hélène. 2013 (Dec 5). À la reconquête de la langue

française. Académie Française. http://www.academie-francaise.fr/la
-reconquete-de-la-langue-francaise [April 15, 2017].

46 d'Ormesson, Jean. 2012 (April 5). Depuis sa fondation en 1635. Académie
Française. http://www.academie-francaise.fr/depuis-sa-fondation-en-1635
[April 15, 2017].

6. Logical Nonsense

1   Bierce 1911, p. 80.

2   As far as I know, this pun is from: @ahuj9 on Twitter. 2011 (Sept 16).
https://twitter.com/ahuj9/status/114745724457074688.

3   Discussed at http://separatedbyacommonlanguage.blogspot.co.uk/2006
/08/tarp-or-tarpaulin.html.

4   Levin 2001, pp. 165–9. The American data came from *The New York Times*
and the *Longman Spoken American Corpus*. The British data came from *The
Independent* and the spoken portion of the *British National Corpus*.

5   Hundt 2009.

6   Levin 2006.

7   Bock et al. 2006.

8   In *NoW: News on the Web Corpus* (Davies 2013b) [Sept 5, 2016].

9   Blunden, Mark. 2012 (Aug 1). Back on home ground: US-based athletes
make the most of competing in London. *The Evening Standard*. http://www
.standard.co.uk/olympics/olympic-news/back-on-home-ground-us-based
-athletes-make-the-most-of-competing-in-london-7998602.html [Aug 8,
2017].

10 Interview: Matt Johnson. 2015 (March 22). *The Big Issue* (London).

11 Quoted in: Tett, Gillian. 2012 (Aug 31). National Identity? Do the math(s).
Financial Times. https://www.ft.com/content/cefe59ca-f238-11e1-bba3
-00144feabdc0 [April 16, 2017].

12 "cmacis." 2007 (May 1). A little rant (math vs. maths). *xkcd* forum. http://
forums.xkcd.com/viewtopic.php?t=4747 [April 16, 2017].

13 Heffer 2014, p. 208.

14 Heffer, Simon. 2016 (March 19). Happy St Patrick's Day to Gerry Adams.
The Telegraph. http://www.telegraph.co.uk/news/worldnews/europe
/ireland/12199040/Happy-St-Patricks-Day-to-Gerry-Adams.html [April
16, 2017].

15 Roxbee Cox, Harold. 1979 (Nov 21). The English language: Deterioration
in usage. House of Lords debate. *Hansard*. vol. 403, cc124–37. http://
hansard.millbanksystems.com/lords/1979/nov/21/the-english-language
-deterioration-in [April 16, 2017].

16 McAlpine, Fraser. 2015 (Feb 10). 10 American words you'll never hear a
British person say. *Anglophenia*. BBC America. http://www.bbcamerica

.com/anglophenia/2015/02/10-american-words-youll-never-hear-british
-person-say [April 16, 2017].

17 Calvert, James. 2002 (Nov 7). Aluminium. *Physics* [personal website].
http://mysite.du.edu/~jcalvert/phys/alumin.htm [April 16, 2017].

18 Wolfram and Schilling-Estes 1998.

19 Heffer 2011, p. 209.

20 Browne, John [former chief executive of British Petroleum]. 2015 (Oct
14). If I ruled the world: John Browne. *Prospect Magazine*. http://www
.prospectmagazine.co.uk/regulars/if-i-ruled-the-world-john-browne [April
16, 2017].

21 Heffer 2014, under "nouns, as verbs."

22 From the online edition of the OED, as it was in September 2016. I chose
these particular initial letters somewhat randomly: they were the first letters
of the surnames of the people sitting closest to me at the time.

23 Franklin, Benjamin. 1828. Letter to Noah Webster. Reprinted in *Lapham's
Quarterly*. http://www.laphamsquarterly.org/communication/proofreading
[April 16, 2017].

24 Rose 2014, p. 113.

25 Meddling with nouns: Who's medalling now? 2012 (Aug 10). *Oxford
Dictionaries*. http://blog.oxforddictionaries.com/2012/08/meddling-with
-nouns-whos-medalling-now/ [April 16, 2017].

26 Zimmer, Ben. 2012 (Feb 10). Downton Abbey: Tracking the anachronisms.
Word Routes. *Visual Thesaurus*. http://www.visualthesaurus.com/cm
/wordroutes/downton-abbey-tracking-the-anachronisms/ [April 16, 2017].

27 Business Diary: A crack in Lego's brick wall. 2010 (Sept 14). *The Independent*.
http://www.independent.co.uk/news/business/news/business-diary-a
-crack-in-legos-brick-wall-2079411.html [April 16, 2017].

28 Heffer 2014: "nouns, as verbs."

29 Gowers, Greenbaum, and Whitcut 1986, p. 184.

30 Heffer 2014, p. 164.

31 Humphrys 2004, p. 117.

32 BBC News 2011.

33 Pearce, Anthony. 2014 (July 4). A pedant's guide to annoying Americanisms.
BT.com. http://home.bt.com/news/uk-news/a-pedants-guide-to-annoying
-americanisms-11363916866278 [April 16, 2017].

34 I searched the *Friends* scripts as published on the fan website *Lives in a Box*:
http://www.livesinabox.com/friends/scripts.shtml [June 18, 2016].

35 Yagoda, Ben. 2011 (March 8). A coffee. *Not One-Off Britishisms*. https://
britishisms.wordpress.com/2011/03/08/a-coffee/ [April 16, 2017].

36 Quoted in Engel 2010.

37 In Murphy and De Felice 2018, we show that British requests—at least in
email—are rather more formulaic than American ones.

38 Amis 1997, p. 87.

39 Trudgill (2003) lists *have* instead of *have got* as a clear example of American grammatical influence on British English.

40 Anthony Burgess, cited in Garner 2016, p. 420.

7. Lost in Translation

1 Juster, Norton. 1961. *The phantom tollbooth*. New York: Random House, p. 35.

2 Blair, Olivia. 2016 (June 24). David Cameron's most controversial moments as UK Prime Minister. *The Independent*. http://www.independent.co.uk /news/people/brexit-latest-news-david-cameron-resignation-uk-prime -minister-career-moments-a7100531.html [April 21, 2017].

   Chumley, Cheryl K. 2015 (Feb 10). U.K. cringes at David Cameron's slang—first 'chillax,' now 'chaterama'. *The Washington Times*. http://www .washingtontimes.com/news/2015/feb/10/uk-cringes-at-david-camerons -slang-first-chillax-n/ [April 21, 2017].

3 "Chael" (Michael Wagner). 2010 (Dec 17). frown. *Prosody.lab*. http:// prosodylab.org/2010/frown/ [April 21, 2017].

4 Full Emoji List, v5.0. 2017 (April 12). *Unicode.org*. http://unicode.org /emoji/charts/full-emoji-list.html [April 21, 2017].

5 Covered at my blog: https://separatedbyacommonlanguage.blogspot .co.uk/2014/09/twang.html [April 21, 2017].

6 Respectively: *Merriam-Webster* online, *American Heritage* (5th ed.), *Collins English Dictionary* online.

7 In the *GloWBE* corpus, Davies 2013a.

8 Hoggart, Simon. 2008 (April 5). Simon Hoggart's Week. *The Guardian*, p. 15.

9 Lawson 1970.

10 Kennedy 1958.

11 Powell, Enoch. 1968. Rivers of blood [speech]. Transcript available at: Enoch Powell's 'Rivers of Blood' speech. 2007 (Nov 6). *The Telegraph*. http://www.telegraph.co.uk/comment/3643823/Enoch-Powells-Rivers -of-Blood-speech.html [April 21, 2017].

12 Lawson 1970, pp. 304–5.

13 I use the scare quotes because the labels don't actually label races of humanity. They label the ways in which we behave *as if there are* races of humanity. We can tell that these "races" are as-if rather than fact because of the extreme culture-sensitivity of the terms. In each of the three English-speaking countries I've lived in, *black* has meant something different.

14 Dickerson, Debra J. 2007 (Jan 22). Colorblind. *Salon*. http://www.salon .com/2007/01/22/obama_161/ [April 21, 2017].

NOTES

15 Black History Month. n.d. *University of Glasgow Library.* http://www.gla
.ac.uk/services/library/collections/virtualdisplays/blackhistorymonth/
[April 10, 2017].

16 Okolosie, Lola, Joseph Harker, Leah Green, and Emma Dabiri. 2015 (May
22). Is it time to ditch the term 'black, Asian and minority ethnic' (BAME)?
The Guardian. https://www.theguardian.com/commentisfree/2015
/may/22/black-asian-minority-ethnic-bame-bme-trevor-phillips-racial
-minorities [April 22, 2017].

17 Numbers from *GloWBE* corpus (Davies 2013a). The "middle class" figure
(US 17,353, UK 9,229) includes hyphenated and plural forms, but the "the
middle class" figure does not.

18 Stewart and Bennett 1991, p. 89.

19 Brown, Anna. 2016 (Feb 4). What Americans say it takes to be middle class.
Pew Research Center. http://www.pewresearch.org/fact-tank/2016/02/04
/what-americans-say-it-takes-to-be-middle-class/ [April 21, 2017].

20 Huge survey reveals seven social classes in UK. 2013 (April 3). http://www
.bbc.co.uk/news/uk-22007058 [April 21, 2017].

21 Park, A., C. Bryson, E. Clery, J. Curtice, and M. Phillips (eds.). 2013. *British
social attitudes: The 30th report.* London: National Centre for Social Research.
http://www.bsa.natcen.ac.uk/media/1144/bsa30_key_findings_final.pdf
[April 21, 2017].

22 Lyall 2008, p. 195.

23 Aitkenhead 2007.

24 Mass Observation panel member, writing in 1948, quoted in Kynaston
2009, p. 145.

25 Aitkenhead 2007.

26 Palmer, Bobby. 2016 (Sept 27). How middle class you are, based on the
things you own. *The Tab UK.* http://thetab.com/uk/2016/09/27/can-tell
-middle-class-based-things-21120 [April 21, 2017].

27 Moore 2015, p. 19.

28 Faul 1994, p. 16; Miall 1993, p. 28.

29 There is some debate about the universality of positive and negative face.
Here, I'm following the basics of a politeness theory developed by Brown
and Levinson (1987).

30 de Tocqueville 1840, p. 506.

31 Hawley, Ellen. 2015 (Jan 16). Manners, American and British. *Notes from
the U.K.* http://notesfromtheuk.com/2015/01/16/manners-american
-and-british/ [April 21, 2017].

32 "Lisa Ng" commenting at Murphy 2012.

33 There may well be regional variations in this, but all the research to date
has compared at the national level. This means that even if some Americans
say *please* more than others, Americans on average say *please* a lot less than

Brits (Biber et al. 1999, p. 1098; Breuer and Geluykens 2007; Murphy and De Felice 2018).

34 "Wyndes" commenting at Murphy 2012.

35 Firmin et al. 2004; Vaughn et al. 2009.

36 Martin, Judith writing as "Miss Manners." 2013 (Oct 2). Miss Manners: Bribery is one way to ensure good behavior in a child. *The Washington Post.* https://www.washingtonpost.com/lifestyle/style/miss-manners-bribery -is-one-way-to-ensure-good-behavior-in-a-child/2013/09/13/7d2c5294 -1c96-11e3-8685-5021e0c41964_story.html [April 21, 2017].

37 "Alberon" and "Tom Lines" commenting at Murphy 2012.

38 Watts 2003.

39 Murphy and De Felice 2018.

40 All cited in Garner 2002.

41 Murphy 2015.

42 Algeo 2006, p. 212.

43 Biber et al. 1999, p. 1098; De Felice and Murphy 2017.

44 Smith 1984, p. 233. I've reformatted the quotation with numbers for clarity.

45 Hymes 1971, p. 69.

46 Hitchings 2013, p. 150.

47 Hollett, Vicki. 2010. The trickiest word in American. *Macmillan Dictionary Blog.* http://www.macmillandictionaryblog.com/the-trickiest-word-in -american [April 10, 2017].

48 Pilkington, Ed. 2007 (April 21). Exchange rate tourists hit the shops of New York. *The Guardian.* https://www.theguardian.com/money/2007 /apr/21/shopping.travel [April 21, 2017].

49 Churchill 1950, p. 609.

50 The *quite* problem only happens for gradable adjectives like these—that is to say, the type of adjective that describes a property that exists to greater or lesser degrees. When we use *quite* with absolute adjectives (where a thing has the property or doesn't), it's interpreted as meaning 'really' or 'exactly' in both nationlects: *quite right, quite dead. Quite* can be used in many other contexts too, modifying noun phrases (*quite a night*), verbs (*I didn't quite hear you*), and especially in the UK, as an affirmative response (*That was a bad idea. –Quite.*) I haven't got quite enough space to discuss them all, but in general *quite* is used considerably more in British English.

51 *Economist* 2010, p. 125.

52 Fox 2014.

53 Barkham, Patrick. 2008 (Oct 2). Comedy. *The Guardian.* https://www .theguardian.com/culture/2008/oct/02/comedy.television [April 21, 2017].

54 Conan show schedule. 2016 (March 16–22). *Team Coco.* http://teamcoco .com/schedule/2016-03-16 [April 21, 2017].

Jacobs, A. J. 2012. *Drop dead healthy.* New York: Simon & Schuster, p. 152.

Rifkind, Hugo. 2011 (Oct 19). I'm too busy to set up schools and regulate industries. Isn't that what governments are for? *The Spectator*. http://www .spectator.co.uk/2011/10/im-too-busy-to-set-up-schools-and-regulate -industries-isnt-that-what-governments-are-for-2/ [April 21, 2017].

55 Damp Squid: The top 10 misquoted phrases in Britain. 2009 (Feb 24). *The Telegraph*. http://www.telegraph.co.uk/news/uknews/4799157/Damp -Squid-The-top-10-misquoted-phrases-in-Britain.html [April 21, 2017].

56 Cruse 1986, p. 270.

8. The Standard Bearers

1 Irving, Washington. 1807. Letter from Mustapha Rub-a-dub Keli Khan, to Asem Hacchem. *Salmagundi* 1(7), 130–40, p. 132.

2 Education in the UK is devolved to the constituent countries—so England can be very different from or very similar to Northern Ireland, Scotland, or Wales, depending on which structures and regulations each has chosen. When talking about education, I stick to talking about England (though some of my points are true of other UK countries).

3 Thoreau, Henry David. 1860 (Feb 3). Journal entry. http://thoreau.library .ucsb.edu/writings_journals_pdfs/J15f4-f6.pdf [Aug 8, 2017].

4 McGovern, Derek. 2006 (Aug 18). *Daily Mirror*.

5 OECD. 2010. A family affair: Intergenerational social mobility across OECD countries. *Economic policy reforms: Going for growth 2010*, p. 185. http:// www.oecd.org/eco/growth/economicpolicyreformsgoingforgrowth2010 .htm [April 23, 2017].

6 North American English. *BBC Academy*. http://www.bbc.co.uk/academy /journalism/article/art20151004130954646 [April 24, 2017].

7 Milroy and Milroy 2012, p. 151.

8 Sampson, George 1925. English for the English. Quoted in Crowley 2003, p. 207.

9 Combs 1931, p. 125.

10 Reith, J. C. W. ca.1924. *Broadcast over Britain*. London: Hodder and Stoughton. Cited in Pointon 1988, p. 8.

11 Quoted in Hendy 2006, p. 83.

12 Quoted in: Viewer offered BBC's Steph McGovern £20 to 'correct' her northern accent. 2014 (Nov 25). *Media Monkey* (blog). *The Guardian*. https://www .theguardian.com/media/mediamonkeyblog/2014/nov/25/viewer-offered -bbcs-steph-mcgovern-20-to-correct-her-northern-accent [April 23, 2017].

13 Dowel, Ben. 2013 (July 15). "Too common for telly" BBC presenter lashes out at Corporation. *Radio Times*. http://www.radiotimes.com/news/2013 -07-15/too-common-for-telly-bbc-presenter-lashes-out-at-corporation [April 23, 2017].

14 This term has never been popular with linguists and increasingly Estuary features are found in what's called "Modern RP." A good introduction to changing RP sounds can be found (and heard) on the British Library's *Sounds Familiar* website: http://www.bl.uk/learning/langlit/sounds/find -out-more/received-pronunciation/ [April 23, 2017].

15 Rosewarne, David. 1984 (Oct). Estuary English. *Times Educational Supplement*, p. 19.

16 Maidment 1994, p. 7.

17 Bradbury, Malcolm. 1994 (Sept 1). Eschew the Estuary. *The Times*, p. 20.

18 Hardy, Rebecca. 2015 (May 23). I've got a northern accent but I'm not working class. So what am I? *The Guardian*. https://www.theguardian.com /commentisfree/2016/may/23/northern-accent-working-class-middle -class-northerner-barm-cake-john-lewis [April 23, 2017].

19 Powell, Keith. 2015 (Oct 13). "You talk white": Being black and articulate. *Huffington Post*. http://www.huffingtonpost.com/keith-powell/you-talk -white-being-blac_b_8284582.html [April 23, 2017].

20 Bonfiglio 2002, Labov 2012.

21 Quirk 1973, p. 76.

22 Gill 2012, p. 72.

23 Ibid., pp. 72–3.

24 *Plan of a Federal University* (1788), in Rush 1947, p. 102.

25 Monaghan 1988.

26 Sokoloff and Engerman 2000, p. 227.

27 Dwight 1823, p. 302.

28 Monaghan 2005, p. 243.

29 Librarian numbers are based on OCLC Global Library Statistics, according to which there is one public librarian for every 6,663 residents in the US and one for every 12,541 UK residents. The UK figure is slightly older than the US one (2009 versus 2013), but given the closing of libraries in the UK due to "austerity" measures, the gap is unlikely to have closed.

30 Kendall 2010.

31 Ellis 1979, p. 175.

32 Chrimes 1967, p. 42.

33 House of Commons, Political and Constitutional Reform Committee. 2014 (July). *A new Magna Carta?* HC 463, p. 24. London: Stationery Office, Ltd.

34 Kirchmeier and Thumma 2010.

35 The UK Supreme Court first sat in 2009, so I searched the decisions between then and the end of 2016, on https://www.supremecourt.uk/decided-cases /index.html [April 23, 2017].

According to the courts' respective websites, the US Supreme Court hears about 80 cases per year. In April 2015–March 2016, the UK Supreme Court heard 92.

36 House of Lords. 1997. *Investors Compensation Scheme v. West Bromwich Building Society*. UKHL 28.

37 Green 1999, p. 130.

38 Greenbaum, Meyer, and Taylor 1984.

39 *Merriam-Webster Collegiate Dictionary, American Heritage Dictionary, Random House Webster's College Dictionary, Webster's New World Dictionary.*

40 Why every American Christian home should have the Noah Webster 1828 Dictionary. n.d. *The Foundation for American Christian Education.* http://www.principleapproach.tv/Bookstore-Homepage/Why-Every-American-Home-1828_Dictionary.pdf [April 23, 2017].

41 James, Clive. 2006 (May). The continuing insult to the English language. *The Monthly.* http://www.clivejames.com/articles/clive/English [April 23, 2017].

42 Ostler 2015, p. 110.

43 Some 19th-century prime ministers didn't go to school—but only because their families were rich enough to employ personal tutors. The well-worn path to the prime ministry is so specific that one can make a good guess at any past PM's school (Eton, maybe Harrow), university and college (Christ Church, Oxford, or Trinity College, Cambridge), and even the degree programme (Classics in the 19th century or Philosophy, Politics and Economics in the 20th century). Margaret Thatcher may be the closest Britain has to a Lincoln-like tale of self-improvement, taking elocution lessons to improve her election chances. But with an Oxford education behind her, it was "feminine shrillness" rather than poor educational opportunities that she sought to overcome.

44 Corbett 1987, North 1987.

45 Hancock and Kolln 2010.

46 Braddock, Lloyd-Jones, and Schoeb 1963, pp. 37–8.

47 *The Newbolt report* (1921). Cited in Hudson and Walmsley 2005, p. 601.

48 Zandvoort, R. W. 1952. A critique of Jespersen's *Modern English grammar,* p. 2. Cited in Hudson and Walmsley 2005, p. 599.

49 Fisher 2001, p. 63.

50 Hauer 1983.

51 *Plan of a federal university* (1788). In Rush 1947, pp. 102–3.

52 Reed and Kellogg 1877.

53 If you'd like to make such beautiful creatures yourself, instruction is available at: http://www.wikihow.com/Diagram-Sentences [April 23, 2017].

54 *United States v Rentz*, 10th Circuit Court, 2015.

55 Cameron 1995, p. 94.

56 Both examples from the government's sample exam papers for Key Stage 2: Standards & Testing Agency. 2015 (July). English grammar, punctuation and spelling. Paper 1: Questions. *GOV.UK.* https://www.gov.uk

/government/uploads/system/uploads/attachment_data/file/439299 /Sample_ks2_EnglishGPS_paper1_questions.pdf [April 23, 2017].

57 American readers might relate this to the Common Core standards introduced in the US in 2010. But note that at the age when English children are expected to use terminology like *subordinate clause*, Common Core only requires that children are able to identify the difference between formal and informal texts. Common Core's goals focus on practicing general literacy and require no particular approach to knowledge about language.

58 Research on the value of any explicit teaching about grammar or writing is mixed, but certain methods offer some promising results. The mere presentation of grammatical information is not enough to improve anyone's writing or speech.

59 Stephen Fry at the Hay Sessions, 2009. *YouTube*. https://www.youtube .com/watch?v=tmVWDAE_hlM [April 23, 2017].

60 Merriam-Webster advertisement in *Time* magazine, Oct 6, 1961, p. 3.

61 Respectively from *The Atlantic, Life, Chicago Sun-Times, Toronto Globe and Mail*. Collected in Sledd and Ebbitt (eds.) 1962.

62 For a good read on the whole story, see Skinner 2012.

63 For more, see Morton 1994, chapter 12.

64 The *Oxford Dictionary of English* (not to be confused with the OED) has followed this US model somewhat, with usage paragraphs for "problematic" words and reliance on a "network of consultants" to make judgments. But it was only with the first edition (1998) that Oxford really advertised the more prescriptive aspects of their dictionary. After that, they hardly mentioned it, perhaps not feeling as comfortable taking on the authoritarian role as *American Heritage* did.

65 Leech et al. 2009, p. 148, using the *Brown* (1960s) and *Frown* (1990s) corpora.

66 Garvey 2009.

67 For example, Leech et al. 2009 and Pullum 2014.

68 Pinker 2014, p. 236.

69 Hinrichs, Szmrecsanyi, and Bohmann 2015, p. 820.

70 Cameron 1995, p. 55.

71 Hommerberg and Tottie 2007, pp. 50–1.

72 Brook and Tagliamonte 2016, p. 321.

73 *American Heritage Dictionary*, 5th ed.

9. *The Prognosis*

1 Letter to Edmund Jennings, Sept 23, 1780. In Adams 1852, vol. 9, p. 509.

2 Younge, Gary. 1996 (Oct 6). Black bloke. *The Washington Post*, p. C9.

3 Stewart, Ryan, and Giles 1985.

NOTES

4 Margolis, Ruth. 2013 (Nov). 8 instances when you should play up your Britishness in America. *Anglophenia*. BBC America. http://www.bbcamerica.com/anglophenia/2013/11/8-instances-when-you-should-play-up-your-britishness [April 18, 2017].

5 The female RP speaker scored fairly low in all categories in this study and the female American fairly high. Because the study had only one voice per accent, it's possible that something about the individual's voice or reading style affected the outcome. Then again, it's very common for the same vocal quality or intonation to be judged very differently in men and women, and that might be happening here.

6 Bayard et al. 2001.

7 Garrett et al. 2005.

8 Gill 2011 provides a very accessible review of the changing role of non-American accents on US television.

9 Dahlgreen, Will. 2014 (Jan 18). It's true! Americans love British accents! *YouGov.* https://yougov.co.uk/news/2014/01/18/its-true-americans-love-british-accents/ [April 18, 2017].

10 Anderson et al. 2007.

11 Stephen Fry at the Hay Sessions, 2009. https://www.youtube.com/watch?v=tk8R2O9ULvs [April 18, 2017].

12 Garrett, Williams, and Evans 2005.

13 I often hear the complaint that Americans talk about "British accents" in spite of the fact that Britain is made up of England, Scotland, and Wales. Well, it goes both ways—in this case, with "North American" standing for any number of accents. But because "North American" includes Canadians, it may have disposed Brits to give a more positive evaluation than if they had been asked about "American."

14 Coupland and Bishop 2007.

15 Engel 2017, order page at Profile Books. https://profilebooks.com/that-s-the-way-it-crumbles-hb.html [April 18, 2017].

16 Skapinker, Michael. 2013 (Jan 9). Thank America for saving our language. *Financial Times.* https://www.ft.com/content/2db09852-58eb-11e2-99e6-00144feab49a [April 18, 2017].

17 Twain 1897, chapter 24.

18 Mair 2006, p. 193.

19 Ibid., p. 17, discussing a 1986 article by Sidney Greenbaum.

20 Mair 2007.

21 For instance, Jenkins (2003) and Trudgill and Hannah (2013) both claim that *different than* is the normal form in American English, with *different from* the British form. But in the *Corpus of Contemporary American English* (Davies 2008–), *different from* outnumbers *different than* by almost four to one.

NOTES

22 Corbett, Philip B. 2009 (June 30) Red pencils ready? *After Deadline* (blog). *The New York Times.* http://afterdeadline.blogs.nytimes.com/2009/06/30/red-pencils-ready-3/ [April 18, 2017].

23 Marsh, David. 2014 (Nov 21). Journey to the center of the global English debate. *Mind Your Language* (blog). *The Guardian.* http://www.theguardian.com/media/mind-your-language/2014/nov/21/mind-your-language-center-or-centre [April 18, 2017].

24 Woolf, Virginia. 1925. American fiction. Originally published in *Saturday Review of Literature.* Reprinted in *The moment and other essays* (1947). http://gutenberg.net.au/ebooks15/1500221h.html [April 18, 2017].

25 Cambridge app maps the decline in regional diversity of English dialects. 2016 (May 26). *University of Cambridge.* http://www.cam.ac.uk/research/news/cambridge-app-maps-decline-in-regional-diversity-of-english-dialects [April 23, 2017].

26 Barber 1964, p. 101.

27 The one non-US/UK word was a scientific term first used in English in the Netherlands.

Butterfield, Jeremy. 2017 (April 21). "American" words in English: Where would we be without them? They own the bulk of the shares. *Jeremy Butterfield* (blog). https://jeremybutterfield.wordpress.com/2017/04/21/american-words-in-english-the-us-owns-the-bulk-of-the-shares/ [April 21, 2017].

28 Thirty words from each year. For the most part, I chose the words by selecting the 49th word on every page of 50 results. If the word began with a capital letter, cited only one quotation, or had a source whose authorship was not clear, I chose the next nearest one. For 1973, I could only get 24 items by this method, so I selected six more by flipping back to previous pages and taking one near the top of each of those.

29 For more on many of these examples, see Ben Yagoda's *Not One-Off Britishisms* blog: https://britishisms.wordpress.com.

30 Bell, Jack. 2012 (June 8). Not-one-off footballisms. Guest post on *Not One-Off Britishisms.* https://britishisms.wordpress.com/2012/06/08/not-one-off-footballisms/ [April 18, 2017].

31 Tan, Rebecca. 2016 (Feb 18). Accent adaptation. *The Pennsylvania Gazette.* http://thepenngazette.com/accent-adaptation/ [April 17, 2017].

32 Stuart-Smith et al. 2013.

33 Watt and Gunn 2016.

34 For example: Dart, Tom. 2016 (Feb 10). Y'all have a Texas accent? Siri (and the world) might be slowly killing it. *The Guardian.* https://www.theguardian.com/technology/2016/feb/10/texas-regional-accent-siri-apple-voice-recognition-technology [April 10, 2017].

35 SATURDAY COMPETITION: The Child Who Went to the "Talkies." *The Manchester Guardian,* Sept 17, 1930, p. 20.

NOTES

36 Hannisdal 2006, p. 195.

37 Badia Berrera 2015, pp. 199–200.

38 Wells 1982, p. 250.

39 Some dialects of American English use a glottal *t* too. My dialect has them before an /n/ sound, as in *mitten* and *button*. One study of /t/ concludes that, at the ends of words at least, "American English is moving toward a more British pronunciation" (Eddington and Taylor 2009, p. 311). Still, though Americans increasingly say *put up* as "pu' up" instead of "puddup," they aren't saying "bu'er." Yet.

40 Badia Berrera 2015, p. 204.

41 On changes to RP, see Harrington et al. 2000; Bauer 1985. On the Northern Cities Shift in the US, see Labov et al. 1997.

42 Wells 1999, p. 38.

43 Gibson 2010.

44 Quoted in: Crystal, David. 2009 (Nov 14). On singing accents. *DC Blog*. http://david-crystal.blogspot.co.uk/2009/11/on-singing-accents.html [Feb 14, 2017].

45 Nosowitz, Dan. 2015 (June 18). I made a linguistics professor listen to a Blink-182 song and analyze the accent. *Atlas Obscura*. http://www.atlasobscura.com/articles/i-made-a-linguistics-professor-listen-to-a-blink-182-song-and-analyze-the-accent [April 18, 2017].

46 For example: Michaels, Sean. 2014 (Jan 10). Wild Beasts take swipe at British bands who sing with US accents. *The Guardian*. https://www.theguardian.com/music/2014/jan/10/wild-beasts-british-bands-sing-us-accents-arctic-monkeys [April 10, 2017].

47 Drummond and Carrie 2017.

48 Quoted in: Topping, Alexandra. 2010 (July 13). First Dizzee Rascal, now the British urban scene is getting crowded. *The Guardian*. https://www.theguardian.com/music/2010/jul/13/british-urban-music-big-hits [April 18, 2017].

49 Quoted in: Hastings, Christopher. 2011 (March 13). How is your English? Research shows Americanisms AREN'T taking over the British language. *Daily Mail*. http://www.dailymail.co.uk/news/article-1365751/How-British-English-Americanisms-ARENT-taking-language-research-shows.html [April 18, 2017].

50 The News on the Web corpus (Davies 2013b; April 19, 2017) has nearly twice as many American *schedule*s as British ones. The *GloWBE* corpus (Davies 2013a) has about 1.5 American *schedule*s for every British one. Some of those British uses are Brits complaining about how Americans pronounce it.

51 Cameron 1995, p. 240.

NOTES

10. Beyond Britain and America

1 In a letter to Edmund Jennings. Adams 1852, pp. 509–10.

2 McCrum 2010, p. 190.

3 Fifty-five countries have English as a de jure official language. That doesn't count the UK, the US, Australia, or New Zealand, which have not made any language legally the official language. So in addition to counting the de jure official English, I include the de facto ones, according to Wikipedia: https://en.wikipedia.org/wiki/List_of_territorial_entities_where_English_is_an_official_language [April 13, 2017].

4 HRH Charles, Prince of Wales, speaking at the British Council, reported in the *Chicago Tribune*, April 7, 1995.

5 IELTS 2017.

6 IELTS reports that 10,000 organizations accept its results, making it the "world's leading test for international migration and higher education" (IELTS 2017). TOEFL reports that "more than 9,000" organizations accept its results (Educational Testing Service, n.d.).

7 It's fairly easy to find statistics on how much the English-language industry (or at least portions of it) contributes to the UK economy. I've not succeeded in finding such data for the US economy. This itself says something about their relative importance to their nations.

8 Different organizations may have different terms. *English as an Additional Language* (*EAL*) is also used in the UK. But *EFL* and *ESL* are, respectively, the most common British and American terms in the *GloWBE* corpus (Davies 2013a).

9 EFL or ESL? TEFL or TESL? *TEFL.net.* http://www.tefl.net/teaching/efl-esl.htm [April 23, 2017].

10 Kohut, Andrew and Bruce Stokes. 2006. The problem of American exceptionalism. *Pew Research Center.* http://www.pewresearch.org/2006/05/09/the-problem-of-american-exceptionalism/ [April 23, 2017].

11 Mark Robson, in: British Council. 2013. *The English effect.* Available at: https://www.britishcouncil.org/sites/default/files/english-effect-report-v2.pdf [April 18, 2017].

12 Paxman 1998, p. 234.

13 Conrad 2014, p. 322.

14 Fink, Lucas. n.d. American or British English on the TOEFL. *ABA Journal.* https://blog.abaenglish.com/american-or-british-english-on-the-toefl/ [April 18, 2017].

15 Zazulak, Steffanie. 2015. American English vs. British English. *Pearson English.* https://www.english.com/blog/inspiredtolearn-american-english-vs-british-english [April 19, 2017].

16 Malaysian students quoted in Kaur 2014. Similar stereotypes about the Englishes can be found in other studies from other parts of the world.

17 Scales et al. 2006, p. 726.

18 Timmis 2002, p. 242.

19 Cited in Scales et al. 2006.

20 Rindal and Piercy 2013, pp. 211, 224, 221.

21 Greene, Robert Lane. 2013 (June 21). A language with too many armies and navies? *Johnson* blog. *The Economist.* http://www.economist.com /blogs/johnson/2013/06/arabic [April 20, 2017].

22 Chia Suan Chong, quoted in Morrison, Lennox. 2016 (Oct 31). Native English speakers are the world's worst communicators. *BBC Capital.* http:// www.bbc.com/capital/story/20161028-native-english-speakers-are-the -worlds-worst-communicators [April 21, 2017].

23 Caulkin, Simon. 2005 (July 24). English, language of lost changes. *The Observer.* https://www.theguardian.com/business/2005/jul/24 /theobserver.observerbusiness6.

24 See Graddol 2006.

25 Jean, Al, Mike Reiss, and Sam Simon. 1991. The way we was. In M. Groening and J. L. Brooks (exec. producers), *The Simpsons,* season 2, episode 12. Fox Broadcasting.

26 Matthew Engel, Feb 28, 2017 on: Like, totally awesome: The Americanisation of English. *Word of Mouth.* BBC Radio 4. http://www.bbc.co.uk /programmes/b08g5533 [April 30, 2017].

27 Robert Siegel, July 7, 2014 on: Nil-ism in America. *All Things Considered.* National Public Radio. http://www.npr.org/2014/07/07/329585162 /nil-ism-in-america-when-you-stare-at-the-pitch-the-pitch-stares-back [April 30, 2017].

REFERENCES

Adams, John. 1852. *The works of John Adams, second President of the United States: With a life of the author, notes and illustrations, by his grandson Charles Francis Adams*, vol. 9. Boston: Little, Brown and Company.

Aitkenhead, Decca. 2007 (Oct 20). Class rules. *The Guardian*. https://www.theguardian.com/uk/2007/oct/20/britishidentity.socialexclusion1 [April 27, 2017].

Algeo, John. 2006. *British or American English: A handbook of word and grammar patterns*. Cambridge University Press.

Allen, Grant. 1890. *Falling in love: With other essays on more exact branches of science*. New York: D. Appleton.

Allport, Gordon. 1979. *The nature of prejudice*. Reading, MA: Addison-Wesley.

Amis, Kingsley. 1997. *The King's English*. London: HarperCollins.

Anderson, Samantha, Samuel D. Downs, Kaylene Faucette, Josh Griffin, Tracy King, and Staci Woolstenhulme. 2007. How accents affect perception of intelligence, physical attractiveness, and trustworthiness of Middle-Eastern-, Latin-American-, British-, and Standard-American-English-accented Speakers. *Intuition* 3, 5–11.

Aristides (Epstein, Joseph). 1997. Anglophilia, American style. *American Scholar* 66, 327–34.

Ash, John. 1775. *The new and complete dictionary of the English language in two volumes*. London.

Badia Berrera, Berta. 2015. *A sociolinguistic study of t-glottalling in young RP: Accent, class and education*. PhD Thesis, University of Essex.

Barber, Charles. 1964. *Linguistic change in present-day English*. Edinburgh: Oliver & Boyd.

Barnes, William. 1878. *An outline of English speech-craft*. London: C. Kegan Paul & Co.

Bauer, Laurie. 1985. Tracing phonetic change in the received pronunciation of British English. *Journal of Phonetics* 13, 61–81.

Bayard, Donn, Ann Weatherall, Cynthia Gallois, and Jeffrey Pittam. 2001. Pax Americana? Accent attitudinal evaluations in New Zealand, Australia and America. *Journal of Sociolinguistics* 5, 22–49.

BBC. n.d. BBC News style guide. http://www.bbc.co.uk/academy/journalism/news-style-guide/article/art20131010112740749 [April 23, 2017].

REFERENCES

BBC News (online). 2011 (July 20). Americanisms: 50 of your most noted examples. http://www.bbc.co.uk/news/magazine-14201796 [April 23, 2017].

Beck, T. Romeyn. 1830. Notes on Mr. Pickering's *Vocabulary of words and phrases, which have been supposed to be peculiar to the United States,* with preliminary observations. *Transactions of the Albany Institute* I, 25–31.

Bennett, Alan. 1977. *The old country.* In *Alan Bennett plays 2.* London: Faber.

Berg, Thomas. 1999. Stress variation in British and American English. *World Englishes* 18, 123–43.

Biber, Douglas, Stig Johansson, Geoffrey Leech, Susan Conrad, and Edward Finegan. 1999. *Longman grammar of spoken and written English.* Harlow: Pearson Education.

Bierce, Ambrose. 1911/2003. *The devil's dictionary.* London: Bloomsbury.

Blount, Roy, Jr. 2008. *Alphabet juice.* New York: Farrar, Straus, and Giroux.

Bock, Kathryn, Sally Butterfield, Anne Cutler, J. Cooper Cutting, Kathleen M. Eberhard, and Karin R. Humphreys. 2006. Number agreement in British and American English: Disagreeing to agree collectively. *Language* 82, 64–113.

Bolinger, Dwight. 1998. Intonation in American English. In Daniel Hirst and Albert Di Cristo (eds.), *Intonation systems: A survey of twenty languages,* pp. 45–55. Cambridge University Press.

Bonfiglio, Thomas Paul. 2002. *Race and the rise of Standard American.* Berlin: Mouton de Gruyter.

Boorstin, Daniel. 1966. *The Americans: The national experience.* London: Penguin.

Boswell, James. 1791. *The life of Samuel Johnson, LL.D.* (reprint of 6th ed.). New York: The Modern Library.

Braddock, Richard, Richard Lloyd-Jones, and Lowell Schoeb. 1963. *Research in written composition.* Urbana, IL: National Council of Teachers of English.

Breuer, Anja and Ronald Geluykens. 2007. Variation in British and American English requests: A contrastive analysis. In Bettina Kraft and Ronald Geluykens (eds.), *Cross-cultural pragmatics and interlanguage English.* Munich: Lincom.

Brockett, John Trotter. 1829. *A glossary of North Country words.* Newcastle-upon-Tyne: Emerson Charnley.

Brook, Marisa and Sali Tagliamonte. 2016. Why does Canadian English use *try to* but British English uses *try and*? Let's try and/to figure it out. *American Speech* 91, 301–26.

Brown, Penelope and Stephen Levinson. 1987. *Politeness: Some universals in language usage.* Cambridge University Press.

Bryson, Bill. 2004. *A short history of nearly everything.* London: Black Swan.

Burchfield, R. W. 2004. *Fowler's modern English usage,* re-revised 3rd ed. Oxford University Press.

Burkett, Eva Mae. 1979. *American dictionaries of the English language before 1861.* London: Scarecrow Press.

REFERENCES

Cameron, Deborah. 1995. *Verbal hygiene*. London: Routledge.

Chancellor, Alexander 1999. *Some times in America*. London: Picador.

Channing, Edward Tyrrell. 1856. *Lectures read to the seniors in Harvard College*. Boston: Ticknor and Fields.

Chicago manual of style, The. 1993. 14th ed. The University of Chicago Press.

Chrimes, S. B. 1967. *English constitutional history*, 4th ed. Oxford University Press.

Churchill, Winston S. 1950. *The Second World War*, vol. III. New York: Houghton Mifflin.

Combs, Josiah. 1931. The radio and pronunciation. *American Speech* 7, 124–29.

Conrad, Peter. 2014. *How the world was won: The Americanization of everywhere*. London: Thames and Hudson.

Corbett, Edward P. J. 1987. Teaching composition: Where we've been and where we're going. *College Composition and Communication* 38, 444–52.

Coulmas, Florian. 1994. Writing systems and literacy: The alphabetic myth revisited. In Ludo Verhoeven (ed.), *Functional literacy: Theoretical issues and educational implications*, pp. 305–20. Amsterdam: John Benjamins.

Coupland, Nikolas and Hywel Bishop. 2007. Ideologised values for British accents. *Journal of Sociolinguistics* 11, 74–93.

Cresswell, Nicholas. 1924. *The journal of Nicholas Cresswell, 1774–1777*. New York: Dial Press.

Crowley, Tony. 2003. *Standard English and the politics of language*, 2nd ed. New York: Palgrave Macmillan.

Cruse, D. A. 1986. *Lexical semantics*. Cambridge University Press.

Crystal, David. 1995. *The Cambridge encyclopedia of the English language*. Cambridge University Press.

Culpeper, Jonathan. 2005. *History of English*, 2nd ed. London: Routledge.

Davies, Mark. 2007–. *TIME Magazine Corpus: 100 million words, 1920s–2000s*. Available online at http://corpus.byu.edu/time/.

Davies, Mark. 2008–. *The Corpus of Contemporary American English: 520 million words, 1990–present*. Available online at http://corpus.byu.edu/coca/.

Davies, Mark. 2011–. *Corpus of American Soap Operas: 100 million words*. Available online at http://corpus.byu.edu/soap/.

Davies, Mark. 2013a. *Corpus of Global Web-Based English: 1.9 billion words from speakers in 20 countries*. Available online at http://corpus.byu.edu/glowbe/.

Davies, Mark. 2013b. *Corpus of News on the Web (NOW): 3+ billion words from 20 countries, updated every day*. Available online at http://corpus.byu.edu/now/.

De Felice, Rachele and M. Lynne Murphy. 2017. *Thanks for your attention: Thanking behaviour in British and American email corpora*. Paper presented at the International Pragmatics Association Conference, Belfast, July 16–21.

Denison, David. 2007. Syntactic surprises in some English letters. In Stephan Elspass, Nils Langer, Joachim Scharloth, and Wim Vandenbussche (eds.),

REFERENCES

Germanic language histories 'from below' (1700–2000), pp. 115–28. Berlin: de Gruyter.

de Tocqueville, Alexis. 1840. *Democracy in America, vol. 2*. Project Gutenberg ebook edition. http://www.gutenberg.org/files/815/815-h/815-h.htm.

Dickens, Charles. 1858. 'Saxon words.' Household Words, vol. 18. Reprinted in W. F. Bolton and D. Crystal (eds.) 1969, *The English language, vol. 2: Essays by linguists and men of letters 1858–1964*, pp. 1–7. Cambridge University Press.

Drummond, Rob and Erin Carrie. 2017 (Feb 7). Why so many singers sound American—but British grime artists are bucking the trend. *The Conversation* https://theconversation.com/why-so-many-singers-sound-american-but-british-grime-artists-are-bucking-the-trend-72328 [Feb 14, 2017].

Dwight, Timothy. 1823. *Travels in New-England and New-York, vol. 1*. London: William Baynes & Son.

Economist, The. 2010. *Style guide*, 10th ed. London: Economist Books.

Eddington, David and Michael Taylor. 2009. T-glottalization in American English. *American Speech* 84, 298–314.

Educational Testing Service. n.d. Who accepts TOEFL scores? https://www.ets.org/toefl/ibt/about/who_accepts_scores [April 13, 2017].

Ellis, Joseph J. 1979. *After the revolution: Profiles of early American culture*. New York: W. W. Norton.

Engel, Matthew. 2010 (June 6). Britain declares war on words that snuck into our skedule. *The Mail on Sunday*.

Engel, Matthew. 2011 (July 13). Why do some Americanisms irritate people? *BBC Magazine*, http://www.bbc.co.uk/news/14130942 [April 8, 2017].

Engel, Matthew. 2017. *That's the way it crumbles: The American conquest of English*. London: Profile Books.

Fairman, Tony. 1994. How the ass became a donkey. *English Today* 10(4), 29–36.

Faul, Stephanie. 1994. *Xenophobe's guide to the Americans*. London: Oval.

Firmin, Michael W., Janine M. Helmick, Brian A. Iezzi, and Aaron Vaughn. 2004. Say please: The effect of the word *please* in compliance-seeking requests. *Social Behavior and Personality* 32, 67–72.

Fischer, David Hackett. 1989. *Albion's seed: Four British folkways in America*. Oxford University Press.

Fisher, John Hurt. 2001. British and American, continuity and divergence. In John Algeo (ed.), *The Cambridge history of the English language, vol. VI: English in North America*, pp. 59–85. Cambridge University Press.

Forster, John. 1872. *The life of Charles Dickens, vol 1: 1812–1842*. Cambridge University Press.

Fowler, H. W. 1926. *A dictionary of modern English usage*. Oxford University Press.

Fowler, H. W. and F. G. Fowler. 1908. *The King's English*, 2nd ed. Oxford University Press. (First edition, 1906.)

REFERENCES

Fox, Kate. 2014. *Watching the English: The hidden rules of English behaviour*, revised ed. London: Hodder.

Freeman, Edward Augustus. 1876. *The history of the Norman conquest of England: Its causes and results*. Oxford: Clarendon.

Freeman, Jan. 2009. *Ambrose Bierce's* Write it right [1909]: *The celebrated cynic's language peeves deciphered, appraised, and annotated for 21st century readers*. New York: Walker.

Garner, Bryan. 2002. *The Oxford dictionary of American usage and style*. New York: Oxford University Press.

Garner, Bryan. 2016. *Garner's modern English usage*, 4th ed. New York: Oxford University Press.

Garrett, Peter, Angie Williams, and Betsy Evans. 2005. Attitudinal data from New Zealand, Australia, the USA and UK about each other's Englishes. *Multilingua* 24, 211–35.

Garvey, Mark. 2009. *Stylized: A slightly obsessive history of Strunk & White's* The Elements of Style. New York: Touchstone.

Gibson, Andy. 2010. *Production and perception of vowels in New Zealand popular music*. MA thesis, Auckland University of Technology. Available at: http://aut.researchgateway.ac.nz/handle/10292/962 [Feb 14, 2017].

Gill, A. A. 2012. *The golden door: Letters to America*. London: W & N.

Gill, Patrick. 2011. The proliferation of English varieties in American television series. In Miguel A. Pérez-Gómez (ed.), *Previously on: Interdisciplinary studies on TV series in the third golden age*. Sevilla: Biblioteca de la Facultad de Comunicación de la Universidad de Sevilla, pp. 743–54. Available at: http://fama2.us.es/fco/previouslyon/46.pdf [April 30, 2017].

Gonçalves, Bruno, Lucía Loureiro-Porto, José J. Ramasco, and David Sánchez. 2017. *The fall of the Empire: The Americanization of English*. Available at: https://arxiv.org/pdf/1707.00781.pdf [Aug 5, 2017].

Gooskens, Charlotte. 2007. The contribution of linguistic factors to the intelligibility of closely related languages. *Journal of Multilingual and Multicultural Development* 28, 445–67.

Görlach, Manfred. 1991. *Introduction to early modern English*. Cambridge University Press.

Gowers, Ernest and (revised and updated by) Rebecca Gowers. 2014. *Plain words: A guide to the use of English*. London: Penguin.

Gowers, Ernest, and (revised by) Sidney Greenbaum and Janet Whitcut. 1986. *Complete plain words*. London: Penguin.

Graddol, David. 2006. *English next: Why global English may mean the end of 'English as a Foreign Language.'* British Council. https://www.teachingenglish.org.uk/sites/teacheng/files/english_next.pdf [April 24, 2017].

Green, Jonathon. 1999. Language: Dictionary wars. *Critical Quarterly* 41, 127–31.

REFERENCES

Greenbaum, Sidney. 1990. Whose English? In Ricks and Michaels (eds.), pp. 15–23.

Greenbaum, Sidney, Charles F. Meyer, and John Taylor. 1984. The image of the dictionary for American college students. *Dictionaries* 6, 31–52.

Guardian style, 3rd ed. 2010. (ed. by David Marsh and Amelia Hodson.) London: Guardian Books.

Hall-Lew, Lauren, Elizabeth Coppock, and Rebecca Starr. 2010. Indexing political persuasion: Variation in the *Iraq* vowels. *American Speech* 85, 91–102.

Hancock, Craig, and Martha Kolln. 2010. Blowin' in the wind: English grammar in United States schools. In Terry Locke (ed.), *Beyond the grammar wars*, pp. 21–37. New York: Routledge.

Hannisdal, Bente Rebecca. 2006. *Variability and change in Received Pronunciation*. Doctoral thesis, University of Bergen.

Harrington, Jonathan, Sallyanne Palethorpe, and Catherine Watson. 2000. Monophthongal vowel changes in Received Pronunciation: An acoustic analysis of the Queen's Christmas broadcasts. *Journal of the International Phonetic Association* 30, 63–78.

Hauer, Stanley R. 1983. Thomas Jefferson and the Anglo-Saxon language. *Publications of the Modern Language Association* 98, 879–98.

Heffer, Simon. 2011. *Strictly English*. London: Windmill.

Heffer, Simon. 2014. *Simply English*. London: Random House.

Hendy, David. 2006. Bad language and BBC Radio Four in the 1960s and 1970s. *Twentieth Century British History* 17, 74–102.

Hinrichs, Lars, Benedikt Szmrecsanyi, and Axel Bohmann. 2015. *Which*-hunting and the Standard English relative clause. *Language* 91, 806–36.

Hitchings, Henry. 2013. *Sorry! The English and their manners*. London: John Murray.

Hommerberg, Charlotte and Gunnel Tottie. 2007. *Try to* or *try and*? Verb complementation in British and American English. *ICAME* 31, 45–64.

Horobin, Simon. 2013. *Does spelling matter?* Oxford University Press.

Horwill, H. W. 1939. *An Anglo-American interpreter: A vocabulary and phrase book*. Oxford University Press.

Hudson, Richard and John Walmsley. 2005. The English patient: English grammar and teaching in the twentieth century. *Journal of Linguistics* 41, 593–622.

Humphrys, John. 2004. *Lost for words: The mangling and manipulating of the English language*. London: Hodder.

Hundt, Marianne. 2009. Colonial lag, colonial innovation, or simply language change? In Rohdenburg and Schlüter (eds.), pp. 13–37.

Hymes, Dell. 1971. Sociolinguistics and the ethnography of speaking. In E. Ardener (ed.), *Social anthropology and language*, pp. 47–93. London: Tavistock.

REFERENCES

IELTS. 2017. New milestones confirm IELTS as the world's leading test of English for international migration and higher education. https://www .ielts.org/news/2017/new-milestones-confirm-ielts-as-the-worlds-leading-test-of-english [April 13, 2017].

Ilson, Robert. 1990. British and American English: Ex Pluro Uno? In Ricks and Michaels (eds.), pp. 33–41.

Ishikawa, Shinchiro. 2011. Duality in the spelling of English verb suffixes *-ize* and *-ise*. *International Proceedings of Economics Development and Research 26: International Conference on Languages, Literature and Linguistics*, 390–6.

Jefferson, Thomas. 1787. *Notes on the State of Virginia*. London: John Stockdale.

Jenkins, Jennifer. 2003. *World Englishes: A resource book for students*. London: Routledge.

Johnson, Marilyn. 2006. *The dead beat: Lost souls, lucky stiffs, and the perverse pleasures of obituaries*. New York: Harper Perennial.

Johnson, Samuel. 1755. *A dictionary of the English language*. London.

Jones, E. E., G. C. Wood, and G. A. Quattrone. 1981. Perceived variability of personal characteristics in in-groups and out-groups: The role of knowledge and evaluation. *Personality and Social Psychology Bulletin* 7(3), 523–8.

Jones, Katharine W. 2001. *Accent on privilege: English identities and anglophilia in the U.S.* Philadelphia: Temple University Press.

Jurafsky, Dan. 2014. *The language of food*. New York: W. W. Norton.

Kamm, Oliver. 2015. *Accidence will happen: The non-pedantic guide to English*. London: Orion.

Kaur, Paramjit. 2014. Accent attitudes: Reactions to English as a lingua franca. *Procedia: Social and Behavioral Sciences* 134, 3–12.

Kemble, Frances Anne. 1890. *Further records 1848–1883*. New York: Henry Holt.

Kendall, Joshua. 2010. *The forgotten founding father: Noah Webster's obsession and the creation of an American culture*. New York: Berkley Books.

Kennedy, John F. 1958. *A nation of immigrants*. New York: Anti-Defamation League.

Kirchmeier, Jeffrey L. and Samuel A. Thumma. 2010. Scaling the lexicon fortress: The United States Supreme Court's use of dictionaries in the twenty-first century. *Marquette Law Review* 94, 77–262.

Kjellmer, Göran. 2009. The revived subjunctive. In Rohdenburg and Schlüter (eds.), pp. 246–56.

Kövesces, Zöltan. 2000. *American English: An introduction*. Peterborough, ON: Broadview.

Kynaston, David. 2009. *Tales of a new Jerusalem 1945–79, vol. 2*. London: Bloomsbury.

Labov, William. 2012. *Dialect diversity in America: The politics of language change*. Charlottesville: University of Virginia Press.

REFERENCES

Labov, William, Sharon Ash, and Charles Boberg. 1997. *A national map of the regional dialects of American English.* Online at: http://www.ling.upenn.edu /phono_atlas/NationalMap/NationalMap.html [Feb 14, 2017].

Laird, Charlton. 1970. *Language in America.* Englewood Cliffs, NJ: Prentice-Hall.

Lawson, Sarah. 1970. Immigrant in British and American Usage. *American Speech* 45, 304–5.

Leech, Geoffrey, Marianne Hundt, Christian Mair, and Nicholas Smith. 2009. *Change in contemporary English.* Cambridge University Press.

Levin, Magnus. 2001. Agreement with collective nouns in English. *Lund Studies in English,* Department of English, Lund University.

Levin, Magnus. 2006. Collective nouns and language change. *English Language and Linguistics* 10, 321–43.

Levin, Magnus. 2014. The bathroom formula: A corpus-based study of a speech act in American and British English. *Journal of Pragmatics* 64, 1–16.

Lodge, Henry Cabot. 1883 (May). Colonialism in the United States. *The Atlantic.* Reprinted in Brander Matthews (ed.), 1914. *The Oxford book of American essays.* Oxford University Press.

Longmore, Paul K. 2005. "They . . . speak better English than the English do": colonialism and the origins of national linguistic standardization in America. *Early American Literature* 40, 279–314.

Lounsbury, Thomas R. 1908. *The standard of usage in English.* London: Harper & Brothers.

Lyall, Sarah. 2008. *A field guide to the English.* London: Quercus.

Maidment, J. A. 1994. Estuary English: Hybrid or hype? Presented at the 4th New Zealand Conference on Language and Society, Christchurch, August. Available at: http://www.phon.ucl.ac.uk/home/estuary/maidment.pdf [April 18, 2017].

Mair, Christian. 2006. *Twentieth-century English: History, variation and standardization.* Cambridge University Press.

Mair, Christian. 2007. British English/American English grammar: Convergence in writing – divergence in speech? *Anglia* 125, 84–99.

Mäki, Johanna. 2015. Organise *or* organize? *The development, use and recognition of verbal endings -ise and -ize in contemporary British English.* Pro Gradu Thesis. University of Tampere.

Marckwardt, Albert H. 1958. *American English.* New York: Oxford University Press.

Maugham, W. Somerset. 1930. *Cakes and ale.* London: Wm Heineman.

McCrum, Robert. 2010. *Globish: How English became the world's language.* London: Viking.

Mencken, H. L. 1921. *The American language,* 2nd ed. New York: Alfred A. Knopf.

Mencken, H. L. 1922. *Prejudices: Third series.* New York: Alfred A. Knopf.

Meritt, Herbert. 1940. The vocabulary of Sir John Cheke's partial version of the Gospels. *The Journal of English and Germanic Philology* 39, 450–5.

REFERENCES

Metcalf, Allan. 2004. *Presidential voices: Speaking styles from George Washington to George W. Bush.* Boston: Houghton Mifflin.

Miall, Antony. 1993. *Xenophobe's guide to the English.* Horsham: Ravette.

Miller, Joshua D., Jessica L. Maples, Laura Buffardi, Huajian Cai, Brittany Gentile, Yasemin Kisbu-Sakarya, Virginia S. Y. Kwan, Alex LoPilato, Louise F. Pendry, Constantine Sedikides, Lane Siedor, and W. Keith Campbell. 2015. Narcissism and United States' culture: The view from home and around the world. *Journal of Personality and Social Psychology* 109, 1068–89.

Milroy, James and Lesley Milroy. 2012. *Authority in language,* 4th ed. London: Routledge.

Mitchell, David. 2010. Dear America. *David Mitchell's Soapbox.* https://www.youtube.com/watch?v=om7O0MFkmpw [April 3, 2017].

Monaghan, E. Jennifer. 1988. Literacy instruction and gender in colonial New England. *American Quarterly* 40, 18–41.

Monaghan, E. Jennifer. 2005. *Learning to read and write in colonial America.* Boston: University of Massachusetts Press.

Moore, Anne Elizabeth. 2007. *The manifesti of radical literature.* Detroit: Pressing Concern Books.

Moore, Erin. 2015. *That's not English: Britishisms, Americanisms, and what our English says about us.* New York: Gotham Books.

Moore, Margaret E. 1997. *Understanding British English,* 2nd ed. New York: Citadel Press.

Morton, Herbert C. 1994. *The story of* Webster's Third: *Philip Gove's controversial dictionary and its critics.* Cambridge University Press.

Moss, Norman. 1991. *British/American language dictionary.* Lincolnwood, IL: Passport Books.

Murphy, M. Lynne ("Lynneguist"). 2012. Saying *please* in restaurants. *Separated by a Common Language.* https://separatedbyacommonlanguage.blogspot.co.uk/2012/08/saying-please-in-restaurants.html [April 21, 2017].

Murphy, M. Lynne. 2015. Separated by a common politeness marker: *Please* in American and British English. Paper presented at the International Pragmatics Association Conference, Antwerp, July 26–31.

Murphy, M. Lynne and Rachele De Felice. 2018. Routine politeness in American and British English requests: Use and non-use of *please. Journal of Politeness Research* (forthcoming).

Norris, Mary. 2015. *Between you and me.* New York: W. W. Norton.

North, Stephen. 1987. *The making of knowledge in composition.* Upper Montclair, NJ: Boynton/Cook.

Orwell, George. 1941. *The lion and the unicorn: Socialism and the English genius.* London: Searchlight Books.

Orwell, George. 1946. Politics and the English language. *Horizon.* Full text available at: https://www.mtholyoke.edu/acad/intrel/orwell46.htm [April 23, 2017].

REFERENCES

Ostler, Rosemarie. 2015. *Founding grammars: How early America's war over words shaped today's language.* New York: St. Martin's.

Oxford English Dictionary, The. *OED Online.* Oxford University Press. http://www.oed.com.

Partridge, Eric. 1947/1969. *Usage and abusage: A guide to good English.* Harmondsworth, Middlesex, UK: Penguin.

Paxman, Jeremy. 1998. *The English: A portrait of a people.* London: Penguin.

Pickering, John. 1816. *A vocabulary, or collection of words and phrases which have been supposed to be peculiar to the United States of America.* Boston: Cummings & Hilliard.

Pinker, Steven. 2014. *The sense of style.* New York: Penguin.

Pointon, Graham. 1988. The BBC and English pronunciation. *English Today* 4(3), 8–12.

Pullum, Geoffrey K. 2014. Fear and loathing of the English passive. *Language and Communication* 37, 60–74.

Queiroz de Barros, Rita. 2007. Spelling standardisation in Shakespeare's first editions: Evidence from the Second Quarto and First Folio versions of *Romeo and Juliet. Sederi* 17, 93–108.

Quirk, Randolph. 1973. The social impact of dictionaries in the UK. *Annals of the New York Academy of Sciences* 211, 76–88.

Read, Allen Walker. 1938. The assimilation of the speech of British immigrants in colonial America. *Journal of English and Germanic Philology* 37, 70–9.

Read, Allen Walker. 1980. British recognition of American speech in the eighteenth century. In J. L. Dillard (ed.), *Perspectives on American English,* pp. 15–35. The Hague, Netherlands: Mouton.

Reed, Alonzo and Brainerd Kellogg. 1877. *Higher lessons in English.* Project Gutenberg edition: http://www.gutenberg.org/ebooks/7188 [April 23, 2017].

Ricks, Christopher and Leonard Michaels (eds.). 1990. *The state of the language.* London: Faber & Faber.

Rindal, Ulrikke and Caroline Piercy. 2013. Being "neutral"? English pronunciation among Norwegian speakers. *World Englishes* 32, 211–29.

Rohdenburg, Günter and Julia Schlüter (eds.). 2009. *One language, two grammars? Differences between British and American English.* Cambridge University Press.

Rose, Kenneth D. 2014. *Unspeakable awfulness: America through the eyes of European travelers, 1865–1900.* New York: Routledge.

Rubenstein, Marv. 2006. *21st century American English compendium,* 3rd ed. Rockville, MD: Schreiber Publishing.

Ruette, Tom, Katharina Ehret, and Benedikt Szmrecsanyi. 2016. A lectometric analysis of aggregated lexical variation in rosewritten Standard English with Semantic Vector Space models. *International Journal of Corpus Linguistics* 21, 48–79.

Rush, Benjamin. 1947. *The selected writings of Benjamin Rush.* (ed. by Dagobert D. Runes.) New York: Philosophical Library.

REFERENCES

Sapir, Edward. 1921. *Language: An introduction to the study of speech.* New York: Harcourt, Brace and Company.

Scales, Julie, Ann Wennerstrom, Dara Richard, and Su Hui Wu. 2006. Language learners' perceptions of accent. *TESOL Quarterly* 40, 715–38.

Scholfield, P. J. 1994. Writing and spelling: The view from linguistics. In *Handbook of spelling: Theory, process and intervention*, pp. 51–71. Chichester West Sussex, UK: John Wiley & Sons.

Schulte Nordholt, J. W. 1986. Anti-americanism in European culture: Its early manifestations. In Rob Kroes and Maarten van Rossem (eds.), *Antiamericanism in Europe*, pp. 7–19. Amsterdam: Free University Press.

Serpollet, Noëlle. 2001. The mandative subjunctive in British English seems to be alive and kicking . . . Is this due to the influence of American English? In *Proceedings of the Corpus Linguistics 2001 Conference*, 531–42. Lancaster, UK: University Centre for Computer Corpus Research on Language.

Shea, Ammon. 2014. A sure uncertainty: On some difficulties using OED online data to establish Shakespearian coinages. *Dictionaries* 35, 121–45.

Skinner, David. 2012. *The story of ain't: America, its language, and the most controversial dictionary ever published.* New York: Harper.

Sledd, James and Wilma B. Ebbitt (eds.). 1962. *Dictionaries and that dictionary.* Chicago: Scott Foresman.

Smith, Charles William. 1866. *Mind your H's and take care of your R's.* London: Lockwood & Co.

Smith, Godfrey. 1984. *The English companion: An idiosyncratic guide to England and Englishness from A to Z.* London: Pavilion.

Sokoloff, Kenneth L. and Stanley L. Engerman. 2000. History lessons: Institutions, factors, endowments, and paths of development in the New World. *The Journal of Economic Perspectives* 14, 217–32.

Stacey, C. P. 1964. The War of 1812 in Canadian history. In Morris Zaslow and Wesley Turner (eds.), *The defended border: Upper Canada and the War of 1812*, pp. 331–7. Toronto: Macmillan.

Stevens, Christopher. 2012 (May 30). Don't talk garbage! . . . or why American words are mangling our English. *Daily Mail* http://www.dailymail.co.uk /news/article-2151922/Dont-talk-garbage--American-words-mangling -English.html [April 17, 2017].

Stewart, Edward C. and Milton J. Bennett. 1991. *American cultural patterns.* Yarmouth, ME: Intercultural Press.

Stewart, Mark, Ellen Bouchard Ryan, and Howard Giles. 1985. Accent and social class effects on status and solidarity evaluations. *Personal Social Psychology Bulletin* 11, 98–105.

Strunk, William Jr. 1918. *The elements of style.* Ithaca, NY: privately printed.

Strunk, William Jr. and E. B. White. 1959. *The elements of style.* New York: Macmillan.

REFERENCES

Stuart-Smith, Jane, Gwilym Pryce, Claire Timmins, and Barrie Gunter. 2013. Television can also be a factor in language change: Evidence from an urban dialect. *Language* 89, 501–36.

Timmis, Ivor. 2002. Native-speaker norms and International English: A classroom view. *ELT Journal* 53, 240–9.

Tombs, Robert and Isabella. 2006. *That sweet enemy: The French and the British from the Sun King to the present.* London: Heinemann.

Trevelyan, George Otto. 1912. *George the Third and Charles Fox.* London: Longmans, Green & Co.

Trudgill, Peter. 2003. World Englishes: Convergence or divergence? Talk presented at Kyushu-Okinawa Chapter of the Japan Association of College English Teachers, Apr 20.

Trudgill, Peter and Jean Hannah. 2013. *International English: A guide to the varieties of Standard English,* 5th ed. London: Routledge.

Twain, Mark. 1869. *The innocents abroad, or new pilgrim's progress.* American Publishing Co.

Twain, Mark. 1897. *Following the Equator.* Project Gutenberg eBook edition. http://www.gutenberg.org/ebooks/2895 [April 27, 2017].

Vaughn, Aaron J., Michael W. Firmin, and Chi-en Hwang. 2009. Efficacy of request presentation on compliance. *Social Behavior and Personality* 37, 441–50.

Watson, Don. 2004. *Gobbledygook: How clichés, sludge and management-speak are strangling our public language.* London: Atlantic Books.

Watt, Dominic and Brendan Gunn. 2016. *The sound of 2066: A report commissioned by HSBC.* Available at: http://www.about.hsbc.co.uk/~/media/uk/en/news-and-media/160929-voice-biometrics-sounds-of-britain-2066.pdf [March 29, 2017].

Watts, Richard J. 2003. *Politeness.* Cambridge University Press.

Webb, Justin. 2008. *Have a nice day.* London: Short Books.

Webb, Justin. 2011. *Notes on them and us.* London: Short Books.

Webster, Noah. 1789. *Dissertations on the English language.* Boston. Isaiah Thomas and Company.

Webster, Noah. 1790. *A collection of essays and fugitiv writings.* Boston: I. Thomas & E. T. Andrews.

Wells, J. C. 1982. *Accents of English* (3 vols.). Cambridge University Press.

Wells, J. C. 1996. Whatever happened to Received Pronunciation? *Jornadas de Estudios Ingleses* 2, 19–28.

Wells, J. C. 1999. British English pronunciation preferences: A changing scene. *Journal of the International Phonetic Association* 29, 33–50.

Wesley, John. 1826. Minutes of several conversations between the Rev. Mr. Wesley and others, from the year 1744 to the year 1789. In *The works of the Reverend John Wesley, A.M.,* vol. 5, pp. 211–33. New York: Emory & Waugh.

342

Whibley, Charles. 1908 (Jan). The American Language. *Blackwood's Magazine*, 117–26.

Whitaker, Alexander. 1613. *Good newes from Virginia*. London: William Welby.

Wilde, Oscar. 1887/1906. *The Canterville ghost*. Project Gutenberg edition (2004), from 1906 John Luce & Co. edition. https://www.gutenberg.org /files/14522/14522.txt [April 30, 2017].

Wilde, Oscar. 1894/1919. *A woman of no importance*. Project Gutenberg edition (2014), transcribed from the 1919 Methuen & Co. Ltd. edition by David Price. http://www.gutenberg.org/files/854/854-h/854-h.htm [April 30, 2017].

Wilson, Thomas. 1553. *The arte of rhetorique*. Text available at: http://pages .uoregon.edu/rbear/arte/arte.htm [April 30, 2017].

Witherspoon, John. 1802. *The works of the late Rev. John Witherspoon*. Philadelphia: Woodward.

Wolfram, Walt and Natalie Schilling-Estes. 1998. *American English*. Oxford: Blackwell.

THE QUIZZES

As discussed in chapter 2, it can be hard to know what's British and what's American. People who read books about language (that's you!) probably know more about it than the average English speaker. Let's see how you measure up. Here are three short quizzes about British and American expressions. The answers follow.

Quiz 1: The following words came into English after 1776. (In some cases, it's a particular meaning of the word that came in.) Put a B next to the ones that originated in Britain and an A beside those that come from the United States.

absenteeism	☐	*acid jazz*	☐	*actorly*	☐
the bee's knees ('fabulous')	☐	*club-hopping*	☐	*to contact* ('get in touch with')	☐
debrief	☐	*ear muffs*	☐	*fantabulous*	☐
foodstuff	☐	*glove box* (in a car)	☐	*to gripe* ('complain')	☐
hinky	☐	*middle-of-the-road*	☐	*nincompoopery*	☐
nitty-gritty	☐	*operatize*	☐	*poppycock*	☐
quad ('square at a university')	☐	*to ramp up* (a price)	☐	*spelunker*	☐
Thermos	☐	*taxi*	☐	*update*	☐

Quiz 2: *Put an X next to the words that have different meanings in the UK and US. (In phrases, pay attention to the bold word.) Only give yourself points if you can give both definitions for the differing ones.*

athletics	☐	blinkers	☐	chugging	☐
daddy longlegs	☐	dungarees	☐	farce (theater)	☐
flapjack	☐	in a **maze**	☐	natty	☐
pacify	☐	pickle (food)	☐	radish (food)	☐
rock (geological)	☐	rote	☐	tipsy	☐
trolley	☐	veil	☐	water park	☐

Quiz 3: *The following expressions are used in both countries. Put an X next to the ones that are used more in the UK.*

excuse me	☐	in and of itself	☐	be up for (something)	☐
ferocious	☐	(please) find attached …	☐	I love your …	☐
in three days' **time**	☐	I reckon …	☐	you're welcome	☐
out **of** the window	☐	please	☐	you poor thing	☐

QUIZ ANSWERS

Quiz 1: *The following words came into English after 1776. (In some cases, it's a particular meaning of the word that came in.) Put a B next to the ones that originated in Britain and an A for those that come from the United States.*

absenteeism		acid jazz	B	actorly	B
the bee's knees ('fabulous')	A	club-hopping	A	to contact ('get in touch with')	A
debrief	B	ear muffs	A	fantabulous	
foodstuff	B	glove box (in a car)	A	to gripe ('complain')	A
hinky	A	middle-of-the-road	A	nincompoopery	B
nitty-gritty	A	operatize	B	poppycock	A
quad ('square at a university')	B	to ramp up (a price)	B	spelunker	A
Thermos	B	taxi	B	update	A

Absenteeism arose in Dublin in the early 1800s. At this point, Ireland was part of the United Kingdom, but it's not part of Britain.

Acid jazz is a British-born style of dance music combining jazz and acid house (1988).

Actorly, meaning 'characteristic of a dramatic actor,' is first recorded in *The Times* in 1957.

The bee's knees is often included in lists of Britishisms that Americans should learn—but it's a Jazz Age Americanism.

Club-hopping ('moving from nightclub to nightclub') is first recorded in 1959 in California.

Contact: In the 1930s, Brits hated this American verbing of a noun. Many Americans hated it too. Now that business jargon prefers *reaching out*, *contact* sounds much more dignified.

Debrief ('gather information from someone after their mission') comes from the Royal Air Force in the Second World War.

Ear muffs are a mid-19th-century American invention.

Fantabulous is first recorded in New Zealand in 1959.

Foodstuff was first used in Britain in the mid-1800s, though at first it was more often *food stuff* or *food-stuff*.

Glove box is first found in the US in 1946. I grew up thinking it must be British because my family said *glove compartment* (US, 1939). I hadn't yet realized how diverse American English is.

Gripe can mean a lot of things, but the 'complain' meaning was first recorded by the American Dialect Society in 1932.

Hinky, meaning 'unreliable' or 'suspect,' comes from African-American and police slang. The first known written use is from 1956. It's not the kind of word that every American would know.

Middle-of-the-road (1894) first described the American Populist Party.

Nincompoopery, meaning 'foolishness,' is a 19th-century British invention, based on the much older *nincompoop*.

Nitty-gritty is originally an African-American colloquialism, first found in print in 1940.

Operatize means 'put into operatic form,' and it's been around since 1785 in Britain.

Poppycock is from Dutch. The first sighting in (American) English is from 1852.

Quad is old Oxford University slang. These days, most American universities have quads.

To ramp up started as jargon in British finance (1970s).

Spelunker started as a jocular term for a cave explorer in early 20th-century American English. It is derived from the Latin for 'cave': *spelunca*.

The **Thermos** was invented by Scottish chemist Sir James Dewar and trademarked in 1907.

Taxi is a shortening of *taximeter*, a German invention that was first used in London in 1903, four years before it made its way to New York.

Update as a verb came into American English in the 1940s. The noun followed in the 1960s.

Quiz 2: Put an X next to the ones that have different meanings in the UK and the US. Only give yourself points if you can say what the differences are.

Same in the UK and US: *farce, maze, natty, pacify, radish, rote, tipsy, veil*, and *water park*.

	UK	**US**
athletics	= US **track and field**	sports in general
blinkers	= US **blinders**, eye shields for horses	= UK **indicators**, lights to indicate a vehicle is about to turn
chugging	a blend of *charity* + *mugging*: fund-raising by stopping pedestrians in the street	from **chug-a-lug**: drinking a whole, large (usually alcoholic) drink without stopping for breath
daddy longlegs	= US **crane fly**	= UK **harvestman**, the *Opiliones* arachnid; also the *Pholcus phalangioides* spider (sometimes called **daddy longlegs spider** in UK)

	UK	US
dungarees	= US **overalls** (UK **overalls** = US **coveralls**)	an old-fashioned word for blue jeans
flapjack	a sweet grain bar made of oats (similar to a granola bar)	= **pancake** (in the American style, thick and fluffy, rather than the more **crepe**-like English pancake)
pickle	= US **relish** (condiment of chopped pickled vegetables)	= UK **pickled cucumber**
rock	must be a relatively large, rugged mass (also the name for a kind of **stick candy**)	unlike UK, can be of any size; for example, an American might complain of a "rock" in their shoe.
trolley	= US **cart**, as in **shopping trolley, drinks trolley**	roughly equivalent to UK **tram**

Quiz 3: *Put an X next to the ones that are used more in the UK.*

excuse me		*in and of itself*		*be up for (something)*	×
ferocious	×	*(please) find attached . . .*	×	*I love your . . .*	
in three days' time	×	*I reckon . . .*	×	*you're welcome*	
out of the window	×	*please*	×	*you poor thing*	×

Shame on you if you said "more British" for all the "polite" words. Chapter 7 has more on those.

ACKNOWLEDGMENTS

I've had great fun writing this book, partly because it has allowed me to learn from so many marvelous people. My thanks to Lesley Jeffries, Jim Martin, and Ben Yagoda for help in getting the project off the ground; to Lynne Cahill and Sandra Jansen, my writing-group sounding board; and to further kind and critical souls who gave feedback on chapters: Sarah FitzGerald, Jan Freeman, Melanie Green, Orin Hargraves, Steve Kleinedler, Justyna Robinson, Rebecca Wheeler, Nancy Wood, and Phil Viner. The book is all the better for the sound advice of my agents, Jane Turnbull and Dan Conaway, and editors, Sam Carter at Oneworld and Kathryn Court at Penguin. Thanks also to Victoria Savanh for her great editorial care.

I am grateful beyond words to the National Endowment for the Humanities, whose Public Scholar Program grant allowed me the time away from my day job to write this book, ten years after starting the *Separated by a Common Language* blog. Any views, findings, conclusions, or recommendations expressed in this publication do not necessarily reflect those of the National Endowment for the Humanities. The School of English at the University of Sussex has generously granted me further support and time. Funding from the British Academy/Leverhulme small grants program aided the dictionary research in chapter 8.

Finally, I thank my bi-dialectal family, who gracefully tolerate my late nights, my grumpy mornings, and my incessant interrogations of their word choices. Phil and Arden, you're all over this book, and I love that.

INDEX

INDEX

Blount, Roy, Jr. 122
"Blue-Back Speller" (Webster) 84, 136, 240
books 253–4
borrowed words 223–6
Bradbury, Malcolm 234–5
"Braddock Report, The" 248
Bragg, Billy 285
Brandreth, Gyles 113
bread 199–201
Britain, *see* Great Britain
British Council 290, 291, 292
British Empire 63–4, 91–2, 289–90
British National Corpus (BNC) 15
Britishisms 20–1, 28–31, 40–5, 61–2, 276–9
    and business 60–1
Broadcast English 231–2
broth 198
Buffon, Count de 9
bumbershoot 39–40, 45
Burchfield, Robert 123, 188
burgers 200–1
Burgess, Anthony 189
burgl(ariz)e 176
Bush, George W. 33
business jargon 1–2, 3, 55–61, 183–4
Butterfield, Jeremy 277

calque 101–2
Calvert, James 177
Cameron, David 6, 191–2
Cameron, Deborah 259
Campaign for Real Ale (CAMRA) 123–4
can I get 187–8
Canada 81, 83
Carnegie, Andrew 137
Case, Jack 257
Chamberlain, Neville 40
Chancellor, Alexander 8
Charles, HRH Prince 1, 180, 252, 269, 290
chat up 224
Chaucer, Geoffrey 99
cheerio 15–16
Cheke, Sir John 130

Chicago Manual of Style, The 259
children 2, 13–14, 171, 287
    and grammar 252
    and politeness 209, 213
China 290
Chitty Chitty Bang Bang (film) 39–40
Churchill, Winston 63, 64, 215
Clarity International 2
class 5, 8, 20, 42, 201–2
    and accent 233, 235
    and middle 204–6
    and pronunciation 113–14, 115, 153–4
    see also aristocracy
Cleese, John 37–8
clever 108
clichés 60
Clinton, Hillary 33
clipping 172–3
closed classes 90–1
Cockney rhyming slang 43–4
cognitive bias 36
colonial lag 97–8
colonialism 79–81, 92, 289–90
colo(u)r 5, 143
comedy 28–9, 45
comma 100, 102
complaints 23
Comprehensive Pronouncing and Explanatory English Dictionary, A (Worcester) 245
computers 3, 281
confirmation bias 37
Conservative Party 251–2
contractions 173
contrastive focus reduplication 26–7
controversy 46
conversion 183
cookie 224–6
Corbett, Philip 122
Corden, James 44, 262
cowboy 58
Crashaw, William 96–7, 98
Creoles 87–8
crime 35–6
Cruse, Alan 224
culture 21–2, 78, 262
Cumberbatch, Benedict 233

354

INDEX

357

INDEX

INDEX

INDEX